NETWORK YOUR WAY TO YOUR NEXT JOB ... FAST

NETWORK YOUR WAY TO YOUR NEXT JOB ... FAST

CLYDE C. LOWSTUTER

DAVID P. ROBERTSON

McGraw-Hill, Inc.

New York   San Francisco   Washington, D.C.   Auckland   Bogotá
Caracas   Lisbon   London   Madrid   Mexico City   Milan
Montreal   New Delhi   San Juan   Singapore
Sydney   Tokyo   Toronto

Library of Congress Cataloging-in-Publication Data

Lowstuter, Clyde C.
    Network your way to your next job—fast / Clyde C. Lowstuter, David
P. Robertson.
      p.   cm.
    Includes index.
    ISBN 0-07-038882-2   ISBN 0-07-038883-0 (pbk.)
    1. Job hunting.   2. Career changes.   3. Career development.
4. Social networks.   I. Robertson, David P.   II. Title.
HF5382.7.L693   1995
650.14—dc20   94-32886
                                                    CIP

1 2 3 4 5 6 7 8 9 0   DOC/DOC   9 0 9 8 7 6 5 4 (PBK)
  2 3 4 5 6 7 8 9 0   DOC/DOC   9 0 9 8 7 6 5   (HC)

ISBN 0-07-038883-0 (pbk)
ISBN 0-07-038882-2 (hc)

*The sponsoring editor for this book was Betsy N. Brown, the editing
supervisor was Caroline R. Levine, and the production supervisor was Pamela
A. Pelton. It was set in Garamond Light by North Market Street Graphics.*

Printed and bound by R. R. Donnelley & Sons Company.

This book is printed on recycled, acid-free paper containing a
minimum of 50% recycled de-inked fiber.

CONTENTS

Secret 3
BE KNOWLEDGEABLE REGARDING THE MYTHS AND REALITIES OF NETWORKING   54

Secret 4

RAISE YOUR TELEPHONE NETWORKING COMFORT   76

Secret 5

USE A COMPLETE NETWORKING MODEL AND INCORPORATE IT AS YOUR OWN   92

NETWORK YOUR WAY TO YOUR NEXT JOB ... FAST

Network Your Way to Your Next Job ... Fast is a highly practical job-hunting system which equips people to effectively make those professional and personal connections necessary to unlock the hidden marketplace and ultimately find their ideal job. *Network Your Way to Your Next Job ... Fast* enables the reader (whether experienced business executive, recent college graduate, professional, or "empty nester" returning to work) to use proven approaches and behavior that have produced distinctive networking results for thousands of the authors' clients. Through powerful interactive exercises and plenty of sample dialogue, people have the opportunity to model an actual client working his way through identifying possible leads into search firms, target organizations, personal contacts, and actual openings while significantly and effortlessly expanding visibility and exposure.

Network Your Way to Your Next Job ... Fast was developed to provide job seekers a positive breakthrough experience in networking, because this critical dimension of careers will mean the difference between a successful well-run career search campaign and one which is perhaps prolonged and may be marked with stutter-start momentum and activity. *Network Your Way to Your Next Job ... Fast* also addresses the many subtle interpersonal nuances, myths, abuses, and trends which have tended to sabotage people's ability to be fully engaged in the process of networking. Think of this book as a state-of-the-art learning system which is an exciting guide to an often misunderstood and poorly executed part of the career search process.

To unlock roadblocks and discover limiting beliefs, ask:

1. What am I assuming about my ability to network?

2. How effective am I, **really,** at networking now?

3. If I do not change how I am networking, what will most likely be the result? In 30 days? 60 days? 90 days? 120 days? What will I gain if I do improve?

4. How will my life and career be different if I learn to network **really** effectively? In one year? Two years? Five years?

5. What am I willing to do to become more effective at networking?

6. What am I willing to commit to for 21 days so I might improve my networking?

INTRODUCTION

Welcome to *Network Your Way to Your Next Job . . . Fast,* a highly practical program which can help you become successful in one of the most important and sometimes most difficult aspects of job changing. If you'd like, you could create a working subtitle: *How to Accelerate Your Job-Hunting Efforts and Produce Your Ideal Job!* After working with thousands of individuals in all walks of life, we know that networking is your key to effective career search. Indeed, networking is essential. **You can have the best résumé in the world and interview superbly well, but without a mastery of networking, you probably are in for a long and difficult search.**

This program is for you if:

- You aren't willing to risk your career future on jobs which just happen to come along. You are committed to more effectively locating and uncovering career opportunities that are right for you.

- You have tried conventional job search methods and have become discouraged; your current job-hunting efforts seem to be stalled, stuck, or not moving as quickly as you would like.

- You are unable to find jobs that truly advance your career or pay the salary you feel reflects your capabilities.

- You want a proven method that will accelerate your getting hired.

- Your networking efforts have not produced the results you desire and deserve, or you are uncomfortable or ineffective in networking.

- You have been terminated, you suspect your job is in jeopardy, or you want to change jobs.

Interestingly enough, many people don't believe that they know how to network effectively. *Networking* sounds so formal and theoretical, even though it increasingly is becoming part of our everyday vocabulary and you, yourself, have networked all your life. Simply put, **networking** is merely contacting other people and communicating what you want to get the information, leads, or advice to help you land the right job.

It's not that you don't know how to network. Of course, you do. You have networked in some form or another to arrange a party, get a movie or play review from a friend, or secure some information quite effectively—even if this is your first bona fide career position right out of school.

So rather than teach you brand new skills, we are intending to reacquaint you with some of the things you already know or those skills which may be a little rusty. We suspect that you will also pick up some additional pointers on how to network even more effectively than you thought possible. Our approach will be decidedly informal and aimed at making you comfortable and confident in your ability to network. We would like for you to pretend that we are sitting across the kitchen table from you and we're old friends talking about networking.

As we progress through these ideas, **we want you to be skeptical**—yes, skeptical. We do not want you to accept or reject everything outright. Rather, we want you to question and challenge the ideas and premises being presented and then adapt and apply them to your own situation. As you do this, these ideas will become your ideas, not ours. While we are asking you to be skeptical, **we are also asking you to be open:** open to the possibility of learning something new that might help you network at a new performance level, open to the possibility that your networking approach could be significantly enhanced if you adapt and adopt some of the recommendations we will cover.

You may find yourself saying, "that will never work!" and perhaps you're right. One of our favorite clients, Steen, used to often say—before he became an expert networker—"I've never done that before and I'm not comfortable with it!" As Steen became more skilled in networking and more comfortable, he would kiddingly observe, "I've never done this before and I am enjoying pushing myself further, as my confidence increases." Other phrases you, personally, may express are "I can't accept charity from my friends" or "I don't know anyone." If these beliefs or others like them stop you from being fully engaged in networking, look for ways you can change the approaches we are presenting so that they might work for you.

Although we know you may feel overwhelmed by all this detail, we intend to walk you slowly through the process of networking so that **you become a master networker.** In addition, there are detailed scripts, charts, models, and experience-based stories from our clients which will help reinforce the ideas presented. This supportive material can be used as a natural extension of these techniques—or these charts and models can be considered to be free standing. You will find specific language, tips, and techniques which you can put to good use immediately. Okay, enough of the housekeeping, let's get into the material.

Clyde C. Lowstuter
David P. Robertson

HERMAN MENDEZ—
A LESSON IN
WORLD CLASS
NETWORKING

Most people acknowledge that networking is a given among peers. But when it comes to presidents, CEOs, chairpersons, national and international figures, and beyond, most people shy away from the prospect. Even for the boldest, networking at this world class level seems too much. At this point, even the best network strategy and personal commitment seem to crash and burn. The following is a perfect example of world class networking as told by David Robertson about one of our clients.

Herman Mendez was extremely well connected as a respected international businessman. He had grown up in his company, a Fortune 100 electronics firm, climbing the sales ladder. Midway through his career, he was promoted into the international sector, doing business throughout the Middle East, Europe, and Asia. Interestingly, he was the creator and initiator of early trade agreements with China which generated excellent revenues and set the stage for additional trade relationships in the area. With his quick mind, charismatic personality, and customer dedication, he excelled in finding unique ways to build client endorsement and to integrate his product lines with the technical needs of emerging nations.

Building upon his strong Peruvian background and education, Herman gravitated toward Latin American business. Always growing, he moved rapidly through numerous sales and marketing roles to regional responsibilities and eventually to the executive level, becoming chairman of his company's Latin American operations.

At the age of 52, Herman, a proud man, was devastated when economic problems at home and abroad led his company to curtail Latin American operations. At home, product obsolescence had caught up with his company. Competitive strikes from Japan had damaged growth, and both profit and cash goals were hurting. On top of that, Latin American inflation and political turmoil virtually destroyed cash transfer from these countries, in spite of heroic efforts by Herman to barter the cash through

European suppliers and markets. Regretfully, Herman's Latin American operation was streamlined, and he was released from the company during a major downsizing.

Herman's decision was immediately to begin an international consultancy. He reasoned that he could help other companies do what he had done for his former company. His friends were supportive, and the climate was ripe for outsourcing. Plus, he clearly had the skills and initiative.

Herman found the headway much slower than at first imagined. He spoke to venture capitalists. He spoke to presidents of corporations both large and small. His three-color brochure displaying a map of emerging nations behind the first page die-cut of the globe was a knock-out. He got on the knife-and-fork professional-speaking circuit. He was a key noter at the world convention in Osaka, Japan, for the electronics industry. He was clearly doing all the right things well.

Still, he needed a mentor—someone in a position of authority who could personally introduce him. Assignments of an ongoing nature eluded him. Although he got plenty of one-time limited projects, no one could quite catch the vision of Herman as the catalyst which could catapult a company into the big leagues internationally. Herman's enthusiasm gradually began to wane, and his mindset shifted from optimism to patience, then to doubt, then to despair. What was missing?

One late evening, as Herman and I sat together in his gracious home in Madison, Wisconsin, we struck upon a plan. I asked, "Who is the most world-renowned international consultant today?" Names came up— writers, business leaders, consultants. Then, after much thought, one of us said Henry Kissinger. Kissinger had just stepped down from his State Department position from the Nixon administration. His name was instantly recognized worldwide. His consultancy, initiated with former Senator Eagleton, was one of the most respected and requested in the world.

It was at this point that a new dimension appeared for the first time in Herman. "I can't call him," he said in genuine shock and dismay. "I'm just an out-of-work business guy in Wisconsin. What makes you think that someone like Henry Kissinger would even give me the time of day—never mind help me? Ha!" Quite frankly, I was stunned by Herman's refusal.

Herman, unlike his bold normal self, simply refused to call Henry Kissinger and ask for help. The leap was just too far, even for this proud, most capable Peruvian. We gave the idea up for awhile. Nothing got better and self-esteem was fading. We met again. "Network!," I urged, "Network." "How do you know Henry through your network? Let's revisit your network. Let's review literally everyone you know." Patiently we went through Herman's list of 1500 people. No one. "Let's go back," I insisted. "Is there anyone you knew in school 25 years ago that might be in politics or international affairs?" Herman thought back. Old names—old faces—all at once he brightened up. A light went on! "There was one person," he said. "We graduated together. He went into the United Nations, I think." Well, the only Peruvian I knew of in the United Nations at that time was serving as the leader of the United Nations. "Not the Secretary General of the United Nations," I heard myself shouting in disbelief. "Yes, that's him," replied Herman.

From then on, things went at warp speed. The next day, Herman renewed acquaintances with his old classmate, who was delighted to hear from him. Herman shared his plans and desires to speak with Kissinger about ideas and introductions which might help him position himself as a valued international consultant. "Of course," replied the Secretary General. "As a matter of fact, there are a number of people in several nations who truly need your help. I shall introduce you and recommend that they call you. I will be delighted to introduce you. In fact, I'll just have him call you. You can work things out together."

Of course, indeed. Later that week, our office received a call from a deep-voiced man with a rich German accent asking for Herman Mendez. It went well. An hour and 15 minutes well. The next week, Kissinger's associate called and spent several hours discussing strategies and arranging a meeting. A high day came when my phone rang. Herman with the best "put-on" Peruvian accent said, "David, I am calling you from a magnificent yacht on the Potomac. We are having lunch with Mr. Kissinger!" Herman Mendez, today, is now a vital resource to emerging nations in wide areas of business, technologies, planning, and international trade. He still lives in Madison, Wisconsin, and proudly identifies himself as a committed networker.

Herman's major networking lessons were:

- **Don't put limits on yourself.**
- **Reach for goals beyond those you think possible.**
- **Maintain your focus and keep your outcome unswervingly in mind.**
- **Involve other, like-minded people in the development of your strategy.**
- **Never, never give up!**

NETWORK YOUR WAY TO YOUR NEXT JOB ... FAST

The Secret to
Networking Success
PART 1

Shaping Your Life the Way You Want _____

Ever wonder why some people have greater success in their careers, network more effectively, have more control over their lives, and appear to be happier than others? If you have, you aren't alone. If you asked these successful people what enabled them to achieve outstanding results, you would probably discover that their personal control and achievements relate to several decisions about how they approach their lives. The decisions concern the kinds of questions they ask, the meaning they attach to things, the clarity of personal and career goals, the extent to which they assume responsibility for how their life and career look, the commitments they make, their willingness to operate flexibly, and their willingness to take consistent and sustained action to meet their desired goals.

Seem out of reach? Not at all. You have been operating that way all of your life—getting what you create; you are just not fully aware of how much (and how often) you are in control. To some people, having to change jobs and having to network is incredibly upsetting, yet for others, changing jobs and networking is a time of renewal and a hope for something better. Granted, everyone's situation is unique, but what makes people react so differently to a similar event? Simply put, it is the **meaning** people attach to the event.

How you represent some event to yourself—how you believe something to be—will significantly influence how you feel about it. For instance, if you were not happy in your job and you found another position more suited to your personality and skills and you left, it's a pretty good assumption that you would feel pleased about your decision and excited about your move. However, if you were terminated from a job that you did not like, by a boss you did not respect, you probably experienced both relief and some pain (anger, sadness, righteous indignation). Some of the upset may be the anxiousness of not knowing what the next step is or the fact that your boss "pulled the trigger" before you did on the company. Who knows? In all likelihood, you may have created leaving the organization yourself, although you were not fully aware of this at the time.

The Secrets to Networking Success _____

While we are not presenting any magic formula for networking success, the material contained in this book represents numerous strategies which, if followed, will help you network far more effectively, confidently, and boldly. You are holding the "secret" to networking success in your hand, and the person who really has the power to implement these strategies is sitting in your chair. The secrets to networking success are as follows:

Secret 1. Understand career search challenges and ground rules for the 1990s and beyond.

Secret 2. Manage your beliefs and behavior that guarantee networking success.

Secret 3. Be knowledgeable regarding the myths and the realities of networking.

Secret 4. Raise your telephone networking comfort.

Secret 5. Use a complete networking model and incorporate it as your own.

Secret 6. Master the four avenues of networking.

Secret 7. Focus on your outcome and you'll produce results.

Secret 8. Effectively conduct an industrywide or geography-specific search.

Secret 9. Write powerful networking letters.

Secret 10. Turn around and beat rejection.

Although this list of 10 secrets may look pretty simplistic, gaining personal mastery of each secret is hardly easy. Indeed, you may feel that mastering these skills will be tough, but let us assure you that it's not impossible. The greater your knowledge, comfort, and experience with each of these "secrets," the more effective your networking. The chapters in Part 2 correspond to these 10 secrets, and we will explore each one in depth.

Secret 1. Understand Career Search Challenges and Ground Rules for the 1990s and Beyond.

This chapter sets the stage for the topic of networking and identifies it as the most important means of the four main avenues to get connected, especially in the tough employment market of the 1990s. These four avenues are explored sufficiently to create the context in which networking occurs. Numerous marketplace trends are highlighted, along with their implications for networking.

Secret 2. Manage Your Beliefs and Behavior That Guarantee Networking Success.

Whether you believe you can or you believe you can't, you're right. The extent to which your beliefs get in the way of effective networking limits the extent to which you will be able to effectively network. Chapter 2 provides an opportunity to identify and experiment with those beliefs and behavior which get in the way of you being fully effective in networking.

Secret 3. Be Knowledgeable Regarding the Myths and Realities of Networking.

As an approach to job changing, networking is the most effective means to reach a wide number of opportunities quickly, yet networking is also regarded with some fear and disdain as taking advantage of others. The pros and cons of networking are explored with a hard-hitting "reality check" as to the abuses of networking and some of its tough necessities. Practical advice is provided to persons who are reluctant to abuse personal relationships; this advice will enable you to powerfully and respectfully network *without* manipulating others.

Secret 4. Raise Your Telephone Networking Comfort.

Presenting yourself professionally, powerfully, and clearly over the telephone is a critical networking skill which must be learned by serious networkers. While we all use the phone, it is surprising how ineffective many of us are when we network. We take for granted the need to be focused and prepared, partially because the telephone is such a common convenience. Practical telephone networking strategies are identified and you have an opportunity to develop your "Verbal Resume"^{SM}, which is a two-minute commercial on your background and capabilities. This "sound bite" of your personal history enables you to effectively position yourself and quickly establish rapport with your network contact.

Secret 5. Use a Complete Networking Model and Incorporate It as Your Own.

Chapter 5 follows an actual client through the nuances of networking as he increasingly becomes more skilled and knowledgeable in networking. The three major steps to powerful networking are detailed, and you will be taught how to effectively prequalify leads that are provided to you. The complex and convoluted process of networking is simplified through an easy-to-follow model with diagrams and script.

Secret 6. Master the Four Avenues of Networking.

The four main job hunting avenues are explored with specific networking language presented to raise your comfort level. The four traditional avenues are: executive search firms/employment agencies, marketing to target organizations, personal contacts or leads, and specific employment opportunities that are in the "public domain" through advertisements.

Secret 7. Focus on Your Outcome and You'll Produce Results.

The key to success in life is having a definite purpose, backed by a definite plan and immediate action executed with unswerving belief and confidence. To succeed in networking, indeed in all aspects of your life, you have to have a goal and to realize that you are completely in charge. This chapter reveals a number of dimensions that will help you to create your career or your life anyway you want and take responsibility for the outcome. The Self-Confidence Formula^{SM} is explored in depth, and a number of worksheets and checklists are provided both to identify skill gaps and to enhance your self-confidence.

Secret 8. Effectively Conduct an Industrywide or Geography-specific Search.

The unique demands of conducting an industrywide search versus those of a local search are identified and explored. Innovative networking strategies are developed for both types of searches, and a number of resources are highlighted.

Secret 9. Write Powerful Networking Letters.

A number of highly effective sample networking letters are included in this chapter. In addition, a number of practical "how-to" tips and techniques cover issues such as meaningful content, communicating "status," announcing position acceptance, and the optimal timing for mailings.

Secret 10. Turn Around and Beat Rejection.

When you look for a job, you will experience more rejection than at any other time of your life. Every letter mailed, every call initiated, every telephone screen, every face-to-face interview, every reference check, and every psychological evaluation represents an opportunity for rejection. This chapter deals with the techniques used to turn around rejection and to gain leverage on your problems to increase your personal drive and motivation. We will address the dreaded "follow-up call" with some highly practical tips and techniques.

The Next Steps

In Part 3 you will explore specific strategies for implementing the "secrets" in Part 2 and how to use your new skills to build organizational endorsement. Sixty-one strategies for networking success are presented which, if followed, will guarantee that you will be more effective at networking. These strategies are the guiding principles that every successful networker applies and consistently follows to ensure success. The list also represents a checklist to audit your performance and evaluate where you may need some additional strengthening.

Ironically, the interpersonal skill sets you use to effectively network are the same skills you will utilize to gain, strengthen, and maintain organization endorsement, so necessary for career survival and advancement. We will explore together the issues of trust building, handling of objections, and promoting your ideas more effectively.

The Secrets Revealed

Revealed

PART 2

UNDERSTAND CAREER SEARCH CHALLENGES AND GROUND RULES FOR THE 1990S AND BEYOND

A Buyers' Market

Finding jobs, really good jobs, in the 1990s and beyond will become increasingly challenging and competitive. More qualified people will be looking for fewer opportunities and facing fewer advancement possibilities given the unabated streamlining and delayering of organizations, domestically and internationally.

The good news and bad news are that hiring organizations have become very selective regarding their selection criteria for new hires—at all levels, it seems. Exacting hiring specifications are no longer found exclusively at the executive level. Rather, companies demand the best qualified individuals with the ideal personality traits to fit their much sought-after open positions, *and* companies are not opposed to waiting for just the right person, regardless of the length of the search. The bad news is that if your qualifications are not a very close fit, you may become frustrated because you are unable to sell yourself as capable of growing into a "stretch" role to make the needed contribution. **You** know that you can do the job (and do it well!) but the company is unwilling to risk a hire from outside the industry or function. Indeed, the company may not need to hire a nonindustry person as there are a dozen equally qualified candidates with exactly the desired background.

That's the bad news. The good news is that, although highly demanding companies often discriminate in favor of industry people, you may get favorable treatment with your work history as your skill set may perfectly match another organization's employment "template."

9

The bottom line is that in the 1990s and beyond, it is a buyers' market, with companies and search firms/employment agencies as the buyers calling the shots. Whoa, wait a minute! Does this mean that it is impossible or hopeless to venture outside of your industry or function? No, not at all. It merely means that exploring alternative functions or industries will probably be considerably more challenging. That's where networking comes in. Whether you are planning to stay within your current function or industry, the personal touch through networking seems to give people an edge. Indeed, employers seem to prefer hiring individuals through personal referrals because:

- More of an individual's background seems to be revealed through personal networking, as a mutual acquaintance will have a better sense of the potential fit. This yields better decisions overall for both the job candidate and the organization.

- Networking can significantly reduce staffing costs, since retainer or contingency search fees may be avoided altogether when new employees are hired as a result of personal referrals.

- Executive positions are often filled through discreet conversations between colleagues who intuitively understand the benefits of ongoing quality networking and of being the conduit of strategic information.

Major Trends on the Horizon _____

The following are the important trends to look for in job hunting:

Trend 1   More than 76 percent of executives are looking for work while employed in their current positions, according to a recent national survey conducted by Cornell University. The economic upheaval in many industries, increasing emphasis on greater margins, the tightening up on benefits, salaries, raises, and bonuses have created a significant shift in employee loyalty. Instead of loyalty toward their employer, people have clearly become much more loyal to themselves, their families, and to their functions. The implication for employers is staggering, ultimately requiring them to be much more responsive to needs of involvement, communication, reward, and recognition.

Trend 2   There will be a large number of chronically unemployed and underemployed people. Tragically, too many people will be permanently underemployed as they either accept jobs significantly below their potential (and previous income levels) or as they bounce from one job to another looking for something stable and financially rewarding. The unemployment rate is clearly an inadequate measure of the true picture. In a recent report, in addition to the 8.8 million people officially counted as jobless, 1.2 million more were so discouraged that they have quit looking or have taken minimal part-time jobs, as that was all they could get—they are no longer counted as "unemployed." Millions more are working at dead-end jobs or jobs that never let them "get ahead" financially.

Trend 3 A large number of executives will become consultants, deliberately or through default as they do not find meaningful employment. Unfortunately, the companies who would not hire them as employees have a tendency not to hire them as consultants even though companies are interested in outsourcing product manufacturing or services, as much as possible. So, from an unemployment statistic standpoint, these executives are the forgotten "shadow labor force." They do not show up as unemployed, rather they are counted as being gainfully employed, notwithstanding that they are earning significantly less than they might have previously.

Trend 4 Approximately 30 percent of college graduates will be significantly underemployed or unemployed through the year 2005, according to a recent Department of Labor study. In addition, starting salaries for new liberal arts graduates are now 3 percent less than the same type of graduate in 1968!

Trend 5 Numerous manufacturing sectors, especially "smokestack" industries, will continue to decline, and the service sector will be responsible for the vast majority of new hires annually. Smaller firms will experience far greater sales and profit growth potential as a percentage of sales than will organizations with more than 500 employees.

Trend 6 Entrepreneurial opportunities will continue to be where true economic growth will occur in the 1990s and beyond. Start-ups, buy-outs, and equity participation will be the business activity that will increasingly occupy the focus of professionals for the foreseeable future. Women will launch new businesses at a pace 1.5 times the rate for their male counterparts. Thus many individuals who have worked only for men will now find themselves working for a woman for the first time. Accordingly, many men and women will struggle with subordinate-manager relationship dynamics never before experienced.

Trend 7 Continued economic globalization has pressured organizations to change their traditional methods of manufacturing to remain competitive. Productivity improvements, automation, cellular manufacturing, just-in-time production, *Kanban* and *Kaizen* systems, cost containment/reduction/elimination, employee communication, focused work teams, and the "learning organization" are all part of the new culture to operate more effectively and profitability.

Trend 8 Be prepared to work for an international organization with its headquarters on foreign soil. Long gone are the economic, trade, and social barriers which effectively kept off-shore companies from competing head-to-head with stateside employers. The steady shift to global organizations with "mobile corporate headquarters" have blurred the cultural lines which have previously delineated international boundaries. To that end, it is increasingly important to become interpersonally and operationally more flexible and adaptive, with the business edge going to people who are fluent in more than one language and who have some international experience.

Trend 9   Partnerships and "value-added" business relationships with vendors and customers are replacing adversarial relationships; all parties have a strong vested interest in each others' success, and everyone is willing to give up some profit to ensure longer-term stability.

Trend 10   To remain competitive, organizations are increasingly outsourcing in-house functions, with many displaced managers establishing consulting or service firms to support the company's outsourced needs. Hence, "cottage industries" are being created to meet the company's desire to lower their overhead and to pass the operating cost vulnerability off to someone else.

Trend 11   The high need for U.S. technology and goods in emerging third-world countries and the former Soviet Union will stimulate the demand for competitively priced products, goods, and services and will create a "boom" economy in certain sectors.

Trend 12   As some type of jobs "go away" forever and as our society moves toward a "full employment economy," due to zero-population growth, the increased demand for qualified and skilled employees will result in companies creating comprehensive training with more displaced people entering into retraining programs.

Trend 13   The personal dissatisfaction which many executives are experiencing with large corporations will lead to an influx of entrepreneurial start-ups as senior executives either exit or do not return to "corporate America." In addition, bright college graduates are increasingly opting for more intimate, faster-paced work environments typically not found in *Fortune* 500 organizations.

Trend 14   As larger companies cut back, streamline, and "delayer" their organization to meet profit objectives (even though they might currently be profitable), the opportunities for career advancement will be increasingly limited as dual management/technical career tracks become the norm.

Trend 15   Employee loyalty, job hopping, individual productivity and performance, employee motivation, and job satisfaction problems will plague firms to the extent that top executives continue to be keenly focused on profits and ignore their investment in human capital.

Trend 16   In a number of polls, the majority of individuals questioned thought it would be harder to find a job in the future than it was to find a job in the past. Indeed, two-thirds believed that job security has deteriorated over the past several years, notwithstanding any economic recovery.

Continued Downsizing

Many economic indicators and forecasts reflect continued company restructuring and workforce downsizing for the foreseeable future. A recent PaineWebber financial release revealed that the latest American Management Association (AMA) report projected ongoing job losses and a lack of consumer confidence. The following are some interesting insights from the surveys conducted by the AMA, the Family and Work Institute, and Time/CNN:

- Close to 50 percent of the companies surveyed nationally indicated that they were currently in the process of downsizing, with 22 percent of them planning to permanently eliminate jobs over the next 12 months.

- Almost 70 percent of these companies anticipate repeated downsizing in both white-collar and blue-collar jobs, with salaried employees being impacted at an increasing rate.

- Given this extent of reorganization, is it any wonder that almost 45 percent of the employees expressed increased fear about employment stability? Fully 54 percent feel that it will be harder to find a job in the next 12 months, and 58 percent of those surveyed know of friends who have lost jobs since the "economic recovery."

- The consensus of all the surveys was that the number of firms that actually downsized in years past were significantly greater than the amount reported. Notwithstanding poor business conditions, organizations downsized because of lowered staffing requirements as a result of productivity enhancements and automation. The result—an increasingly competitive marketplace for the unprepared job seeker.

A Personal Challenge—Getting Prepared and Mastering Networking

One of the most frequently expressed comments made that causes some people to shy away from networking is that they do not want to "ask others for jobs" nor impose upon the relationship. Certainly, your perspective on networking will be decidedly negative if you feel networking is merely contacting people and, in effect, demanding "You got a job?" If people believe that networking is a tactic of pressuring friends and relatives and acquaintances to produce job openings and leads, then their concern is quite justified. No wonder many people are reluctant to contact others because of the fear of rejection and the loss of face. Effective networking, however, is much more than "asking for a job." You network for:

- Information
- Advice
- Leads

Critical Information

If you are contemplating switching industries or even functions, you will find that you must quickly become knowledgeable in this other field to be credible in the marketplace with personal contacts, search firms, employment agencies, and hiring companies. We tell our clients who are looking for work that before each interview at the least they need to get information on the company being interviewed, its competitors, and marketplace conditions (social, economic, demographic trends) affecting this industry and this target company. Ideally, through personal discussions, annual reports, market forecasts (such as Dun & Bradstreet reports or PaineWebber financial analyses or Value Line reports), employee newsletters, product literature, online computerized library services (like InfoTrac), professional associations, industry trade magazines/releases, and newspaper/magazine articles, you can get information on the following:

- Company sales and employee size and the main businesses (domestically and internationally)
- Organization structure
- Significant issues confronting the company (its business units), its competitors and industry, such as pending litigation, expiration of significant patents, or the addition (or departure) of key executives
- Senior executives' backgrounds, operating styles, and results achieved and the corporate culture, mission, values, and major "drivers" of the business
- Significant current or potential products, market trends, or emerging technologies
- Recent or planned acquisitions, mergers, divestitures, expansion, re-engineering or restructuring
- Factors that contribute to success (or inhibit success) in this company, in its competitors, or in this industry

Format for Collecting Target Organization Data

You need to get in the habit of collecting some basic information on each of the organizations you "target" as a potential employer. Having this data will help you be more knowledgeable in your conversations with key people. The following is a format which will enable you to collect valuable company information.

```
Company Name
Address
City                          State        Zip Code
Telephone (    ) _____   FAX (    ) _____
Key Executive Name                         Title
Key Executive Name                         Title
Key Executive Name                         Title
Products/Industry
Annual Sales
Significant Co. Challenges
```

Questions You Might Ask a Prequalified Target Organization Contact

In the process of collecting pertinent company background information, you might identify a key figure in your targeted company or industry and initiate a contact. To this key executive, you may indicate that you are in the process of exploring alternative career fields and you'd like an opportunity to discuss the executive's function, the company, and the industry.

Prior to visiting with an informed contact you should be prepared to answer (and ask) a series of questions related to alternative career paths. Keep in mind that you should ask the questions which follow only *after* these executives have agreed to help you explore your career options. It would be highly presumptuous of you to begin to ask many of these questions without having first legitimized it with the other person.

1. What has been your career path? Please briefly describe your work history.

2. What skills are required to effectively perform in this role or industry?

3. What are the **positive** aspects of this job? Function? Industry?

4. What are the **negative** aspects of this job? Function? Industry?

5. What skills, abilities, and contacts **should one have** to succeed in this role?

6. What skills, abilities, or contacts do you think **I lack?**

7. To be fully equipped to function in this role, what is required?

8. Who do you know who is already successful in this ideal role?

9. What specific actions have they taken to be successful?

10. How would I establish credibility for this role, given my background?

11. How much of a market is there for your goods and services? How would you describe your competition, and to what extent will you be able to capture business?

12. Who else might you recommend I contact, as an expert in this area, who might share his or her perspective?

Questions That May Be Asked of You by Your Network Contacts

Here are 15 critical questions you ought to carefully answer and share your responses with your family or relationship partners when preparing yourself to enter a career search involving a shift in your career field. Your network support person and organizational contacts may also ask you some of these questions, so be prepared.

1. With few or no limitations placed upon you, what are your ideal career dreams?
2. What are you willing to do to be successful? By when?
3. How does one know when he or she has acquired the necessary skills for this job?
4. What appeals to you when you see yourself in this role?
5. What are the real drivers and motivators behind your wanting to do this?
6. What do you **gain** by pursuing this dream?
7. What do you **lose** by pursuing this dream?
8. What do you **gain** by **not** pursuing this dream?
9. What do you **lose** by **not** pursuing this dream?
10. As you pursue this career option, how might you support you and your family financially if you had to take a significant cut in pay? How would you feel about that?
11. If you were someone else, would you invest in you? Why? Why not?
12. Are you truly enough of an expert with your current skills to be successful in the role that you are asking me about? Why?
13. How will you create a sufficient distinction for you to succeed in this new role?
14. Given that you are going to shift careers, how will you earn enough to support you (and your family) in both the short term and long term?
15. How extensively are you prepared to risk your worldly possessions in pursuit of this?

Key Advice

Advice seeking from networking contacts is really more **strategic** than information gathering. Seeking advice presumes that you are beyond the initial exploration of alternative career options and have considered all the questions about your desired change, such as those on the preceding pages.

You are now at the point in which you are fully prepared to ask for valuable insights and opinions about your specific proposed plan from others more experienced. Securing advice is a somewhat intimate process, as you are engaging your contacts at a deeper level by asking them to understand what you are currently doing right as well as those areas you might improve.

By way of example, we have the privilege of working with an extremely talented board of directors which acts as our advisory group at Robertson Lowstuter, Inc. The board is our sounding board, and our meetings represent a forum in which we can safely present our strategies and concerns. Fundamentally, our advisors (our advice givers) help us maintain our perspective by performing "reality checks" on our plans. Our meetings are always stimulating, and sometimes uncomfortable, as our respected colleagues challenge our preconceived ideas, offer alternative thinking, and help us to safely explore options we might not have considered without a little prodding on their part. **No matter who you are, how knowledgeable you are, or how skilled you are, you can benefit from some form of advice, counsel, or coaching.** Even world class athletes have coaches, trainers, and assistants who help them operate at a peak performance level, so don't feel that you are immune to the value of advice and counsel from others. Asking someone's opinion may be the best thing you could do for yourself—if you genuinely want honest feedback. It is very easy for us to become defensive when we are provided straightforward feedback. This is understandable. We all want others to think well of us. We get very good at defending our views or showing how we really are capable and in full command of everything. Relax. Everyone knows that you (and we) are not perfect. It's really not all that important to look good all the time at the risk of not getting genuine feedback. When we respond positively to criticism, great! We have significantly improved the probability of enhancing our outcome. If on the other hand, we respond to feedback with justifying or defensive statements, it looks as though all we really wanted is confirmation of how good our plan is. We run the risk of appearing as if we really do not want to change it. So, before you crank up the creative juices of your friends after asking them for input, be absolutely clear about what you want. Do you want an emotional stroke? Fine. Then enthusiastically *inform* people what you are doing, rather than asking for input. However, if you are truly interested in their feedback, then be prepared for some constructive criticism, indeed, push for it if all you get is that emotional stroke. Although it's great when people tell you how marvelous you are and how wonderful your plans are, it brings very little clarity to your strategies. Changing careers is a serious step with far-reaching consequences. It deserves your honest and open seeking of the best advice and counsel you can gather. The hurt of some immediate constructive criticism is nowhere equal to the pain of making a long-term mistake in the planning and execution of your career direction.

Leads You Want to Secure

The third dimension of networking is securing leads from your contacts into search firms, target organizations, and personal friends or business colleagues. Generating leads requires much more networking skill than getting information or securing advice. In this dimension of networking, you are asking—in effect—for your colleagues to share more of themselves, to be more at risk, to be vulnerable, if you will. By asking your contacts to provide leads, you are asking them to entrust in your care the relationships they have with others. Your contacts are trusting you not to violate those relationships, not to embarrass them or to be inappropriate. You may not have thought about it this way, but providing names to you is truly a leap of faith on their part. Is it any wonder that some people are reluctant to share? If you do encounter some resistance or reluctance, rather than being judgmental or quitting too soon, ask yourself:

- "How am I perceived by this person?"
- "To what extent am I seen as powerful, resourceful, effective, and appropriate?"
- "If the other person's perception of me is less than favorable (how could that even be???), how can I, then, earn the trust necessary to secure the leads I want, given that I know this person is well connected?"
- "What do I need to start doing? What do I need to stop doing? What should I continue to do to reinforce for this person that I will be a responsible guardian of her or his leads?"

With the flood of careering books on the market and the outplacement support extended by employers or other support groups, such as churches, synagogues, or community centers, people are becoming better prepared to look for work than ever before. The challenge, therefore, is how to distinguish yourself from others vying for the same opportunity. To that end, you need to be increasingly sophisticated (though not overly smooth or glib) in a broad repertoire of job-hunting skills, especially networking.

In Search of the Perfect Employer: Job Sources _____

You never know how, when, or where the perfect career connection will be made. Although there are many nuances to finding a job and leads seem to ricochet all over the place, the four traditional avenues for finding a job are as follows (entrepreneuring is the fifth nontraditional job-hunting method):

- Entrepreneuring
- Advertisements
- Search firms/employment agencies
- Target marketing to organizations
- Personal networking

If you are interested in developing an effective job-hunting strategy, which includes exploring each of these avenues in depth, then we suggest that you pick up our book, *In Search of the Perfect Job*. Recently published by McGraw-Hill, this book has been receiving high marks from seasoned executives to recent college graduates as the most complete, credible, easily understood careering "guidebook" in the market. It has become an authoritative resource in the careering field, and we are confident that you, too, will appreciate its practicality.

Proven Ways to Get Connected

Responding to ads or getting connected through search firms involve what we call the "visible job market," in that opportunities are known to exist; they are "visible." The "hidden job market" deals in the realm of possibilities and potential—not certainty, as in a bonafide job opening. Such career opportunities are "hidden" and are uncovered through the avenues of personal networking or marketing yourself directly to selected target organizations. To conduct a well-rounded effective career search, you must become intimately familiar with the various strategies outlined in *In Search of the Perfect Job* for approaching both the visible and the hidden job markets.

The Hidden Job Market

While all the four traditional career search avenues are important, we feel that personal networking is by far the most important strategy for you to master. Although open positions in the visible job market are theoretically known to everyone, you will invariably find yourself in very stiff competition for a desired job. Career opportunities in the hidden job market, however, will not be as widely known and will emerge largely out of your own efforts. To that end, you will not experience the same level of competition. You uncover these career possibilities for your own job search by diligently networking with your personal contacts or by identifying specific target organizations.

Interestingly, more than 70 percent of all jobs are found through the efforts in the hidden market. Ironically, most people spend the majority of their job-hunting time in less effective activities such as responding to ads and writing "cold call" letters to companies. Often job seekers have no intention of personalizing the contact with a follow-up phone call or personal visit. "Why is that?" you ask. Excellent question. Conducting a campaign in the hidden job market is much more difficult and requires more persistence—not more skill or talent. Well, perhaps a little more self-marketing skills. Certainly, personal networking requires more guts and personal commitment than does merely responding to ads.

Another reason that people spend so much time, effort, and energy in the visible market is because of a genuine misconception that most jobs are filled by locating and responding to declared or advertised job openings. There is strong support for this misconception. We frequently are asked by well-placed executives, when asking about our outplacement support, how many actual job leads we would create for them. Although we do a lot to help focus job leads, we are always amazed at how strongly entrenched is the belief that most jobs are filled by a well-planned job-requisitioning process that funnels people through successive hurdles of advertised openings or search firm efforts. That's how the majority of people both look for and connect in their new jobs. We have a different approach. A recent review of our Robertson Lowstuter outplacement candidates who were participating in our executive programs revealed the following:

- Eighty-seven percent were hired into jobs which did not actually exist as recognized openings when they contacted the organization for the first time.
- The majority of the people got their jobs well within four months after beginning their search.
- Ninety percent secured positions at the same or better compensation packages than those had in their previous position.

Perhaps you may not be able to achieve this kind of track record in your search, but we are confident that you can significantly improve your job-hunting skills. To produce these results, you may have to reexamine (and get beyond) the traditional corporate thinking which does not recognize the extent to which good jobs are often filled through more informal network channels which "prequalify" you for previously unknown opportunities.

Your goal is to effectively balance your efforts in both the hidden job market and the visible job market.

Career Search—by Level, by Avenue

Many people ask us what is the expected probability of success by organization level for the various career search avenues (personal networking, search firms, target organizations, and advertisements). Although **all** avenues work and should be utilized, the following reflects our experience of people getting connected:

Type of Job	Personal Networking	Target Organizations*	Search Firms	Advertise-ments
Executive	Very high	High	Moderately high	Low
Managerial	High	Moderately high	Moderate	Moderately low
Professional-technical	High	Moderate	Moderately high	High
Administrative-secretarial	Moderately high	Low	Moderate†	High

* Includes both target marketing to organizations and mailings to selected companies. The yield for direct mailings to organizations is exceedingly low, less than 5 percent.

† Although only a moderate number of administrative-secretarial positions are filled through employment agencies, a *moderately high* percentage of these positions are filled as a result of offers being extended through **temporary help agencies,** with the agency charging a fee.

MANAGE YOUR BELIEFS AND BEHAVIOR THAT GUARANTEE NETWORKING SUCCESS

Whether You Believe You Can or You Can't, You're Right! _____

The extent to which you have beliefs which enhance your ability to network, that's the extent to which you will be able to effectively network. Pretty profound isn't it? Most universal truths are simple. Your brain is a truly remarkable instrument, as it will respond directly to the programming you provide it. Indeed, your brain does not distinguish between the positive, empowering images or the negative, self-limiting images you provide. Ironically, it takes as much energy to believe negative thoughts as it does affirming ones. So why do we have a tendency to believe that our capabilities are limited versus limitless? Why do we sabotage our best intentions, efforts, and desires? Good questions. People who limit themselves do not deem themselves capable or worthy of success. They sabotage their efforts and they have "belief tapes" which they unconsciously play when confronting a challenging or risky venture. These self-defeating beliefs tend to be **core beliefs** and create the context in which the difficult is truly impossible and fear is a common emotion. Examples of negative core beliefs might be that a person thinks he or she is stupid or fat or clumsy or ugly or klutzy or unattractive or weak or poor or fearful or a failure. Positive core beliefs might include beliefs that a person is strong, athletic, handsome or beautiful, effective, resourceful, innovative, bold, assertive, wealthy, credible, bright, articulate, confident, or capable of accomplishing anything.

Core beliefs are different from opinions, though they may seem very similar. Most of us are able to change our opinions when we encounter sound logic that is irrefutable though different from our previously held positions. However, we unknowingly operate as if our core beliefs are inviolate and unchanging. It's almost as if these core beliefs are some kind of universal truth, like the force of gravity, unchanging and unyielding, and you can't do anything about them. Yet, where did our core beliefs come from? They were formulated very early in our childhood from the countless reinforcements which we received from our parents, older siblings, relatives, teachers, and playmates and the daily input we receive from others. As you know from first-hand experience, whether the reinforcements were negative or positive, your personality was influenced and shaped by these interactions. So, inasmuch as these core beliefs were **learned,** they can be unlearned or replaced by new beliefs which are more supportive and congruent with what you want for yourself. You **can** decide what core beliefs you operate with—you're not "locked in" to always running with the same beliefs if you want to change. Remarkable!

Fred—a Diamond in the Rough

Let us give you an example of what we mean by how firmly our core beliefs hold us in their grip. The other day we had lunch with an old friend, Fred Jones. He was vigorously complaining about what a jerk his boss was. (Fred contends he was merely reporting and observing, but he was really complaining.) His boss was new to the company, and the boss and Fred got into a heated argument the very first day they met. Fred's new boss made the "near fatal" mistake of telling Fred, a long service employee of 25 years, what he expected from Fred now that Fred worked for him. We were sure that it was pretty intense, as Fred knows his stuff and gets quite emotional when he is confronted or if he thinks he is being taken advantage of or depreciated. The term *detonate* pretty well captures how it must have been. We could almost see the scene at lunch as Fred punched the air with his fist and jabbed his finger in our faces as the air around us in the restaurant embarrassingly turned blue with Fred's loud and colorful expletives. In the retelling, Fred was both angry (at his obviously short-sighted boss) and delighted (at how he intimidated this new executive and put him in his place). After we had allowed the emotional storm to blow past, we pointed out that there might be some benefit from a more moderate approach to his boss, one that might even be thought of as reflective or accommodating. To Fred, however, operating flexibly was for ". . . spineless, gutless, round-heeled, do-nothing bureaucratic, pencil-pushers! It's a good thing he leaves me alone so that I'm able to do my job for the company! Besides, I can't change. I've always been this way and I'm too old to change at this point, even if I wanted to!" Inhaling deeply, we gently tried to point out an alternative approach to operating, one that might appeal to Fred's sense of fair play, justice, and company loyalty. Unfortunately, Fred "Yes, but!" all the way through our attempts to illustrate that his behavior was directly related to his beliefs and image he has of himself and that it really wasn't working as well as he thought. He conceded that he could change his behavior instantly if he wanted. "But," he said with a wink and a grin, "I enjoy being a scrapper. That's my reputation. That's who I am. If I change, then what am I known as? Being a bit unpredictable and scary is fun; people don't mess with me. As long as I don't get fired, I'll be OK. After all, I'm a 'be.' " "What's that?" we asked. Fred laughed. "I **be** here before you and I'll **be** here after you. I'll survive and I'm not changing to suit this guy. Maybe I'd change for someone else I respect—who respects me first—at some other time, though not for this person."

Even after Fred acknowledged that he knew that he could shape his behavioral response and life any way he chose, he continued to operate as if on automatic: You got in his face, he ate you for lunch! We fully understood Fred's delight in how he defined his "persona," and we had absolutely no illusions about our ability to change him at lunch. Why? Simply put, we had no leverage. There was not enough "attention-getting pain" in his life to get him to pause and commit to shifting his behavior. No pain, no gain—on change. Fred, as yet, had no reason to change. He didn't see how his behavior had cost him promotion after promotion, in spite of his superior technical know-how. He didn't link up being difficult with the small annual raise he got, which over the years had cost him tens of thousands of dollars, even though he had made major financial contributions to his company. He really didn't understand why he was by-passed for key task forces and committees and why so many younger, less experienced people were constantly being moved up around him. Fred just didn't "get it." So why should he consider changing his beliefs? It would take a major job loss before Fred finally woke up.

Creating What You Want _____

Why do some people have greater "luck" in their lives than do others? Is it simply being at the right place at the right time? Does opportunity really "knock," or does it merely lie there waiting for someone to recognize it as something more than a problem?

The meaning which you choose at such times is a direct result of your "personal enabling" or "self-defeating" beliefs. It is important to pay attention to these beliefs and to change them when they are detracting from your ability to react creatively and positively to situations. Several good questions which you may wish to ask yourself are, "Is my life working the way I'd like it to right now? To what extent am I able to get my needs met? To what extent am I frustrated in my attempts to persuade others or work comfortably and smoothly with others?" If your life isn't as full as you'd like it to be, you may be a candidate for change of some limiting beliefs.

It isn't necessary to hold onto limiting beliefs. You have at your command a whole range of powerful, enabling beliefs. If you have read our book, *In Search of the Perfect Job,* you may recall that Clyde told his story of how he dramatically "expanded his career options" and created leaving his company in a similar kind of situation as Fred probably will experience unless he changes. In Clyde's words,

> . . . *so in effect, I got exactly what I had created in the relationship; I wrote the script and my boss played out his role. I'm convinced that he did not see me endorsing him, so why should he endorse me. . . . Once I pushed through all the blame, I realized that there was much more personal power in my accepting complete responsibility for how my career and life looked, rather than rationalizing my termination by assessing fault. The "context" of fault requires that someone be wrong, that blame be levied, and that roles of victim and persecutor be assigned. I didn't want to blame anyone anymore.*

Clyde transformed a disabling belief into a new, empowering belief. Clyde simply recognized that his boss was "one of the good guys." To be sure, each had a different perspective as to how the department ought to function. This, of course, led to their split. But now, Clyde experienced the split as "no fault." There was no persecutor, so there was no victim. Now Clyde could handle the inevitable change powerfully and constructively.

Taking Control and Responsibility for Your Life

In the context of assuming complete responsibility for how your life looks and shaping your own destiny, we want to present a metaphor. Let's say you were involved in an automobile accident in which the other (unfortunately, uninsured) driver was clearly at fault. Your car was totalled and you were injured. With regard to your feelings, you could justifiably have a multitude of choices. You can feel incredibly angry (or sad) at the injustice of the situation or you can take the position that this unfortunate situation was merely an accident and there should be no emotion attached to it. After all, you "chose" to be driving your car on this particular road, at a given speed, at a given hour, which put you in the precise spot to be clobbered by another vehicle. Had **you** been driving just a little bit slower or a little faster or taken a different road, **you** could have avoided the collision all together. Nonetheless, **you** made a number of choices, albeit unconsciously, to be at that intersection at a most unpleasant time. Hence, the crash. Clearly, in the "legal context," the other driver was at fault. However, in the "responsibility context," you can, if you wish, choose to be responsible for you being in the intersection. One reason that you might elect to make this choice is that at the precise moment you choose to be responsible, you suddenly are able to be fully responsible for and in control of the emotions you have surrounding the event. It's true, you do not have to choose the responsibility option. For example, you can choose the "blame" option. You can blame yourself for not driving a different route or a different car, you can be angry at the other driver and blame that person for being both uninsured and for running the red light. You can blame your boss for giving you a lukewarm performance review which distracted you from your concentration, you could be furious at your spouse for the starting an argument at breakfast to which you were formulating a rebuttal when—WHAAAMMM!!!—out of nowhere the other car plowed into the side of your vehicle. These are all possible choices. Neither one is right. Neither one is wrong. Simply notice that when you elect to be victim and select the anger and blame option you continue to experience the pain of these emotions and the disruption to your life. When you simply select to be responsible for the way things are—for no other reason than you just choose to see things that way—you gain control and balance and begin to powerfully move forward again. The point is that you have a choice in our auto accident metaphor. You can **fixate blame** and be emotional toward the other driver or you can **assume responsibility** for this and move on unemotionally and unblaming.

You can apply this model to virtually every aspect of your life. By being aware of your choices and your ability to quickly assume control over your life and emotions, you have a substantial advantage in how you respond to life's inevitable challenges. In your job search, this advantage becomes a major competitive edge over other competitive job seekers in winning the perfect job.

The extent to which you are "sleepwalking" through life, not fully conscious of your emotions and choices, is the extent to which you have unknowingly placed limits on yourself and your ability to network powerfully and effectively. For our friend, Fred, since he chooses to limit his repertoire of interpersonal skills with a whole barrage of excuses, he will continue to be a victim. He will forever be upset "because of" some event, some person, or some circumstance. Unfortunately, Fred has unknowingly limited his ability to interact effectively with diverse personalities and challenges. He has clearly undermined his promotability, job security, and economic welfare by limiting his ability to influence others and contribute to the organization. What a waste of talent, expertise, and passion! To assess the extent to which you feel you're in control, please turn to Worksheet 1.

Again, there are no right or wrong choices—only ramifications. If you find that you are able to contribute fully, be as innovative as you'd like, and have the unqualified support from your colleagues, then you must be making the right choices for you. If you are experiencing discord in your personal or professional life and are not able to fully utilize your skills or produce the results you desire, you may be unconsciously making disempowering choices and not assuming responsibility for how your career and life look. If you are interested in operating differently, you may wish to ask others whom you respect for feedback on how they see you and ask for their help by having them point out dysfunctional behavior when it occurs. Please turn to Worksheet 2 for additional insights.

If the intensity you once felt *and* the enthusiasm you once exhibited about people, programs, projects, or things is consistently less than before, then we contend that you have already made the decision to withdraw or disengage from being 100 percent committed at your workplace. Although it may be time to move on, you might still have an option. **Another strategy would be to acknowledge your insights to your boss and commit to turn the job and your attitude around.** This might very well be the maturing opportunity your boss has been hoping for as you express your willingness to operate more flexibly and responsibly. The point is that this is a choice over which you have a great deal of control if you are aware of what is going on and make the choices consciously.

At some conscious or subconscious level, you "manage" your job and the people around you the way you want. If you are unaware of your choices or choose not to be responsible for what you do and say, in retrospect, a decline may appear like career sabotage in the inevitable way in which it resulted in you being criticized or even terminated. By the way, if you have always known of your choices but are now just beginning to deal with them, welcome to where the rest of us are; grudgingly accepting that we both represent the problem and also the solution. Depending upon the meaning you attach to this revelation, you might be bummed out that you might have to change (which includes no more blaming) or really excited by the prospect of regaining control over your life and the relationships in it.

Gaining Insights through the Questions You Ask

The quality of your life and how you manage it will depend upon the quality of the insights you have and the commitment which you have or are will-

WORKSHEET 1
You Create Where You Are!

To examine the extent to which you are in control and managing your life the way you'd like, please complete these questions candidly. Work quickly and spontaneously. Your first response is usually your best response. Use this exercise to reaffirm that you are, indeed, in control of your emotions, your career, and your life.

Check one response for each of the following questions.

1. When you lose an argument with your boss, do you
   a. Criticize the boss.
   b. Get upset and hold a grudge.
   c. Get upset, then lighten up later.
   d. Immediately compromise and move on.

2. When you get a raise considerably less than you feel you deserve, do you
   a. Assume that you lost out because you did not "kiss up."
   b. Go in and complain, vowing to get even.
   c. Complain and then try harder on the job.
   d. Go in and gain clarity on your next performance goals with your boss.

3. When you are very unhappy with circumstances surrounding your job, do you
   a. Isolate yourself, feeling hurt while subtly letting people know of your upset.
   b. Act out your upset and attack others.
   c. Initially act out your upset, then try to work things out.
   d. Begin an initiative to reestablish your credibility or begin a well-organized plan to leave your organization.

4. When you are criticized by someone, will you most likely
   a. Attack back, citing examples from the past when the other person was wrong.
   b. Become emotional, not fully accepting the validity of the criticism.
   c. Become emotional and then later work to understand the criticism.
   d. Welcome it as a learning opportunity and solicit more.

5. When a colleague's behavior is very different from your own, do you
   a. Avoid him all together and make demeaning remarks about him.

(Continued)

b. Minimize your dealings with her while keeping your comments to yourself.

c. Slowly accept his behavioral quirks over time and learn to live with them.

d. Immediately seek to understand more fully what her motivations are.

6. When you are not as innovative or as productive as you would like, do you

a. Blame others' interference and cite other circumstances which affirm this.

b. Voice what needs to be done but do not take action as it's useless to try.

c. Have a ready excuse about your situation and begin to work to resolve it.

d. Assume complete responsibility and immediately act for a turnaround.

Interpreting Your Responses.

Worksheet 1 is not meant to be a scientific measure of the extent to which you assume responsibility for your life and choose disabling or enabling options. Rather, this exercise is designed as an opportunity for you to learn how you may be functioning and give you the option of choosing what outcome you want to create. The key to the exercise is as follows:

a responses   These responses are blame-oriented with the behavior strongly vested in maintaining the status quo. People who live their lives in blame will tend to find themselves upset quite often as they are unwilling to be flexible and adaptive to the trials and tribulations of everyday living.

b responses   These responses represent destructive blame in that the behavior and the emotion seem to be directed at "getting even." Individuals who are engaged in destructive blame expend quite a bit of energy fanning the fires of discontent (theirs and others) with their inflammatory rhetoric and actions which undermine positive action. There are no discernable positive empowering behavior choices, only disempowering and disabling choices.

c responses   These responses reflect behavior in which positive, empowering choices are made, but they may be made too slowly for a smooth recovery and for an effective operating style. Individuals who get upset, complain, and resist change initially then slowly modify their behavior may be

(Continued)

unknowingly inhibiting their careers. Certainly, they run the risk of being seen as persons who may not be approachable and are possibly difficult to deal with.

d responses These responses reflect beliefs and behavior in which people assume responsibility for their lives and consciously choose empowering and enabling options. These choices are usually made quickly by people who have very strong biases toward action, problem resolution, and helping people meet their needs.

WORKSHEET 2
How Close Are You to Changing Jobs?

This worksheet will help you look at the factors which we feel generally precede a job change. By not being aware of them, it is possible to subconsciously think and act in a way which has career-threatening ramifications. Your unconscious behavior can lead to involuntary separation often without you being aware of all the interactions going on.

To help you see if there are some career circumstances occurring which could cause you to abruptly change careers unless immediately addressed, please answer the following questions. If you have been involuntarily separated, please consider these questions in the past tense.

Yes   No

_____ _____ **1.** Are you as happy as you would like to be on the job?

_____ _____ **2.** Are you as productive as you know you could be?

_____ _____ **3.** Are you as creative as you know you have been previously?

_____ _____ **4.** Is your advice sought after as much as it once was?

_____ _____ **5.** Do you get along with your boss as well as you would like?

_____ _____ **6.** Do you trust and respect your boss?

_____ _____ **7.** Have you updated your résumé or thought that perhaps you should?

_____ _____ **8.** Have you ever thought about what it would be like to be employed somewhere else?

_____ _____ **9.** If you could conduct a very discreet search without anyone finding out, would you do so?

_____ _____ **10.** If you had access to a foolproof game plan for successful job changing, would you be interested in it, so that you might make a change without pain or hassle?

(Continued)

Scoring the Worksheet.

If you answered *no* to two or more of the questions from 1 to 6 or *yes* to two or more of the questions from 7 to 10, then chances are very good that you have already left your organization—psychologically and emotionally, that is. A series of beliefs and behavior which you have associated with separation and loss of relationship are already actively at work in your daily interpersonal relations and business dealings. You may be physically still in residence at your company, but your heart and mind are probably somewhere else. Because of this, your commitment to turn the situation around or complete the project or reestablish the relationship with your boss may seem less important than it once did. What is worse is that as time progresses others will increasingly see your shift in commitment. As this happens, the unanticipated "departure process" accelerates and becomes less and less recoverable.

ing to make to change that which isn't working. If you are willing to consistently take action and follow through on your goals, then your life will probably be more closely aligned with your dreams than if you never seem to get around to changing.

As we have mentioned before, your brain is a remarkable computer that not only has a tremendous capacity to store and retrieve data but also can provide sound solutions to your most puzzling issues, provided you ask good questions. You need to learn how to ask empowering questions if you:

- Have chronic problems
- Are unable to stick with a commitment
- Always seem to have bad things happen to you
- Often experience an emotional "roller coaster"
- Are not achieving the results you know you have the capability of producing

Here's a great way to look at how you phrase questions or state affirmations to yourself about situations which trouble you. You may ask yourself, "What is the difference between poor questions and affirmations and good ones?" By "good" questions or affirmations we mean those questions or statements which stimulate you into action, provide a sense of well-being, are uplifting and positively reinforce the best you have to offer. By poor questions or affirmations we refer to those questions or statements which tend to undermine your self-image, depreciate your personality, and keep you stuck. Interestingly, if you ask poor questions or make poor affirmations to yourself you will get poor answers which will not promote a powerful and effective you. Indeed, poor questions or statements will promote you being "stuck."

Examples of poor questions or affirmations are:

- "I'm no good at managing my boss."
- "I just can't talk to _____ (groups or top executives)."
- "I can't successfully promote myself or network on the phone. It's way too uncomfortable."

See Worksheet 3 for examples of self-defeating affirmations.

Why is knowing these questions important and what is the impact of them? What's the big deal? How can simple questions influence how you operate? Valid questions, as those seemingly innocent questions in Worksheet 3, hardly seem worth any trouble or fuss.

WORKSHEET 3
Self-Defeating Questions and Affirmations

The following are further examples of poor questions and of affirmations which are negative, reinforce a poor self-image, and perpetuate your being stuck:

- "Why can't I do _____?"
- "I just can't _____."
- "Why am I always doing _____?"
- "No matter how hard I try, I'm always _____!"
- "I'll never be _____."
- "I'm no good at _____."
- "I can never learn _____."
- "Only _____ can do this."
- "_____ always makes me too uncomfortable."
- "I don't deserve _____ because of _____."
- "When will I ever be able to _____?"

Please write in some of your favorite self-defeating or self-limiting questions. You know—the ones that you use that reinforce you being stuck. The ones you use whenever someone challenges you to stretch and grow in your personal and professional life. You know them. Chances are they are "old friends" which have been limiting you and your potential for a long, long time. Let's list them now so that once and for all you can "blast" them out of your way and power up your career to reach your full potential.

- _____
- _____
- _____
- _____
- _____
- _____

The big deal is that they control your life much more than most of us realize. Your self-defeating beliefs restrict you in ways in which you would never tolerate restriction by another person. They limit you in all aspects of your life, your relationships, and your career, inhibiting your contributions and your income and promotions.

If you ask yourself a negative question as you try to address an important issue for yourself, you will invariably experience the very behavior or condition you are trying to avoid. How is that? If asked a question your brain will supply an answer, regardless of whether it is real or fantasy. To illustrate this dynamic, let's move on.

A Proven Weight Loss Method: A Metaphor

Let's say for example, that you are overweight and you ask the question, "Why can't I lose weight and be beautiful?" Your brain will immediately respond as directed and will begin to provide all the possible reasons that it is impossible for you to lose weight. The result is further proof that you are out of control in your cating and exercise strategy and you can do nothing about it! Your brain willingly accommodates the negative inquiry by responding:

> **You're overweight because you are slothful; you eat too much; you don't exercise; you have no willpower; you have fat cells, it's genetic—your whole family is big; you have a condition known as "over-active knife and fork." You are pleasantly plump and have big bones—you're not fat. You are never going to lose weight—you've tried before and you only gain more back. Like some people are tall, some people are fat—you're fat. Learn to live with it, besides—you like to stuff yourself, so you must like being overweight.**

Whoa! Talk about your mind running away from you and "taking no prisoners"! Since most overweight people have associated eating with some meaning of feeling good, if their brain provides answers which makes them feel bad, they will have a tendency to immediately overeat to feel good about themselves again. Unfortunately, after gorging themselves, it is not uncommon for these same people to ask another poor question. They lament, "Why do I do this to myself?" At this point, what does the brain do? Right! It dutifully kicks in another set of responses which further reinforce that this person will never lose weight, short of a miracle. Actually, the miracle is a better set of questions. If you want to shed a few pounds, instead of asking negative questions, try asking yourself questions which have a high probability of yielding positive, affirming, and motivating feelings. For instance . . .

Ask the question, "**What are the good things which I can do right now which will help me to lose weight and enjoy the process?**" Can you feel the difference? To this new question, the brain rushes to establish a completely different context, one which is empowering, affirming, and action-oriented. The brain says, "Here's what you can do!"

Make an appointment with your physician for a complete physical, join the health club, go on those early morning walks with your neighbor, study up on the impact of high-fat foods and throw out all junk foods, make a long list of your strengths, do not dwell on your weaknesses—rather commit to constant improvements and positive changes, listen to super upbeat music when you exercise, commit to exercising (no matter how little) every day, do not beat yourself up for being out of shape, pat yourself on the back for any forward progress, identify a stretch goal for yourself, and associate a positive reward for yourself.

See the huge difference the quality of the question makes? Note the positive affirmations which seem to flow effortlessly from such a "good" question. It's actually a bit mind-boggling the different perspective you get when you ask an empowering question versus a disempowering question. By the way, do you know how you can tell if your questions are positive or negative? It's easy and simple. **If a given question makes you feel good, stronger, and more capable, then it is probably a positive one.** However, if a question is demotivating, undermines your relationships with others, makes you feel smaller, weaker, less capable, or more hesitant—chances are that you are engaging in negative questioning. Indeed, you may not even be aware that you have been asking yourself questions, all you are experiencing is the result of feeling uplifted or feeling discouraged.

If you are feeling positive, powerful, and happy ask yourself: "**What can I do to reinforce and enhance this positive feeling?**" As your brain gives you an answer, write it down, commit to acting on it, and do it! If you are frustrated or discouraged ask: "**What can I do right now to feel good about this, turn it around, and enjoy the process?**" Write down the ideas your mind provides and act on them as soon as practical. Complete Worksheets 4 and 5 to enhance your positive affirmations.

We have only listed several self-defeating questions in Worksheet 3, but we know you have your own which we want you to list. Why? Once you are aware of the negative questions you ask yourself, you will function more powerfully and achieve the results you want. Knowing these questions will help you get a handle on how, when, and why you become disempowered and sabotage your best efforts and intentions.

WORKSHEET 4
Positive, Affirming Questions

If you ask positive-yielding questions, you will become more powerful and effective, regardless of who you are, your job, your education, your organizational level, or how much money you make.

In the space provided below, identify a problem that you'd like to solve:

_____

_____

_____

Address your problem and create constructive action by answering the following positive, affirming questions:

1. "What might be a logical, nonemotional reason for this problem or condition?"
2. "What are 10 positive things I can do right now?"
3. "What are 5 positive things I can do in the future to prevent this from happening?"
4. "What am I grateful for in my life?"
5. "How can I begin to take control over my career, relationships, life today?"
6. "What good can come out of this?"
7. "What positive things have I learned as a result of this experience?"
8. "Who has done what I want to accomplish and how might I learn from them?"
9. "What am I willing to do to achieve my desired goal?"

WORKSHEET 5
Identify Your Own Positive Affirmations or Questions

We know that you have a number of positive affirmations that reinforce your efforts and keep you focused on your outcome and keep you going. Below is a list of positive affirmations or questions which you may find helpful in developing your own list.

- I relate well to all kinds of people all the time.
- What can I do to create a higher more positive profile in my company?
- I am capable of achieving anything to the extent I am committed to it.
- I can learn something positive from every experience.
- How might I create richer, more abundant relationships with people?
- I am able to earn and save as much money as I want.
- How can I get in shape and enjoy the process?
- I am well-liked, respected, and have many people who support me

Get the idea? Now it's your turn. In the space provided below, **write down as many of your positive affirmations or questions which make you feel strong, confident, and effective.** Work quickly; your first response is probably your best response. Don't worry about the order or how they sound; just get them down.

- _____
- _____
- _____
- _____
- _____
- _____
- _____
- _____
- _____
- _____
- _____
- _____

Beliefs That Empower You and Your Networking Efforts _____

Consider the questions we ask or the affirmations we make about the way we operate as road signs depicting an event, like children playing. We don't actually see children playing, rather the sign represents children playing so we are alerted to the possible presence of kids and are cautioned about careless driving. Similarly, our questions or statements can be considered to be the tip of an iceberg, which conceal a **belief** below the water line of our consciousness. **Questions, like road signs, alert us to a belief, attitude, or feeling which directly influences how we behave.**

Unfortunately, many of us carry around a lot of excess baggage, in the form of dysfunctional ideas, which holds us back and keeps us from operating as fully as we might otherwise. We call these thoughts "disempowering beliefs."

Disempowering beliefs erode our confidence and inhibit us from fully tapping into our potential, let alone asking good questions. A disempowering belief is any thought or condition you believe to be true which limits you, makes you feel less whole or less powerful. In this next exercise, you will have the opportunity to identify those disempowering or negative beliefs and the cost to you, in general and specifically regarding networking.

Empowering beliefs are invigorating and vibrant, stimulate us into action, and help us expand beyond our immediate situation. Have you ever felt really alive, excited, and in touch with people and the world around you? In that moment, when your confidence was high—be it an instant, a day, or a week—things really seemed to come together well. In those times, you believed that you could accomplish just about anything you focused on, if you wanted it badly enough. Those feelings and beliefs which allowed you to stretch and achieve beyond what even you thought possible are your empowering beliefs. Someone once said: "**If you think you can or you think you can't, you're right!**" Your mind is very good at doing what you tell it. If you tell it, you can't run a 10K, then you won't. However, if you are a "nonathlete" and in good health and you begin to increase your daily walks and runs just a little bit, then you can run a marathon (26.2 miles), if that is your commitment. If you feel you are too old to launch a new business, then you are, even though Harland Sanders didn't launch Kentucky Fried Chicken until he was 65! If, however, you approach age as an attribute versus a liability, a whole new world of new options will open up for you. Instead of being too old, you would now recontextualize that disempowering belief into an empowering belief that says, "**I am a seasoned professional with a wealth of experiences any employer would be proud to have!**" And your questions? You can use questions to mobilize you into action or to develop new empowering beliefs. **"What are three ways my experience gives me a superior edge over everyone else?"** And so on. See what we mean?

As your partners in this process, let's see if you have any disempowering beliefs which block your careering success. Please complete Worksheet 6, "My Perceived Networking Roadblocks," and circle the responses you feel apply to you.

Stop the Destructive Cycle: Recontextualize Your Disempowering Roadblocks

Disempowering roadblocks stop you or, at the very least, slow you down from achieving the kinds of gains of which you are capable and which you desire. It is as if you own an incredibly powerful $80,000 sports car and you deliberately put a governor on its engine so you won't be able to drive it more than 37 miles an hour—hardly the 125-mph top speed the car was capable of obtaining. You protest, "I would never do that. It would be a tragic waste of money, notwithstanding the automotive engineering and performance." However, we contend that you, along with the rest of us on the planet, do not use our God-given talents, skills, and abilities fully and joyfully. Like the metaphor of putting a governor on the car's high performance engine to inhibit its performance, so do we also put a governor on our own performance and capabilities. Albeit, unconsciously.

It's important when dealing with roadblocks which limit your potential in life to be able to make the invisible visible. It's critical, indeed, vital, to your own well-being that you visualize (and make real) these roadblocks. Positive change starts with awareness. Some people are comfortable with the metaphor of a roadblock, others prefer metaphors depicting governors on car engines, or ropes that bind, or anchors weighing them down, or the sense of always operating in slow motion. Whatever the most appropriate metaphor or association is for you, the reality is that your disempowering beliefs are like lens filters through which you view the world in a different context. They are truly barriers or impediments to your success. Although your psychological and emotional roadblocks are invisible, they are as real as if they were made of wood and steel.

We want to help you break loose from the bonds of dysfunctional behavior and ideas by helping you recontextualize your self-defeating beliefs. We want to help you redefine how you think about things and enhance your ability to operate in a more powerful manner which supports you achieving your goals. Interestingly, a disempowering belief recontextualized always becomes empowering.

In consultations with thousands of employees, both those who have been displaced from their companies and those who are failing to reach their true

WORKSHEET 6
My Perceived Networking Roadblocks

Review and **circle** those statements which you feel are potential road-blocks to your effective networking. On the bottom of this sheet, write down any additional dysfunctional roadblocks missing on this list.

I don't know how to ask for leads.

I don't know many people.

I don't earn much money, so why would someone help me?

You need to be employed to be credible and to be able to network effectively.

My former boss may not provide a good reference.

I was terminated.

I am switching industries and that's difficult.

I worked for an organization which downsized.

I am too old.

I am handicapped.

I don't have a college degree.

I don't have enough education.

I have too much education.

Some career moves have been lateral.

I've only worked for one company.

I do not like to talk on the phone; I have never been much of a talker.

I need to change careers.

My grades were poor.

I have been unemployed before.

I have employment gaps.

I am unemployed now.

I need/want to relocate.

I am reentering the job market after raising a family.

I have changed jobs a lot.

I don't have much business experience.

Asking people for help is asking for charity and a handout. I won't do it!

I'm embarrassed to tell people I need to change jobs again.

Other roadblocks you might have:

_____

_____

_____

_____

_____

potential within their organizations, we have seen the effects of disempowering beliefs or roadblocks which significantly eroded these individual's confidence, self-esteem, assertiveness, hope, courage, and belief in themselves. Tragically, these employees created and lived within the confining limits of dysfunctional make-believe worlds and genuinely believed them to be reality. Talented, wonderfully capable individuals believed the self-defeating stories they had been conditioned to believe about themselves rather than operate differently to produce the kind of feelings and results they longed for. We have been privileged to play a part in facilitating the transformation of many a person. We're sure it's not surprising to you that individuals who were most successful in turning around their self-defeating perspectives and beliefs were also the people who were most effective in securing new careers. These were the individuals who successfully accelerated their professional performance and achieved their business and personal stretch goals.

Please turn to Figure 2.1, "Recontextualizing Your Roadblocks" and note how several disempowering beliefs which would definitely inhibit networking, once recontextualized, can be transformed into empowering beliefs which can liberate and mobilize a person into action. In this exercise, we are asking you to **identify your top three disempowering beliefs or roadblocks** which get in the way of your being as effective as you would like to be in networking. To identify your top three, you may wish to develop a much longer list of dysfunctional beliefs and then rank them. You may also wish to refer to the earlier exercise and familiarize yourself with the roadblocks which you previously identified. It's been our experience that you may have several global, all-encompassing disempowering beliefs which manifest themselves in a number of "subordinate" ways so that, in truth, you have several major and minor issues.

Gaining Leverage to Eliminate Life's Negative Influences _____

Eliminating disempowering beliefs which you may have had almost all of your life is both simple and easy, provided you are able to get enough leverage or motivation to change. Someone said, "Give me a long enough lever and I can move the earth." The point is, you might want to do something or desire something, but until you have leverage on yourself, until you have a burning motivation and an unswerving commitment to **make it happen,** all you have are wishes. Fervent wishing to win the lottery is a far cry from launching a business and meeting demanding customer needs to such an extent that over time you generate sales revenues equal to winning the $5 million lottery. On the one hand, the money is secured by random

Recontextualizing Your Roadblocks

Roadblocks stop you or, at the very best, slow you down from achieving the kinds of gains of which you are capable and which you desire. Although your psychological and emotional roadblocks are invisible, they are quite real. What we want to help you do is to recontextualize your roadblocks so you might redefine how you think about them. A recontextualized disempowering belief always becomes empowering and liberating!

ROADBLOCK/ DISEMPOWERING BELIEF	RECONTEXTUALIZED	EMPOWERING BELIEF

Roadblock	Recontextualized	Empowered Belief
I'm too old. . . .	becomes . . .	I'm seasoned!
I'm unemployed. . . .	becomes . . .	I'm free to search for the perfect job!
I'm a job hopper. . . .	becomes . . .	I'm experienced in many companies!
I'm too young. . . .	becomes . . .	I have plenty of energy and years of productive work ahead!
I don't have a college degree. . . .	becomes . . .	I have plenty of "hands-on" practical experience, more than the equivalency of an undergraduate degree.

My Top Three Roadblocks

1. _____	becomes	_____!
2. _____	becomes	_____!
3. _____	becomes	_____!

Figure 2.1.

chance with little direct involvement on your part, aside from buying a ticket, with the odds of 1 in 200 million that you would ever realize your goal. This is what we would consider a passive strategy or a nonstrategy. If, on the other hand, you created a burning desire to generate the $5 million and were 100 percent committed to its achievement, then the likelihood of securing it is more an issue of probability than chance.

To help you gain the much-needed leverage on your disempowering beliefs, we encourage you to complete Worksheets 7 and 8.

Gaining and Losing from Behavioral Change

In the next two exercises, Worksheet 9, "Discovering What Works and What Doesn't Work in My Career" and Worksheet 10, "Gaining and Losing from Behavioral Change," you will be asked to respond to the question, "What do you **gain or lose** from changing and what do you **gain or lose** from **not** changing?" Interestingly, some of the basic laws of physics are equally applicable in the realm of human dynamics and provide clues as to why we operate the way we do.

A body at rest will remain at rest until acted upon.

A body in motion will remain in motion until acted upon by an outside force.

For every action, there is an equal and opposite reaction.

All of us are motivated to behave in a given manner until something or someone influences us otherwise. If we are behaving in a dysfunctional manner, out of our disempowering belief, we are both gaining and losing something in the process. Remember Fred? While Fred is a very gracious and generous person with a tremendous amount of common sense, do you recall how he is his own worst enemy? If Fred is upset, he might behave in a loud, overly bold, and assertive manner. He may **gain** recognition and attention and get his way, as he intimidates everyone around him. However, Fred also runs the risk of **losing** the respect from others, and he misses the opportunity to learn from them because he pushes people around and he doesn't listen. We have filled out Worksheet 9 for Fred, as an example for you to follow.

We are not suggesting that you are overly loud, push people around, or are generally obnoxious—heaven forbid. Rather, we are acknowledging that all of us operate with our own special set of behavioral rules or beliefs, sometimes consciously, many times unconsciously.

- People who make quick decisions **gain** rapid action and reinforce their images as bold leaders, yet they may **lose** out on better options because they acted precipitously.

- People who do not speak up on important issues **gain** or maintain their anonymity and do not have to risk being confronted, yet they **lose** the opportunity to grow and have their opinions influence others.

WORKSHEET 7
Gaining Leverage on Disempowering Beliefs

To gain the much-needed leverage on your disempowering beliefs to eliminate them and replace them with empowering beliefs, please complete the following questions:

My top disempowering beliefs:

1. _____

2. _____

3. _____

If I don't change, the following impact is possible on my:

Family: _____

Career: _____

Relationships: _____

Earnings: _____

Confidence or self-esteem: _____

Personal power: _____

Company endorsement: _____

Networking: _____

Other: _____

WORKSHEET 8
Your Disempowering Beliefs Recontextualized

Please look at the previous exercise where you identified your top disempowering beliefs. In this exercise, we want you to gain the much-needed leverage on your disempowering beliefs to eliminate them and replace them with empowering beliefs. Please take care in completing the following questions fully.

My top three roadblocks recontextualized:

1. _____ becomes _____!

2. _____ becomes _____!

3. _____ becomes _____!

If I *do* change to these new beliefs, the following impact is possible on my:

Family: _____

Carecr: _____

Relationships: _____

Earnings: _____

Confidence or self-esteem: _____

Personal power: _____

Company endorsement: _____

Networking: _____

Other: _____

WORKSHEET 9
Discovering What Works and What Doesn't Work in My Career

This exercise will help you break through some of your roadblocks and identify actions which will positively influence your career and help you manage it better.

1. What are the top three things that are **working well** in my career, and how can I strengthen them?

2. What are the top three things that are **not working well** in my career, and what can I do to turn them around *and* enjoy the process?

3. What **three actions** can I take to develop and strengthen a trusting and respectful relationship with the people I work with, especially my boss?

4. What are the top three **disempowering** or **negative beliefs** I have about my ability to really succeed in my job now or in my search for the perfect job and the **price I pay** for holding onto these beliefs?

Disempowering Belief	What It Costs Me
A.	A.
B.	B.
C.	C.

(Continued)

5. What are the top three **empowering** or **positive beliefs** I have about my ability to really succeed in my job now or in my search for the perfect job and the **gain I receive** for holding onto these beliefs?

Empowering Beliefs	How I Benefit
A.	A.
B.	B.
C.	C.

6. What three **beliefs** can I hold and what **action** can I take to become more confident, happy, helpful, supportive, and valuable to the people around me (subordinates, peers, bosses) **while** enjoying the process?

Beliefs	Action
A.	A.
B.	B.
C.	C.

7. What are **six ways** I can keep my commitment to positive action and reduce self-sabotage in my job or career?

A.

B.

C.

D.

E.

F.

WORKSHEET 9
Discovering What Works and What Doesn't Work in My Career

Sample—Fred Jones

We asked Fred Jones, our old friend who had such a difficult time with his boss, if we could see his responses to this exercise. This is what he gave us. If you recall, this exercise will help you break through some of your roadblocks and identify actions which will positively influence your career and help you manage it better.

1. What are the top three things that are **working well** in my career and how can I strengthen them?

    Many people like me and turn to me for advice. I was selected by my professional association to serve on its board, and I am beginning to teach a college course. I continue to make significant contributions to the company—last year I saved more than $5 million.

2. What are the top three things that are **not working well** in my career and what can I do to turn them around *and* enjoy the process?

    I was passed over for promotion again. I was told that I was too hard on my people and I had difficulty fitting in with senior management. My new boss and I do not get along well, and we fight all the time. I can slow down and not be so driven to be right. Seek the opinions of others, especially my boss. Learn to respect everyone more.

3. What **three actions** can I take to develop and strengthen a trusting and respectful relationship with the people I work with, especially my boss?

    Listen more attentively when people talk to me. Don't jump in with the answer, rather ask others what they think we should do. Determine what my boss is good at and seek his advice on some topic.

4. What are the top three **disempowering** or **negative beliefs** I have about my ability to really succeed in my job now or in my search for the perfect job . . . and the **price I pay** holding onto these beliefs?

Disempowering Belief	What It Costs Me
A. I'm too old to change now.	A. I may have lost some $ and promotions because I'm unwilling to change.

(Continued)

B. My boss is out to get me fired!

C. No one will hire me because I'm too old and make too much money.

B. I do not have the support of my boss in even the simplest of things.

C. I'm starting to resent feeling like I'm stuck here and have no escape.

5. What are the top three **empowering** or **positive beliefs** I have about my ability to really succeed in my job now or in my search for the perfect job and the **gain I receive** holding onto these beliefs?

Empowering Beliefs	How I Benefit
A. I'm a seasoned pro and can really make a significant contribution.	A. I'm really confident in my abilities to do a phenomenal job.
B. There's not much I haven't dealt with.	B. I am able to make sound decisions quickly because I am able to anticipate what will most likely happen technically.
C. The company would be lost without me.	C. I don't worry about my job or my future, so I just do my job to the best of my abilities.

6. What three **beliefs** can I hold and what **action** can I take to become more confident, happy, helpful, supportive, and valuable to the people around me (subordinates, peers, bosses) **while** enjoying the process?

Beliefs	Action
A. My boss likes me and respects me.	A. Spend more time with him, acknowledge some of my biases, and work through them while getting to know him better.
B. My colleagues appreciate my straightforwardness and communication skills.	B. Confidently approach my colleagues and ask them for their opinion on something I'm working on, listening respectfully.
C. I am highly adaptive, flexible, and possess well-developed leadership skills.	C. Volunteer for task force assignments where I will gain greater visibility and deal with diverse personalities.

7. What are **six ways** I can keep my commitment to positive action and reduce self-sabotage in my job or career?

A. As I begin to get angry with my boss, I need to immediately stop and apologize and ask for clarification as to how he sees things differently than me.

(Continued)

B. Involve others in my "personal growth experiment" to positively reinforce when I interact well and to quickly point out for me when I blow up.

C. When I am with others, I can benefit greatly if I continually ask myself the question, "What can I learn from the people around me and what might the logic of their position be?"

D. Have someone from Human Resources or Robertson Lowstuter facilitate the resolution of some of the interpersonal "challenges" I have with others.

E. Ask the executives who have the best developed organizational skills to coach me.

F. Get some intensive interpersonal training with ongoing follow-through support.

WORKSHEET 10
Gaining and Losing from Behavioral Change

Fill in the matrix below, identifying those things which you **gain,** maintain, or protect and those things which you **lose,** avoid, or miss out on.

What Do I Gain	What Do I Lose
from changing?	
from NOT changing?	

BE KNOWLEDGEABLE REGARDING THE MYTHS AND REALITIES OF NETWORKING

SECRET 3

I Can't Ask Anyone for Help.
I Don't Do Charity!

Talk about setting yourself up for failure! This is a frequently stated disabling belief. Although well-intended, the above mindset reflects two problems. The first is a misunderstanding of what networking really is. The second is a tremendous undervaluation of others. This belief is neither very realistic nor very forgiving. "I don't do charity!" has as its premise that networking is somehow associated with the idea that you are needy and something valuable is given to you with no involvement or investment on your part. It certainly projects the feeling that you haven't earned the right to expect cooperation from others because you have not added value to them. People who initially feel this way intuitively seem to know that because they may have not established strong, supportive relationships with others, so why should others support them? If you feel this way and have been operating in somewhat of an isolationist manner, now may be a good time to open up more to others, at home and at work, adding value—giving of yourself. You will be absolutely amazed, yea even astounded, at the positive response you will get. Come on. Join in. Be prepared to meet some truly wonderful people. Because many have gone through exactly what you are now experiencing, they would love to help. The challenge is to find them.

The belief "**I can't ask anyone for help; I don't do charity**" sets the stage for this chapter, which deals with the beliefs, assumptions, biases, stereotypes, myths, realities, and abuses of networking. People's opinions about the job search process in general and about networking specifically are like noses—most everyone has one. We are always fascinated about the origins of many of the myths folks have about networking, in particular, as it is often seen as the most difficult element of the career search process to do well. One thing is certain. Networking is tough for "stuffed shirts." Egos are most easily wounded, one's capabilities are readily challenged, relationships are questioned, and confidences are shaken.

You might compare the humbling experience of networking to jogging. You can be the most powerful person in the world and wear $1000 suits, but when you put on your running shoes and shorts none of your wealth or position power will help you run any better. It's just you and your body, huffing and puffing along the trail at the most basic and profound level. You're either in shape or you're not. Period. When you network, you quickly discover in those quiet moments before you dial your contacts the extent to which you are confident and in "networking shape." The discipline to exercise on a consistent basis is not unlike the discipline to network effectively. You have to be focused on your goal and be committed to it regardless of how you feel about it. Commitment is a decision, not a feeling. We go to work, we pay our bills, we travel on business, we work long hours not because we want to always but because we said we would. It's out of our word that things get done; it's out of our commitment. The best reason in the world for ever doing anything has always been, "Because I said so!"

By the way, being able to effectively network does not require some kind of innate skills set. The "born networkers" are individuals who **learned** over time to quickly build rapport with others in such a manner so as to have people want to help them. These "natural networkers" have learned to add so much value to people that their contacts would feel disappointed if they didn't have an opportunity to lend a hand. Although these "born networkers" make networking look easy, it's learned. Our goal is to help you to learn these highly effective networking skills on an accelerated basis. Accelerated learning **does** work if you have the desire and commitment. Are you ready?

Let's get personal. **Your** opinions about networking are formed through stories you've heard, techniques you've read, as well as good and bad personal experiences (yours and those of others) and your tolerance for risk-taking. If you have strong negative beliefs about how you interact and operate with others and if you are unwilling to change, then your ability to network may be unnecessarily limited. Remember our friend Fred? He had this problem. While he was talented technically, he was unwilling to be flexible, interpersonally. He was a prisoner, held captive in some assorted beliefs that later on in life he discovered that he didn't even fully believe! Don't wait for disaster to strike as Fred is, rather step back and reexamine your beliefs about how you operate with others, especially in this arena called networking, as we review them here.

Our intent is to identify a number of these opinions, beliefs, convictions, or points of view which inhibit your ability to effectively network. We will then present a perspective which helps you recontextualize them. We hope that this "reality check" will prove useful for you as you sort through your own ideas and fears. We know that we will not cover every unproductive bias, myth, stereotype, or belief which you or others have. Indeed, you will have an opportunity to "flesh out" your own list of self-defeating myths or assumptions and decide if you are going to hold onto them or shift.

The Top 16 Myths

Myth 1: It's Better to Look for a Job When You Have a Job.

Reality

Au contraire! This is perhaps one of the most persistent and strongly held beliefs which we encounter. It's so common that most people accept it out of question. It is certainly understandable that we **do** feel more confident and secure when we have a job as opposed to when we do not. However, if you operate confidently, it really doesn't matter if you're employed or not. In fact, most of us who have learned to really network, now see being unemployed as a decided advantage if you properly conduct your career search.

> **Myth's Assumption:** The basis for this myth is the belief that you are more powerful and can be more selective when you are employed because you will not be forced to accept a job if it isn't right.

Interestingly enough, after years of testing, we have discovered that **this myth just isn't valid anymore.** First, let's deal with the facts, then look at a possible reason that it might be so strongly held. The facts are that unemployed people, with 40 to 50 additional "prime-time" job-hunting hours per week:

1. Have access to more job-hunting avenues than when they were employed.
2. Are free from being secretive so they can access valuable resource people who may have "gotten them in trouble" with their job while they were working.
3. Can initiate and go on five times (or ten times) more interviews and therefore generate more offers from which to choose and leverage a better position and salary than their working colleagues.
4. Are more likely to be selective in the quality of the job which they take, thus having a longer and more productive stay in their new job.

Surprised? It's absolutely true. The stigma of losing a job, which used to frighten off employers, is virtually gone. Job loss of qualified people for all manner of reasons is now so common that the fact that you are out of work is of minimal importance as long as you do not appear to be upset and damaged yourself. Clearly, employers do not want to hire someone "dragging a lot of emotional baggage around." Oh, of course, there are still a few dinosaurs out there who still think as they did in the 1950s, but they are fast becoming extinct.

The reason that this myth is so widespread may have more to do with people's sense of personal worth and value when out of work than it does with reality. Let's think about it for a moment. How powerful are you in a job when it clearly isn't working or when you are "on the bubble"? First, you may truly need to escape the "clutches" of a disempowering employment relationship to be at your best power level. This myth can be somewhat "comforting" (though not very productive) when we have a wounded ego. This myth can also fuel our upset when we are uncertain about long-term finances. In actual fact, however, it is considerably easier to conduct an active career search campaign if you are **not** employed. Whenever you hear yourself saying this myth, just consider the facts and the logic we presented. Think about how tough it is to look for a job when you are gainfully employed. It is nigh unto impossible to initiate (and receive) more than 20 phone calls to your networking sources, mail out dozens of résumés, and go on three to five interviews on a weekly basis without always looking over your shoulder.

Also, think of what "still-employed" job hunting does to your sense of integrity. How do you feel when getting paid by a firm while you sneak around answering calls on company time, hiding behind the leafy plant in your office so people won't know that you are on a networking call or on a phone interview? **You never have a better opportunity to be more powerful and effective at job hunting than when you are unencumbered by work and free to conduct your career search full time.**

Myth 2. If You Are Over 45, It Will Be Very Tough to Get a Good Job.

Reality

Well, yes and no. We've seen companies be reluctant to hire a talented person because she was over 45 and we've also seen companies gravitate toward another person because he was 61, as they wanted a mature, seasoned professional who could bring a calming presence to the organization and be a mentor to others.

> **Myth's Assumption:** This dysfunctional belief is that companies only want individuals under age 40, as they are the ones who have the new ideas, energy, and drive to make things happen and lead the organization to its next level of performance.

Granted, if you are 55 you might presumably work only another 10 years until retirement. But remember, the average length of service for a young high potential person these days is 5 years or less, so is that argument very realistic? Since the probability of staying in a job for more than 10 years for anyone is low, given today's economy and the "throw-away mentality" of many larger companies, the "retirement window" argument just doesn't seem to hold much credence. Also, age is so relative. You can be young and think old, or you can be old and think and act younger than your years. Several years ago we had one 48-year-old overweight client named Warner, who at first glance people thought he was in his seventies. He had two speeds; slow and stop. Warner would slowly shuffle along the corridors with his head bowed, shoulders slumped, and a somber expression on his face. His eyes were devoid of any life, certainly no sparkle or joy. He could be best described as a negative, embittered man old well beyond his years whose lack of enthusiasm and self-confidence distanced himself from others, especially search firms and potential employers. Since Warner graduated from a prestigious "think tank" university with an MBA, he operated as a pseudointellectual, hoping against hope that his aloof, snobbish style would appeal to an employer's intellect and that he would be hired. As you might suspect, he was unemployed for more than two years, in large part, because of his steadfast refusal to change and "brighten-up" so that he was more acceptable to employers and search firms. If Warner would have spent the same amount of energy on empowering behavior and a confident image which he spent on reinforcing his "tired, old man act" he would have long since been connected. He was certainly intelligent enough! We would love to report a happy ending to this experience, but we can't. The simple truth of the matter is that sometimes we are not able to change people who stubbornly refuse to accept help and guidance from others, even when it becomes painfully obvious to everyone that their way is not working. What happened to Warner? Today he is employed in an unchallenging and low-paying job with people he constantly puts down as not being very bright. He is miserable and genuinely mystified and angry that people do not just hire him because he is "smart." We wonder if someday on his tombstone will be the words "Here lies Warner. He never 'got it.' "

Much of the bias against older employment candidates is that older employees are seen as not able to physically maintain a demanding work schedule or they are not very flexible thinkers or they have outmoded technical knowledge or they have old-fashioned operating styles, or that they expect younger employees to defer to them as more wise and experienced.

What to do? If you are over 45, our counsel to you is to pay attention to your appearance. Dress smartly and attend to personal grooming. Go to an upscale clothing store and place yourself in the hands of a knowledgeable, well-dressed salesperson for both clothes, as well as hair styling. Keep in good physical condition, given your health and circumstances. Use positive, upbeat, and forward-thinking language. Avoid "history lessons" which tend to perpetuate your being stuck, no matter how much you enjoy them when talking about others. Brush up on your technical skills including computer literacy. Meet people's eyes with a friendly, outgoing smile. Be genuinely pleased to be there. Offer a firm handshake. Exude a sense of well-being, confidence, and energy. If you do, then you will find that the vast majority of line executives actually prefer seasoned veterans who can jump right in without training, make reliable judgments which only come from experience, and who keep the younger "troops" settled down during turbulent times. The bottom line: Learn to operate more flexibly and effectively and live joyously, for enthusiasm and confidence are contagious.

Myth 3: People Aren't Going to Help Me, a Stranger, Network.

Reality
Will Rogers was noted for saying, "A stranger is a friend I just haven't met." If there is anything that we have learned during our years of helping people to effectively transition through difficult career and job changes, it is that there are a multitude of people out there who will befriend you in this process. All you have to do is initiate the contacts. Time after time, we have found that if you extend yourself, add value to others, be straightforward and nonmanipulative, be of good cheer, confident, and enjoy yourself—you will do just fine. "What?! Easy for you to say, Dave and Clyde! You aren't the one looking for a job, having to network." Sure, we are. We have to network in our business every day. Like every other business which depends upon customer relationships and new or repeat sales we must constantly expand our circle of contacts. We are not asking you to do anything that we aren't doing every day of the week, every week of the year. We understand very well how to network, its problems, its challenges, and its joys.

> **Myth's Assumption:** People feel that others are so busy with everything else in their life, they will not stop to help you with your little "job hunting project." Unless they know you, others do not have any vested interest in your well-being. Why should they? They do not know you or care to know you. Your career search issues are your career search issues—not theirs.

> **What to do?** Remember: The basis of all networking is relationships. If you have solid relationships with others, people will not feel that you are abusing the friendship, rather your friends will welcome the opportunity to support you. Likewise, your friends and colleagues have equally good friends who would support them if **they** needed help. If your contacts are solid citizens, doesn't it stand to reason that they would have equally strong friends who would be willing to extend themselves to others in need, provided you handle yourself appropriately? Even strangers? Sure, it happens all the time. Think of a networking introduction as a metaphor: The time is

the early seventeenth century and you are friends with the king of the land. Since means of communication is somewhat limited to carrier pigeons or hand-delivered messages, letters of introduction take on great significance. A letter of introduction is considered to be a strong endorsement, and the bearer is to be afforded the same level of respect and assistance as would the originator of the note. So it is with you. Consider a networking lead to be an introduction to a contact who will extend to you the same courtesies and support he or she would extend to your mutual friend.

Myth 4: Companies Discriminate against People Who Have Been Terminated.

Reality

The fact that companies might be hesitant to hire someone who has been recently "zapped" has less to do with his or her employment status and more to do with the extent to which the person may be emotionally "beat up."

> **Myth's Assumption:** Because involuntary termination is usually so painful, most people experience a tremendous range of often conflicting emotions during their job loss. Anger, depression, or even trauma will show up in the workplace and make working with a previously terminated employee difficult.

Regardless of your own rationale surrounding your exit from a previous company, a potential employer is interested in what went wrong and the reason for some of your choices. (What led you to this company in the first place? What are some of the choices you made? What have you learned in the process? What could you have done differently and why didn't you? What prevented you from operating more effectively at this time?)

No company wants to hire a person who is demonstrably defensive or upset (bitter, sad, angry, or vindictive). The extent to which you communicate or telegraph your upset and defensiveness is the extent to which organizations will, at the very least, zero in on specific problem areas. Don't count on this though. It is much more likely that the company will simply drop you from employment consideration without telling you the reason for the rejection or isolation. Although you might be justifiably angry or hurt that they would drop you with no real "reason," you can be assured that it is a rare company, indeed, which would straightforwardly communicate their fears and concerns to you. Unfortunately, you are left in the dark with little feedback and even less insight.

What to do? Review the earlier sections in this book on taking responsibility and be sure that you have consciously chosen things to be as they are. Unless you deliberately choose things to be a certain way life may not reflect what you want, as you are not "in charge." Have your close and trusted friends observe and evaluate your behavior and language for emotionally ladened words and dysfunctional behavior. Drop these immediately. Review Myths 1 and 2 and make certain that you have incorporated this perspective in your job-hunting efforts and your life. "Power up" your sense of urgency. Make sure that you contact enough people every day so that the occasional rejection doesn't loom out of perspective.

Myth 5. Having to Look for a Job Is a Sign of Failure.

Reality

Welcome to the 1990s! Don't buy this myth for a moment. There aren't too many people who haven't been adversely impacted by an economic downsizing, directly or indirectly or by a personality "mismatch" at some point in their careers.

> **Myth's Assumption:** This assumption is rooted in the feeling that you have obviously done something significantly wrong to have gotten zapped, or you must have a major personality flaw to have to actively look for work. If you didn't work out in your previous employer, then it is only a matter of time until your problems surface in the new job.

It's been said that if you haven't been fired at least once in your career, you haven't been doing your job or that you have been operating too cautiously. In these days of so-called rightsizing there aren't too many people who haven't themselves gotten zapped, know someone who has gotten zapped, been bounced around involuntarily within a company, or been concerned about job security, at least **once** in their careers. Being out-of-work happens to the most talented and most capable. In fact, if you have been zapped, then you are in the company with some of the country's leaders, including a few presidents.

What to do? Review your strengths, your credentials, your experiences, and your past successes. Take time to quantify and write down your accomplishments and responsibilities. List the valuable contributions which you made to your organizations. Start with the present and go back as far as you need to demonstrate to yourself how good you are and what your skills are. When you very proudly declare that based on these accomplishments and capabilities, you'd hire yourself—then you are ready.

Myth 6. If Companies Know You Are Actively Looking, They Will Take Unfair Advantage of You.

Reality

We suspect that there will be some organizations who will try to deliberately underpay you because you are unemployed or desperate to leave your current employer. An analogy might be that we have been admiring your car and we want to buy it from you for $1200. You snort—"Don't be ridiculous, it's worth $12,500!" While our example may seem far-fetched to you, many of us unwittingly fall into this trap when it comes to employment relationships if we are not careful and forget our ability to negotiate a better deal.

Myth's Assumption: If you are unemployed or having to look for work, you'll be lucky to land a job, what with all these downsizings, layoffs, and job eliminations. You do not have many options, you may not have any other employment opportunities, and you aren't in a position to argue. "A bird in the hand is worth two in the bush!"

What to do? When extended an offer, you do not have to accept any employment offer unless it is reasonable and makes sense to you. "Yes, but what if it is the ideal job for me?" you exclaim. Well, perhaps it is and perhaps it is not. If it is the "ideal" job for you—hopefully, the organization views you as the "ideal" person to fill the job which means you have some leverage to negotiate for additional monies, bigger title, company car, delayed start date, extra vacation—whatever you need to do to make it an acceptable offer.

If you are more in love with the organization than it is in love with you, you run the risk of being taken advantage of as you are entering into an imbalanced relationship. It is our recommendation that you closely evaluate the reason for the disparity in the relationship and see what company objections or misconceptions you can uncover, then dispel them. Several of our outplacement clients fell victim to blind loyalty, in that they were much more forgiving of the offenses of others in their company, while their colleagues were extremely critical of them. Fundamentally, our clients accepted positions in organizations where they did not have solid support and endorsement **before they were hired,** and things got even worse as time went on. Hopefully, no one is going to coerce you into taking a less-than-acceptable position. However, if you feel you are being bullied **now,** when everyone is supposedly on their best behavior, you have to wonder what these people will be like when you are part of the "family" and they can "abuse" you behind closed doors. **Listen not only to your head, but also to what your "gut" and heart are telling you.** Is this the place for you? Are you being welcomed and made to feel a part of the team or do you feel like an intruder? While it is not uncommon for the negotiations to become strained if the offer is not great, you may need to assess the extent to which **you** are being unreasonable. Put yourself in your potential boss's place and critically look at your behavior and demands. If you think you might be seen as unreasonable, modify your demands and behavior to still communicate what you want but do it in a highly supportive manner so as to create a "win/win" context. To create a "catch-up" strategy, to remain whole compensationwise, you may wish to take advantage of the salary negotiation ideas presented in Step 11 of *In Search of the Perfect Job.*

Myth 7. Résumés Should Be Only One Page. Your Résumé Can Be Any Length.

Reality

Although issues about résumés don't technically fall into the category of networking, you will hear plenty of well-intended advice from your networking friends, colleagues, and search firms. This advice won't all be restricted to the length of your résumé; the advice will cover every conceivable element from the type font to its paper weight, color, details to include, details to exclude—everything! You will find that everyone in the whole world is an expert in résumés, and they want to give you their authoritative opinion.

Myth's Assumption: The assumption is that there is only one kind, style, length, or format for a résumé. Another assumption is that employers and search firms really do want to know everything about you. If full disclosure requires you to create a 4-page résumé, then that is what you should create and send out indiscriminately to everyone.

What to do? Your resume should be short enough to pique the interest of the receivers and not overwhelm them and long enough to communicate the breadth of your abilities, capabilities, and results achieved. The simple truth of the matter is that your résumé should be a highly telegraphic marketing tool (and not a "tell all" document). It should be long enough to powerfully highlight your background and results achieved—and no more. You are dealing with résumé "scanners"—not readers. To that end, your marketing cover letter has 5 to 8 seconds to "hook" the scanner and your resume has 10 to 15 seconds for the scanner to determine if your résumé warrants a more in-depth screening. Clearly, that's not much time to have your hard-earned credentials be evaluated and thrown into the "A" pile. Nonetheless, that is reflective of the stiff competition which you face when you venture forth on the marketplace. To that end, **normally your résumé should be no longer than 2 pages!** If you are a recent graduate with fewer than five years of experience, then you might wish to consider a 1-page résumé which is normally associated with people at the beginning stage of their careers.

Myth 8. I Can't Get a Good Job Because No One Is Hiring.

Reality

Protests to the contrary, when it comes to the complex, multilevel market channels which must be used when looking for a job today, not many people really know how to market themselves in the most powerful and effective manner. You may have changed jobs before and learned a lot about job hunting, but you did not necessarily capture all the offers which were available for individuals with your background. In that last "go-around" how many offers did you receive? Did you get all the money which you could possibly have wanted and dreamed about? On a percentage scale of 1 to 100 percent, what percentage of your last job represented the perfect career move for you?

The phrases "No one is hiring" or "Everyone is cutting back" are used as the ultimate excuse for poor job-hunting results. We have never, ever found it to be so, even in the worst of economic times. The belief that there are no jobs reminds us of the phrase, "Yes, but." "Yes, I really am doing everything possible to find a suitable career position, but there are no jobs. Why should I continue to look, there are no jobs!" When a person operates his or her life with an escape clause this big, then it is easy to avoid assuming accountability for how that person's career and life looks. It's no wonder some of us don't accomplish much. These are the individuals who say that the market is terrible and, indeed, can cite statistics which seem to prove their point. These people know what they want, yet are unwilling to work for it. "Yes, but!" is the opposite of "When the going gets tough, the tough get going!"

> **Myth's Assumption:** Most jobs are going to show up as openings or opportunities. Position needs are clearly recognized by the hiring company and are generally advertised or put out to search. There is another assumption that believes that these "openings" are really very hard to find and that you need to spend a lot of time, effort, and money to discover them. Many job-hunting clubs or groups, database systems, newsletters, and company recruiters perpetuate this myth. Above all the myth assumes that if you have the formula that others have used effectively, that should be sufficient to coax the jobs from hiding without having to invest much time, effort, or work in the job-hunting process.

Boy, talk about being further from the truth! As we observed earlier, declared "openings" account for a minority of all the jobs filled. A whole world of hiring is going on, outside the formal process, which fills 70 to 80 percent of all job needs. Companies are always hiring for hundreds of reasons—even during the worst of economic times. They just don't appear as advertised openings. That's why conventional job hunters sincerely believe that "no one is hiring." George Burns was once asked, "Why is that you are always finding money?" George responded, "I look down." If you look in the right place and in the right way, there are plenty of good jobs openings and closings every day in the hidden market. But you do have to look and dig for them and risk talking to people when they do not have any bona fide openings. Job hunting takes disciplined work.

Just knowing how to get a job isn't enough. Even when there **are** openings, just because you **know** what to do does not mean that you are doing it well. Just because you **know** you should contact search firms and supply them with a résumé, doesn't mean that you have developed a powerful résumé which distinguishes you from your competition nor does it mean that you are able to effectively vault over the hundreds of others who are also vying for attention from the recruiter. An underlying premise to this myth's assumption can be seen in the analogy of visiting Paris for a week and declaring that you now know what the French are like. In these difficult employment times, you must work hard and diligently to improve and hone your job-changing skills. The question is—have you done so? To what extent are you physically, mentally, emotionally, and psychologically performing at your peak? Unless your industry or skill sets have been made completely obsolete, there is a high probability that you can secure one of the good opportunities out there waiting for you, somehow, somewhere. As we will remind you often throughout this book—there are two things which you can't control: timing and luck. However, to enhance the timing of your connection, and your luck, be prepared! As the late Earl Nightingale used to say, "Luck is preparedness meeting opportunity."

What to do? While you may be working harder and may even be exhausted, you may not be working as effectively as you could. Please do not be offended by this or feel we are picking on you. This idea of "no jobs" is simply not accurate. If you are having a tough time in your job search, then you may wish to shift *where* you look and also improve the effectiveness of *how* you look. None of us operate fully to our potential. . . . Your challenge and strategy is to learn what you are doing right and discover what you can do differently or do better. In addition, our experience is that even in the midst of significant economic downsizings some companies actually hire individuals with unique skills to "back fill" those positions created by the shrinking organization. As inconceivable as this is to departing employees, it is not that uncommon to hire one person with a multifaceted skill set to replace two or more employees, thus lowering the overall payroll costs. Who knows, someone else's misfortune may be your golden opportunity.

Myth 9. Job Hunting Is Inconvenient, Difficult, Time Consuming, and No Fun.

Reality

The extent to which you view job hunting as laborious and a hassle, that's the extent to which you will have difficulty being enthusiastic, having a positive expectancy, and building rapport.

> **Myth's Assumption:** Any time you change jobs, there is always a lot of stress involved, problems seem bigger and more difficult to handle, it costs more than you imagined, and you lose a little more confidence each time you have to look for a job.

Truly, it is as simple as getting what you create. If you envision your career search as a positive, challenging process which will undoubtedly stretch you to be the best you can be, then you will have a completely different experience than if you see this as a terribly gruelling time. Please don't misunderstand. We are not naively saying that you might not have some rough spots in your career search. Rather, we are just being realistic. Try an experiment with us. Repeat the follow phrase out loud, louder and louder each time until you are shouting it. **GET EMOTIONAL!**

"I can't do it!"
"I can't do it!"   Louder
"I can't do it!"   LOUDER
"I CAN'T DO IT!"   LOUDER!
"I CAN'T DO IT!"   LOUDER STILL!!
"I   CAN'T   DO   IT!"   SHOUTING!!!

Question. Do you think you can do "it"? On a scale of 1 to 100 (with 100 being 100 percent confident in your ability to do "it" and 1 representing almost zero confidence), how would you rate your ability to accomplish "it"? By the way, it doesn't matter what "**it**" was, your mind filled in the blank. So, our question remains unanswered—do you believe you can do "it" after all those powerful negative affirmations? We think not. If you **really** put yourself into these negative affirmations to the extent that the last one was presented in almost a shouting, argumentative tone trying to convince someone of one of your core beliefs, perhaps the existence of gravity: "Listen, gravity does exist, no matter how you feel about it!!!!" Job hunting can be a drag and no fun and the biggest pain—if you let it. We recently overheard one of our usually optimistic senior executives lamenting to a search firm contact that, "Boy, this job hunting is terrible. It's so demeaning and demoralizing. People don't return your phone calls, it's next to impossible to stay positive and motivated, and people ignore you. I can't seem to spark any momentum in my campaign, and my networking has dried up completely. I hate it." Soooo, how effective do you think this executive was in creating a positive result in his networking and career search? You are absolutely right! Not very effective. He spoke what he believed and got what he created! (To put your mind at ease, so you won't worry, we helped him recontextualize how to think, feel, and act so as to create a much more powerful result.)

What to do? Just so we don't leave you hanging with a belief that says you can't do "it" and to illustrate the **positive power of your focused mind,** we want you to repeat the following phrases as you did before—out loud, louder each time until you are shouting this out: Get emotional!

"I can do it!"
"I can do it!"   Louder
"I can do it!"   LOUDER

"I CAN DO IT!"	LOUDER!
"I CAN DO IT!"	LOUDER STILL!!
"I CAN DO IT!"	SHOUTING!!!

Now how would you rate your ability to do "it"? On a scale of 1 to 100 (with 100 being 100 percent confident in your ability to do "it" and 1 representing almost zero confidence), how would you rate your ability to accomplish "it"? Have you noticed any shift in your personal power and self-confidence? You should have been able to both create a heightened sense of confidence and to distinguish between the levels of your personal power when you were negative versus when you were positive. For some, the distinction between their negative beliefs and their positive beliefs need to be made crystal clear before any change can occur. For others, the distinctions may not be very great (or nonexistent). If that is your case, you might wish to repeat this exercise again, but this time really put your emotions into it until you can flip out of negative self-defeating beliefs into an outrageously positive and confident emotional state.

One last point. A well-run career search campaign doesn't necessarily have to be fun to be successful. It's like exercise. Sometimes exercising is fun, sometimes it's not. It isn't always comfortable. But then, comfort isn't the goal. Physical fitness is the goal. The goal in exercising is to do it to the best of your abilities and physical condition and be disciplined enough to do it regularly, regardless of whether you are having fun. If you want to get or stay in shape, you **have** to exercise. Period. In the same manner, networking isn't always comfortable. But then comfort isn't the goal either. Getting a really good job is the goal. **To conduct an effective career search, you** *have* **to learn to network well and do so to the best of your abilities. Period.**

Myth 10. Networking Is the Only Way to Go— It Is the Most Effective Avenue to Locate the Perfect Job.

Reality

Obviously, we are advocating networking as a powerful and effective means to connect with your ideal job. However, lest we be misunderstood, let us state that we feel that networking is only **one** of four main avenues to getting connected.

> **Myth's Assumption:** For some people, their myth is that networking is the best way to get connected. It is clearly action oriented and a great way to reach a large number of people directly. Being face-to-face with a network contact is much more personable and can produce multiple leads if handled well. The majority of managerial opportunities and many lower-level jobs are filled through the connections made through networking.

If you recall, the four main job changing paths are: personal networking, search firms/employment agencies, target marketing to organizations, and advertisements. There is merit in *each* careering avenue. The point is that you should not forget to utilize all four means to getting connected, though networking is one of the most effective ways to tap into the contacts of others to gain the much-needed careering visibility.

Myth 11. Your Credentials Are More Important Than Your Ability to Sell Yourself.

Reality

You can have the best credentials in the world, have accomplished a great deal, and have a tremendous amount of raw talent—and still not get connected because you don't sell yourself well.

> **Myth's Assumption:** An old tradition of the 1950s and 1960s had as its premise, "If you work hard, are loyal, and do a good job, you will be noticed, your company will take care of you through promotions, handsome salary increases, recognition, and you will have lifetime job security." That was an appropriate premise for an expanding postwar economy. It is no longer a reliable rule for today's economy. This myth is based on the idea that the **rule** still exists and is valid. The myth says, "you don't have to sell or market your ideas, your projects, or yourself. Just get good results and you will be sought after in the marketplace."

Clearly, this old rule no longer applies in our current fast-changing economy. It's interesting that some of the conflict between older and younger employees stems from the disparity from the way things used to be and the way they are now. Older employees often see their younger colleagues as shamelessly "politicing," and the younger employees perceive their older business associates as naively waiting for the company to take care of them. The truth of the matter is "**People hire people they like. People hire people that are like them and with whom they are comfortable.**" Connections are everything; if you have them—great! If you don't build connections, you may be in for a possibly long and tedious career search.

In networking, and in interviewing, personal chemistry has a lot to do with whether two people will make the connection, share leads, develop the synergy important to innovation and creative energy, and want to spend time together. Marketing yourself is every bit as important as having good abilities and a record of accomplishments.

In interviews, company decision makers will be evaluating you on the basis of:

1. **Can you do the job?** Do you have the technical competency, skills, and track record that would lead me to conclude that you have the capability to do the work?

2. **Are you interested in the job?** Are you enthusiastic and excited to be here? To what extent have you done your homework on the company, its competitors, the industry, the socioeconomic trends, and other factors that might demonstrate your interest, your capabilities, and your drive.

3. **Will you fit in?** Do you have the personality to relate well to me, to the team, to the corporate culture, to the others in the organization, and to what extent will you reflect the values of the company to our customers, vendors, and suppliers?

While all the above questions are important, the third question is the most critical, as it addresses the issue of personal chemistry and your ability to establish the much-needed rapport to effectively market your skills and abilities. Try as you might, if you and the other person are not in synch, you aren't going to sell yourself well at all even if you have excellent accomplishments and capabilities. As our good friend Rod Deighan of Patrick Douglas was fond of saying, "There are two ways to move a string. You can either push it or you can pull it. It's a lot easier to pull the string than to push it." You will be much more credible when talking about your accomplishments, if at first you have built rapport. This means taking the time to have thoughtfully and carefully made your network contact (or an interviewer) comfortable with you. As we will see later, it will be much easier to secure networking contact information when you first establish rapport and sell yourself than to push for leads before legitimizing your request for information.

Myth 12. There Is Little Support and Gratification When You Look for a Job.

Reality
If you believe your career search will be long and hard with little support from others, than it will be. **You get what you create and you get what you focus on.** As a way to help his daughter cope with the loss of her leg after a skiing accident, Reverend Robert Schuller challenged her to "look at what she had left, not at what she had lost." Dr. Schuller's premise, and ours, is that if you focus **only** on your job loss, your slow and difficult career search, or the extent to which you are emotionally upset or drained, then you will be operating largely out of the context of job loss or upset.

> **Myth's Assumption:** Many people believe that after all is said and done, you are alone in this world (and in your job hunting) to manage the best you can. No one is going to hand you a good job on a silver platter. Besides, people are looking out for themselves, and they will care and help out only when it is convenient. Also, the work of job hunting is disagreeable, demeaning, and unpleasant.

Pretty disheartening and pessimistic assumption upon which this myth is based, isn't it? As with all of these myths and their assumptions, there is some truth in this myth. It is true that you are ultimately alone with your choices, decisions, and beliefs. If you believe that people are not supportive and will not help, then they won't. However, if you believe that there are people who you know (and some that you haven't yet met) out there who are more than willing to extend a listening ear, an empathetic shoulder to lean on, and a Rolodex file that they are willing to peruse through with you—then they will.

Before others can even remotely begin to support you, you need to support yourself with affirming beliefs *and* actions. Your **internal support system** is composed of those beliefs, images, messages, and psychological and emotional "tapes" that seem to run your life, as if it is on automatic. As we have referenced before, if the images and messages rattling around in your skull communicate to you that you can't count on others for support, guess what? You are going to be one lonely, cynical person who has an uncanny knack for driving people away at the exact time when you need them the most. **Ironically, the time when you need to reach out to others the most will be the time when you are least likely to do so. The time when you need to be most open and receiving will be the time when you will be most closed and defensive.** Sounds pretty desperate and scary, doesn't it? You might even think, "This could never happen to me! I'm too much in control to ever allow this to occur." Well, welcome to reality. This debilitating crawl into isolation is very common, slow, insidious, and experienced by most of us at some time. You rationalize that your friends do not want to be burdened with your problems, so you tend to bury the issues and not address them while ignoring your friends and the very resources you need.

What to do? If you are interested in shifting from the above-described negative state to one which is more positive and powerful, we recommend the following. Ask yourself the following questions to shift your focus from negative to positive, from lack to abundance, from sickness to health. Ask yourself these questions at least four times a day (before breakfast, before lunch, before dinner, and before drifting off to sleep). By the way, if you find yourself saying, "I have nothing to be grateful for!"—keep looking for something in your life for which you are grateful, no matter how small and seemingly insignificant.

RECONTEXTUALIZING FOR SUPPORT

1. How confident am I? How can I increase my confidence and boldness?
2. What am I grateful for in my life? How can I enrich this?
3. Who do I love and who loves me? How might I love more?
4. What am I happy and excited about? What can I do to be more joyous?

5. When am I peaceful and content? How can I enhance my peacefulness?

6. What am I most proud of? What else am I proud of and how can I be more proud?

7. How have I served others today and how have I been served? How can I increase my support and service to others?

8. What have I learned today? What other things do I need to learn to be even more effective?

9. What am I committed to doing? How can I increase my commitment to ensure the accomplishment of this task?

10. How have I been successful? How can I be more successful and contribute more? To myself? To my family? To my employer? To my friends?

11. How am I in control of my life and my career? How can I accomplish more of my personal and business goals?

Myth 13. Only the Strong Will Survive the Rejection and the Wide Emotional Swings That Accompany the Job Search Process.

Reality

"Only the strong will survive" is a pretty scary concept. You might find yourself asking, "Am I strong enough to survive?" Even the most confident of us can experience some emotional setbacks if we repeatedly come in second for the job we wanted. "Strong" does not refer to physical stature or social boldness, rather it references the discipline one draws upon to handle life's challenges. Interestingly, some people who appear to be the "meekest" actually have a steel core. They are resolute in that life's adversities will not defeat them and "if it doesn't kill 'em, it will make them stronger!"

> **Myth's Assumption:** Only a special breed of person is able to withstand the onslaught of emotions that are present during job changing. If you have any kind of emotional instability, you are going to suffer a lot of pain when rejection comes your way.

Now let's look at this realistically. We have all heard (or seen) the moaning and groaning of people who seem to surface in groups, in magazines or on the TV, who have been unemployed for years and can't find work. One thing we have always observed is that these are the people who never have a clear careering goal or networking strategies or activities. These folks do not have a well-organized search campaign to locate and build strong relationships with hundreds of target firms or networking contacts. If you see these people on TV, you see them involved in some form of household chore casually dressed with little sense of urgency or focus. These are the individuals who declare job hunting to be so tough and the marketplace so bleak. You, personally, do not have to experience this level of discomfort or desperation in your job search. Granted, you will potentially experience more rejection (and highs and lows) in your search than during any time of your life. For every call you make, every letter you send out, and every advertisement you respond to has the potential of a rejection. However, nothing ventured, nothing gained.

What to do? So, rather than dreading rejection, say "**next!**"—the phrase one of our most successful networkers used to help himself not take any turndowns as personal. We will cover some of the practical ways you can manage rejection, stress, and strain in more detail in Secret 10.

Myth 14. There Will Be a Big Problem in My Family as a Result of Having to Look for a Job.

Reality

Really? Why? We understand that there might be, but why declare it to be a foregone conclusion? Announcing it to be so is a little like the person who says, "Every year on December 1st I always have a bad cold, so I'm working overtime in preparation for when I am going to miss several days of work. I've got to get busy, since it's only two weeks away." We acknowledge that there may truly be some added stress and that a career search can generate a lot of anxiety, especially if finances are tight. If your financial picture looks a bit bleak, then you should take immediate corrective action. Get on a budget, pay off your credit card bills, hide your credit cards and only pay cash, avoid unnecessary spending, cut back on "luxury" items like movies, ice cream, booze, and dinners out. While you might feel that these moves are dramatic, it's really taking control of your life and safeguarding the long-term emotional well-being of you and the ones who live with you.

> **Myth's Assumption:** There is a belief that if you are out of work or "forced" to look for work, there will be significant upset in the family. It's unnatural to be upbeat and of good cheer. If there is a smooth transition it's obvious that everyone is suppressing their true feelings.

If your finances are OK, keep in mind that people (especially your family) will take their behavioral cues from you. If you are an emotional wreck and out of control with anger or overwhelmed with grief, then others will also be, understandably, upset. It's very common for your loved ones to feel even greater outrage, betrayal, and sadness than you feel. In fact, it is unfair to them if you don't try to regain control. It's terribly upsetting for your family and friends to see you upset. You being upset naturally heightens their upset.

What to do? Instead of viewing your termination, for example, as a betrayal, thus upsetting you and making your family even more upset, try viewing it as a business decision that just **feels** personal. Communicate the following thoughts in the sentences which are below often enough so you can speak about your departure without any negative emotion around the telling. We recommend something like the following: **"As you may be aware, my company recently reorganized, and my position has been affected. Although I am a little saddened that my time with _____ (your company) has ended, as I accomplished quite a bit while I was there, this is the time to move on. I am excited about the next step and my careering options."** In fact, as you begin to generate networking results, you might even indicate that you have had some employment interest from companies already, that you have received requests for interviews, or even an offer or two.

Your success and positive expectancy will elevate the spirits of everyone around you and, in turn, will lift your enthusiasm and spirits. Those around you will settle down tremendously if you are able to maintain the position that you will be alright and that you appreciate everyone's support and that you will call on them for networking purposes later.

Myth 15. You Need to Know Many Senior Company People to Network Effectively.

Reality

Well, it certainly helps. However, it's the **quality** of the contacts which you have and make, not necessarily the quantity of your contacts. Like anything else, you start slow and build. You begin with your first networking contact and then branch out from there. The old adage, "the journey of a thousand miles begins with the first step," was never truer than in networking. A quality list is made one phone call at a time, one visit at a time, one networking interview at a time.

> **Myth's Assumption:** This myth is rooted in the belief that unless you have a huge list of great contacts, your search will be long and arduous. In effect, the quality of your networking is directly related to the length of your list. In addition, only senior-level contacts are of any use. Individuals in lessor jobs can't possibly know anyone or anything to help you.

Ironically, the senior managers whom you know to be well connected often are the least helpful and the folks who occupy "lesser" positions are often flattered by your request and will usually try to help the most. Unless you are a high-visibility executive, interestingly, the very senior executives may seem to be the most reluctant to open up their personal files to you, given the fact that you do not operate at their level!

What to do? To create a long list of high-quality network contacts, begin by brainstorming all the people you know—your business colleagues (past or present), friends, neighbors, relatives, college or university contacts, fellow congregation members from church, synagogue, or mosque, and so on.

After you develop your initial list of names, go back through it and prioritize these names on an A, B, or C priority basis, with an A name representing a person who might have really good contacts, be receptive to a call from you, and be supportive of you. To develop business contacts with executives senior to yourself, we recommend a two-step approach. First strengthen your confidence, personal power, boldness, as well as your networking technique with others whom you are comfortable. Second, visualize success in these networking phone calls to senior executives, in much the same way you visualized success with less senior executives. Envision the behavior, thoughts, and feelings of one of your senior executive contacts networking with a peer. Slowly it dawns on you that the confidence that these senior executives have when they network amongst themselves is exactly the level of confidence and personal power you feel when you are networking with one of your old friends and colleagues. The nervousness that we sometimes feel when we "network up" is of our own making. The trick is, therefore, to recapture and reexperience the confidence and boldness when you felt unbeatable—before you make your calls.

Myth 16. If You Are Terminated, You Will Become Cynical, Less Trusting, and Highly Suspicious of People and Their Promises.

Reality
"Once burned, twice shy," is an operating philosophy which many people seem to adopt if they have been zapped. If you have been really burned, you may have cause to have a high level of mistrust.

> **Myth's Assumption:** People will take advantage of you if you do not take a "hard and fast" position on things. In addition, if you have been terminated, you will never trust anyone again, ever.

Caution: There is a major "red flag" hiding in this myth. If you do not overcome and rise above your (perhaps, justifiable) negative feelings and eliminate them, your whole being may be poisoned. Anger and bitterness can and often will corrupt you physically, emotionally, and psychologically. You literally put at risk all your relationships in order to hold onto your self-righteous anger—no matter how "right" you may be. As a result of your behavior, you may unwittingly isolate yourself at the very time when you most need the support, care, understanding, and contacts to others. Notwithstanding, if you are hesitant and highly guarded while networking, your contacts may suspect that there is some hidden agenda and feel (unnecessarily) manipulated. If you allow your friends, colleagues, and family to experience your anger and upset, you run the risk of irreparably damaging your relationships because you are seen as a person who cannot be trusted. You might also be seen as a person who might be awkward or inappropriate with a close friend or a delicate network contact. If you are emotionally "out of control," people won't share leads with you, and your greatest networking fears will be realized.

What to do? Clearly there is a balance to be struck as we strive to assume responsibility for our lives and live in a nonblaming, nonvictim manner, as well as maintaining a high sense of urgency and career focus. When contemplating what you can do about managing the normal emotional "roller coaster ride" attendant to most career searches, please seriously consider the counsel we are sharing out of our clients' (and our own) experiences throughout this book. To specifically get a handle on how to handle stress, pressure and rejection, you may wish to review the comments in Secret 10, "Turn Around and Beat Rejection."

RAISE YOUR TELEPHONE NETWORKING COMFORT

―――――――――――――――――――――――――――― SECRET 4

Telephones are extremely potent search tools. Although the telephone can be your greatest ally, it can also stop you dead in your tracks before you get to first base. Presenting yourself powerfully, professionally, and clearly over the telephone is a critical marketing skill which must be learned by committed job seekers. Most all of us are very comfortable using the phone on personal matters, but many people have serious reservations about using the phone to generate leads and interviews. Let's take some of the mystery out of those first few moments on the phone and raise your telephone networking comfort level.

The "Verbal Résumé℠": Your 2-Minute Commercial ―――――――――――――――――――――――――

Obviously, your written résumé is a vital part of your job search campaign. Your résumé covers your entire career, highlighting important aspects of your responsibilities, accomplishments, and abilities using language that reflects your capabilities to contribute to another organization. It is critical that you develop the capability of quickly highlighting who you are during your networking calls.

Your "Verbal Résumé"℠* is a 2- to 4-minute, tightly worded, brief and punchy presentation that concisely presents a clear and interesting summary of you. It parallels your written résumé as it also highlights your key qualifications and how you can contribute. Think of your Verbal Résumé as

―――――――――

*The concept of the Verbal Résumé℠ was developed by Robertson Lowstuter, Inc., 104 Wilmot Road, Deerfield, Ill. 60015.

an advertising commercial filled with "sound bites," quickly gaining the listener's attention and with enough interesting benefits to make it worth the person's while to continue to listen. It is a well-prepared way to lift your listener away from your paper résumé and directly into communication with you. Just as your written résumé was scripted and clarified, your Verbal Résumé is also written out. Then it is revised and refined until it becomes an interesting, relevant, and action-oriented career synopsis which you can deliver in a nonhurried verbal style within 2 to 4 minutes. When you practice, "deliver" rather than merely read your Verbal Résumé into a tape recorder. That means speaking and gesturing as if you were in front of your network contact (or an interviewer). Use the full range of facial and hand gestures and tonality—raising and lowering your voice, as well as pausing for effect, altering the speed and pitch of your voice. Use all the vocal tools you would when trying to be convincing to another person. Practice it with your close friends, family, or friendly bathroom mirror. A great time to rehearse your Verbal Résumé is while driving in your car to appointments. Don't worry about the people in cars next to you, everyone has their own agenda, and yours is to powerfully deliver your Verbal Résumé.

Many experienced job searchers make photocopies of their initial presentations to keep near all their telephones as visual support. They find that these copies help their self-confidence and reduce worry about what to say next on the phone if they happen to get stuck for a loss for words.

When you do not have eye contact with an interviewer, you miss all the guiding signals of body language and facial expression available in a personal interview. A well-rehearsed written summary enhances your confidence as to what to say about your background. This frees you up to listen even more intently on the telephone to what your network contact might be saying and to notice voice changes or important leads.

The Six Elements of Your Verbal Résumé

Your Verbal Résumé consists of six distinct sections. Follow this format as you write out your Verbal Résumé.

1. Introducing Your Verbal Résumé

Take advantage of the first few critical moments of a network connection or interview to introduce your Verbal Résumé, since this is the time in which first and lasting impressions are made. After you have appropriately "linked up," established rapport, and, perhaps, learned something from the other person, you might consider using language similar to the following:

> **I wonder if it might be helpful if I were to briefly sketch-in my background, what I have been doing, what I'm looking for in my next position, and why I am leaving my company. Would that be helpful?**

In most situations your focus is very much appreciated and will meet with an immediate approval. Proceed immediately to deliver the rest of your Verbal Résumé which is highlighted in the following sections.

2. Career Focus

In a single sentence, concisely focus your primary career orientation. If you are an accountant you might begin by saying, **"I have a strong financial and accounting background and over 10 years experience in managing general accounting."**

If you are an engineer you might say:

I'm a registered professional engineer with fifteen years of mechanical and electrical instrumentation experience.

Or, if you are changing career focus, you might say something like this:

Although I have yet to manage my own sales territory, I have excellent work experience. I am able to successfully present ideas to managers, I'm persistent, and I have quickly learned every job I've been given.

3. Born and Raised

In a single sentence, briefly outline where you were born and raised. Do not go into detail. The purpose is to focus yourself geographically (East Coast, Midwest, West Coast, for example).

4. Education and Special Training or Skills

Briefly state your degrees, major subjects, and school name in about 5 seconds. Do not elaborate on your college experiences or choices unless you are a recent graduate. It is not necessary to fit this information chronologically into your presentation. Quickly cover the information here, so that you can concentrate on your experience. This handles "tickets":

I have my Bachelor's in Psychology from Aurora University and my Master's in Labor Relations from the University of Illinois.

You may also wish to cover special credentials in this section such as a CPA, PE, or RN. Relevant special nondegree or noncollege training can be included such as seminars or workshops. Be careful to only include those items that are relevant to this interview, as this can take up valuable time in your 3- to 4-minute limit.

If you have not completed your formal education, this section is ideal to focus your best skills and talents gained through on-the-job experience or apprenticeships.

5. Work History and Significant Accomplishments

Unlike your written résumé, your Verbal Résumé starts at the beginning of your work career and proceeds chronologically up to the present, without mentioning every position change and dates.

The reason for reversing this procedure is to quickly skip through your early years so that you can finish your presentation by talking about your most recent work experience.

Of the time allocated to this section, spend two-thirds of the time on the last five to eight years of your career and one-third on all preceding time. If your earlier experience is more important to the position you are seeking than your last five to eight years, then, of course you should shift your emphasis accordingly. Begin with your early position or positions in summary fashion and move up to the current time, listing companies, titles, key responsibilities, and accomplishments. A good rule-of-thumb for accomplishments is to provide no more than about four results for your entire Verbal Résumé. If you provide more, you will probably get bogged down in detail and your delivery will lengthen unnecessarily. The accomplishments which you select should be significant and represent a "mosaic" of your skills and capabilities.

Pay particular attention to your transitions from company to company. They should be reasonable and believable. Refer to new skills, responsibilities, or experiences which each new job has provided. Keep track of your time. Two to 4 minutes go by quickly, so diligently watch your tendency to provide more data than needed when the interviewer reinforces you with a comment (or an affirming smile, if you are face to face).

6. Reasons for Leaving

Until you discuss your reason for leaving your current employer, your entire discussion remains under a cloud. If you do not bring it up, your secondary network contacts (or the interviewer) will or should. When the other person raises the issue, it may be asked in an investigatory manner which may sound as though there is some suspicion about your circumstances.

If you bring it up, the issue of your departure is presented voluntarily and you are able to use language which clearly reinforces your candidacy. The result is usually quick recognition and understanding of economic, political, interpersonal, or organizational events, and you have the freedom to continue the discussion, further exploring your background. If you confidently reveal this potentially damaging information, everything else you say probably is believable. When you are using this information in an interview, conclude by asking the interviewer if he or she would like you to explore any of the preceding areas in more detail. If you are using your Verbal Résumé to introduce yourself to a network contact, conclude by offering a concise statement about your networking activities. The following example illustrates how one of our former clients, J. Michael Commons, introduced his reasons for leaving his current employer to one of his network contacts:

I have had a very challenging career with the TCA Company. I've been involved in every stage of the sales and marketing function and have advanced to National Sales Manager.

The business has recently consolidated its operations, with my division being impacted. As such, the need for two sales managers is not present. So given the limited opportunities now, I've decided that it's a good time to move on, and I am doing so with the full knowledge and support of the company.

While I'm uncertain about my next employer, I'm excited about the prospects in the marketplace. To that end, I certainly appreciate you taking the time to help me with some networking contacts.

Preparing Your Verbal Résumé

In conclusion, the six elements of a Verbal Résumé for your use in designing your introduction presentation are:

1. Introducing your Verbal Résumé
2. Focus
3. Born and raised
4. Education, training, skills
5. Work history and accomplishments
6. Reasons for leaving and current networking status

Before preparing your Verbal Résumé, review Figure 4-1, an example of an introductory summary utilized by another job seeker. The speaking time of this example is approximately 2 minutes and 55 seconds. Read this example out loud, with a watch, so you can experience an optimal delivery speed. Then, turn to Worksheet 11 and create your own Verbal Résumé.

At no point, should your uninterrupted Verbal Résumé be longer than 4 minutes. You'll have time for greater elaboration later, but not now in this capsule summary of your credentials.

Break through to Your Target Organizations _____

The eight tips which appear on p. 84 will help you break through to your target organizations:

A Verbal Résumé

I am an experienced corporate photographer with experience in all aspects of technical, product, advertising photography, and lab work.

I was born in the Kansas City area and was raised in California and the Midwest.

My education includes Photo Journalism at UCLA, and Commercial/Industrial Photography at Dresden School of Professional Photography and at Kodak Educational Center in Rochester.

My first assignment was as a photographer with the *News Tribune* in Long Beach, California. I covered news, sports, and fashion events and developed a strong sense of urgency in meeting deadlines. It was a challenging and creative position, but it didn't give me much variety, so I applied to several publishing companies.

I held several positions with publishing houses, completing many on-location commercial assignments. I also had the opportunity to manage a photography department with Durant Drug Company, where I also had supervisory responsibility and retail sales duties. I enjoyed managing the department as well as the special photography assignments.

I have a strong personal attraction to photography, especially in scenic and natural environments, and I have had exhibits and a one-man show of my work in New York.

Since 1974, I have been Corporate Photographer for Acco Brothers Co., a leading manufacturer in the specialty chemical field. I have managed all corporate in-house photography including:

- Catalogue, product, and advertising photography
- Public relations and executive portraiture
- Extensive on-location field assignments for product shots

I am experienced with most photographic equipment and in both black-and-white and color lab processing.

Recently Acco Brothers has chosen to close its corporate photography department and use outside services as a cost reduction move, and I am affected by this transition.

While I had no desire to leave the company, this transition allows me the opportunity now to look for another excellent company that has a strong interest in having a quality, in-house photographic capability. That brings you up to date on my background.

I sincerely appreciate the opportunity to network with you. Any questions about my background? No? OK. Let me ask you if I might— what search firms or employment agencies might you know of?

Figure 4-1.

WORKSHEET 11
My Verbal Résumé

Using the guidelines of the preceding pages write out your Verbal Résumé.

_____

_____

_____

_____

_____

_____

_____

_____

_____

_____

_____

_____

_____

_____

_____

_____

_____

_____

_____

_____

_____

_____

_____

(Continued)

1. **Prepare an opening statement.**   Write it down on paper and see how it sounds to you. Make it interesting and attention getting. If you bore listeners, chances are they will either politely dismiss you or hang up. Be prepared, confident, and enthusiastic.

2. **Practice.**   Practice delivering your Verbal Résumé until you can recite it without sounding sing-song or monotonous. If you get someone on the telephone who is interested, you can launch into it. Learn how to enthusiastically delivery your Verbal Résumé with the same high-level energy you use to talk about something of great importance to you. Keep the concept of "sound bites" in mind.

3. **Pick up the telephone and ask for interviews.**   To get network interviews, you must pick up the telephone and ask for face-to-face interviews. But this means knowing to whom you would like to speak, what you want to ask them, and where they can be reached.

4. **Prepare a plan of attack.**   After you have decided on your plan of action, prepare specific questions, and decide how you will answer some of the common questions which you may be asked.

5. **Record a few calls.**   Use your tape recorder to record a few calls. Listen to your voice and decide how you can improve your phone manner.

6. **Relax.**   Learn to relax on the telephone, listen, and react to what the person on the other end is saying. Take notes which you can read and refer to later. You need to get the facts the first time. Do not be afraid to have your network contact repeat or spell out a person's name, the name of a company, or an address. These facts are crucial to your job search.

7. **Describe who you are, what you want, and what you have to offer.** Keep in mind that all you will be asking for is an opportunity to meet for purposes of introduction and networking.

8. **Establish follow-up.**   Communicate your commitment to follow up on this initial phone call within a few days to either confirm the interview schedule or press for another meeting "for purposes of introduction."

A Practice Method to Build Telephone Confidence

Preparation is the key to building self-confidence in telephone self-marketing. Successful telephone communication is not achieved by luck but is the result of practice. Luck is what we call the effortless coming together of carefully practiced and executed skills.

You never know what people may say when you call them. If you are not prepared or have not practiced your telephone techniques, some of their questions can "throw you for a loop" and limit your successful introduction.

Review carefully the following four-step approach used by many job searchers to build their confidence on the telephone.

Step 1   Research

Step 2   Primary network contacts

Step 3   Secondary network contacts

Step 4   Target organizations

Step 1. Research

Build your confidence early in the job search by using the telephone for nonthreatening, low-risk information gathering or research. You are going to require a quality target list of companies which match the profile of your job objectives to contact about your availability, including such specifics as name of decision maker, title, telephone number, perhaps even sales size of company. Clearly, you would not want to send out your résumés to organizations on an impersonal "occupant" basis. You know how you treat such mail. Knowing that you are contacting the right person by name is a great confidence builder. It also significantly improves the quality of your contact, the company's perception of you, and the rate of response to your résumé.

So begin by calling companies on the telephone. Use the receptionist, other department people, or clerical people to get the correct name and title of the person whom you wish to contact later. Normally the best person for you to contact in a target company is your potential boss's boss—at least two levels up in the organization. If you just target the person to whom you might report, conceivably your credentials might represent a threat to this person. Obviously, this will require some creative research on your part; sometimes, however, it is well worth the effort.

This is the RL Research Group and I am verifying some data on your company. Can you please tell me the name of your company president? Can you spell that last name please? And her correct title, please? Thank you very much.

As you research your target firms in this manner, you will begin to feel your comfort level improving and your telephone skills becoming stronger. With very little risk on your part, you are able to get the "feel" of how to introduce yourself and your purpose quickly, to be creative in overcoming objections, and to use the telephone as a job search tool.

As an aside, while you may wish to also research the personnel officer of a company, it is important to note that the personnel representative may not be aware of job opportunities which may only be at the "conceptual stage" in the boss's mind. Since most bosses these days ponder a job need for months before actually activating a search, you miss a tremendous opportunity to gain an edge on your competition if you limit yourself only to personal contacts and do not entertain target organizations.

Step 2. Primary Network Contacts

Next begin using the phone to inform your primary network of personal friends, business and professional colleagues, neighbors, and acquaintances of your status and your career objectives. This shouldn't be too difficult. After all, these people are not strangers. They are people you know well and who would want to help you succeed. Introduce your job skills quickly to them. Ask them if they have any information or can provide leads into target companies, search firms, personal contacts, or if they know of any specific employment opportunities.

This activity is not at all like begging for a job. In fact, it is not even selling! **Do not even ask your network friends if they know of anyone who is actively hiring.** If you do a good job describing your skills and abilities, you will not have to ask. If they know of something current, they will volunteer that. Remember, if your contacts seem to "stiffen up" and say "I do not know anyone who is hiring" you have somehow miscommunicated your intentions. You need to clarify that:

> **Pardon me. I wasn't very clear. Let me try again. I am not asking *you* for a job. I am sorry if you feel as if I was putting you on the spot. Rather, I am interested if you know any companies (and search firms and leads) I might contact which fit my career direction. What are the firms you would call or the colleagues *you* would contact if you were looking to network?**

What you are after now is contacts—companies and people who might, from time to time, have a need for people with your skills. Here are the key things to say to your network contacts:

1. Crisply focus your basic skills, abilities, and career objectives.

2. Ask if your friend can suggest good **target organizations** that you should include in your target list which might have a future need for someone with your skills. They may even know the right person to contact by name or someone who would be able to "introduce you to the firm."

3. Ask if your friend knows anyone in **your list of target organizations.** Again, these organizations are ones you specifically want to have a relationship with, even though there might not be any current openings.

4. Ask if your friend can suggest any **search firms** or **employment agencies** through personal experience or through his or her company's personnel department.

5. Ask if your friend would provide the names of **personal contacts** for you, who might be willing to suggest companies, people, or search firms which might help you.

When you have called 20 to 30 friends and discussed your abilities and goals with them, you will find your competence and confidence level reaching new heights. Read the following sample to prepare for Worksheet 12.

SAMPLE NETWORK INTRODUCTION

As you may be aware, my company recently went through another reorganization, centralizing its operations, and my position was eliminated. I might have had the opportunity to remain in the organization in a lesser capacity, but I was not interested in putting my career on hold for 3 to 5 years. As such, I am looking with the full knowledge and support of the company for a challenging sales and marketing management position.

To recap, in my capacity as Regional Sales Manager I am skilled in new product introduction, field sales, account penetration, and dealer development. My strengths lie in creating distinctive promotional campaigns and training approaches which quickly produce results and improve sales and profits.

Step 3. Secondary Network Contacts

It is now time to contact your secondary network contacts. These people are the individuals your personal friends have recommended that you contact. This still isn't cold calling. Initiating these calls is a little bit tougher, but by now you should be getting really good at this. Actually, it is simply following up with people who will be happy to talk with you on the basis of your mutual friend's suggestion. When you call, immediately make the linkage back to your mutual friend. This makes your contact a bit easier and more comfortable. Then follow the same steps you used with your personal friends in Step 2.

Let's review how one of our job searchers, Jean Dorn, introduced herself to a secondary network contact:

Hello Mr. Reynolds, my name is Jean Dorn. You don't know me, however, I am a friend of Bill Gentry. He suggested that you might be able to briefly help me on a subject he and I were discussing. Have I caught you at a good time?

Mr. Reynolds, I am an experienced manufacturing manager, with an excellent engineering background and a solid track record of increasing productivity and reducing manufacturing costs in the consumer packaged goods industry.

WORKSHEET 12
My Network Introduction

Using information from the preceding page, write out your own introduction to your network contacts.

_____

_____

_____

_____

_____

_____

_____

_____

_____

_____

_____

_____

_____

_____

_____

_____

_____

_____

_____

_____

_____

_____

_____

_____

Because of some recent ownership changes over at Drexel Corporation, I am going to be looking for a new assignment. Bill said that you have good knowledge of your industry and he thought you might be able to suggest some good consumer product firms that I should send my name to so that they will know about me in case they have any future openings.

Continue making secondary network calls in this manner until you have made 20 to 30 calls. Since the use of your mutual friend's name minimizes resistance, concentrate on quickly introducing your skills, abilities, and accomplishments. Concentrate also on smoothly and comfortably shifting from introduction to your request for information. At this point you have now become a seasoned telephone networker. You have spoken to dozens of people. Your confidence level should be excellent. Now is the time to step out and follow through on all solid secondary contacts throughout your campaign and to call your target organization contacts.

Step 4. Target Organizations

Prepare a written outline to help you make direct contact phone calls to potential employers. Place it by your phone and refer to it to get started or if you think you might forget something.

Stand up and gesture when you talk to people, especially on the telephone. People will catch your enthusiasm and sincerity. Smile. Imagine the interviewer as a friend. If you knew you could not fail, how would you act? See Figure 4-2 "The A,B,Cs of Telephone Contacts" for a summary of good telephone skills.

Hello, my name is (name). I am the (title) at (company).

Recently my company has _____ and my job has been impacted.

I am interested in a position as a _____ or a _____ because of my experience and skills. While you might not have any appropriate opportunities at this time, I am interested in becoming known to your company should a need develop.

I am an experienced _____ skilled in _____, and my strengths lie in _____ and _____.

As I am just beginning to conduct a job search, I have identified your company as one I would like to get to know better. That is why I am calling. I am interested in (company) and any current or future needs you might know of within your company or others in our industry.

Highlights of my accomplishments include _____, _____, and _____.

Can we set up a brief meeting on _____ or _____ of this week, or would next week be better for you?

Thank you very much. I sincerely appreciate it.

The A,B,Cs of Telephone Contacts

A telephone contact has three parts:

A. Identifying who you are

B. Positioning what you want

C. Adding value

A. Identifying who you are.   Letting an employer know who you are is crucial. Pronounce your name slowly and understandably. Start with a greeting. For instance:

> **Hello, my name is _____. I am the (title) at (Company).**

B. Positioning what you want.   Get to the point quickly with an employer. Do not keep him or her guessing. Indicate that you either want to be considered for a position inside the company, or you are calling to network because your company's restructuring, (if that is the reason). Be specific and get to the point.

> **Recently my company has _____ and my job has been impacted.**
>
> **I am interested in a position as a _____ or a _____ because of my experience and skills. While you might not have any appropriate opportunities at this time, I am interested in becoming known to your company should a need develop.**

Read this out loud to yourself and be certain that you can be clearly understood. Speak up clearly. When you make the first few calls you may be nervous. However, after several practice calls, you will probably find your introduction becoming more relaxed, natural, and conversational. **Practice, practice, practice** will get you relaxed and feeling powerful.

C. Adding value.   This is the most important part of your conversation. The employer needs to see your potential as a valuable contributor. If you add value, doors will open.

- What do you have to offer that this company cannot do without?
- What are your skills, experiences, good qualities, and results achieved?
- How are you different from all of the other job seekers?

Tell the employer what you have done, what you can do, and what you would like to do. Use the qualities that you have already assembled, but **present them conversationally**—as if you were talking to a friend.

(Continued)

> I am an experienced _____ skilled in _____ and
> my strengths lie in _____ and _____. As I am just
> now beginning to conduct a job search, I have identified
> your company as one I would like to get to know better.
> That is why I am calling. Highlights of my accomplish-
> ments include _____, _____, and _____.
>
> Read the qualities you have listed out loud. You may want to make
> some changes in wording so that they are easier for you to repeat.
>
> **People take their cues from you.** If you believe in yourself—that
> you can contribute significantly to an organization, regardless of your
> role or level—then others will believe in you also. You will get what
> you create not only in life but also in your job search.

Figure 4-2.

Telephone Follow-Up

An integral part of your initial conversation with prospective employers or
networking contacts is positioning yourself for follow-up phone contact.
Often, your first connection with people will not yield the results which you
would like. You must plan to recontact them numerous times to gain meaningful leads or exploratory interviews. At the close of your conversation, ask
if you may follow up with a second call to keep your contact posted on the
progress of your search. When you do this confidently, provided you have
not made your contacts uncomfortable by pressuring them into providing
leads, most people will graciously indicate their acceptance of a recontact.

USE A COMPLETE NETWORKING MODEL AND INCORPORATE IT AS YOUR OWN

For every person actively conducting a career search and doing a good job networking, there is at least one "story" that illustrates how powerful and miraculous networking is. The truth is, you never know how your connections are going to develop or from whence they come. As soon as you figure out all the angles, another dimension will develop. Long ago we've stopped trying to predict **exactly** how things materialize through networking. Let us share with you a number of actual networking experiences. You'll note that in every case, these **people were effective at networking, using a strategy to create the outcome they desired.**

Thibault's Strategy

A few years ago, an architect friend of Clyde's from France wanted to explore the possibility of working in the United States, notably Chicago, because it is one of the leading architectural centers in the world. So his friend, Thibault Pigelet (pronounced "Tea-boe Pea-jol-lay"), networked with him. As a result of this networking contact Clyde agreed to help him in getting interviews with a number of Chicago architectural firms. Since architecture was not his field of expertise, Clyde had to develop a **strategy** which would enable him to successfully sell himself first, then Thibault, to these firms. Clyde's strategy was to start with **any** architectural contact. Let's hear the story in Clyde's words.

> *I thought to myself, "Who do I know who is an architect or who may know someone who is an architect?" As luck would have it, the property manager in our office complex was an architect. Since Mike was trained as an archi-*

tect, I knew he would know many of the firms in Chicago and the directories identifying the major architectural houses for me to contact. Indeed, my property manager had two leads into quality firms. With the directories he graciously provided and these two leads, I leveraged introductions into quite a few firms which resulted in 12 bona fide interviews with the partners of Chicago's leading architectural firms in four days! That's right. Twelve scheduled interviews in four days. What a madhouse. Thibault averaged three interviews a day. My wife, Carolyn, became his chauffeur, ferrying him from one interview to the next with the minimum amount of wasted motion. Carolyn had every route mapped out and even had alternate routes memorized if there was an unexpected delay. Talk about interviewing frenzy! From these interviews, Thibault generated several second interviews, two of which resulted in offers. Thibault was so talented and convincing, coupled with his natural ability to quickly develop rapport with people, that one of the offers was for an equity partnership in a small, rapidly growing regional firm in the city. Unbelievable! It was amazing how in a span of four days Thibault could generate two offers. It boggled my mind. How was I, a nonarchitect, able to convince twelve of Chicago's leading firms to set up interviews? Simple. I believed passionately in the quality of the product (Thibault) and I knew beyond a shadow of a doubt that once firms knew of his breadth of experiences and talent, they would be well pleased that I insisted on an introductory meeting. I believed in Thibault to such an extent that others did so as well. After he got the second offer, I asked Thibault how he was able to generate these offers. While he is fluent in English, he created these offers out of thin air, for these firms had no open positions. They had no plans to hire anyone—let alone a foreign national. Thibault in his usual modest way shrugged one shoulder and said, "Why not? It was what I wanted to do. I set my sights on it, I willed myself to concentrate powerfully on my goal to get an offer, and I wasn't going to be satisfied until I demonstrated what I could do."

If Clyde could do this for someone else, **you** can certainly do it for yourself—for who knows you better than yourself? What happened to Thibault? Well, as luck would have it, through this experience he created such an aura of confidence and competency, that he generated a virtual avalanche of new work when he returned to Sallanches, France, in the Mont Blanc Alps region before making his decision on which U.S. firm to join. That was a few years ago and he has elected to remain in France for a few more years until his children are a little older, then he and his family may start the campaign again for an opportunity in the United States. In Thibault's case, he fully utilized one of his many stateside contacts (namely, Clyde) to open up introductions in Chicago **target organizations** and **search firms** specializing in the architectural community.

The Perceived Difficulty of Networking _____

Many job seekers spend a disproportionate amount of time on low-yielding job search activities because they see networking as difficult. Why is networking seen as difficult? One of the reasons is a belief that networking is cold calling, and folks don't like to make or receive cold calls. How do **you** feel when you receive unsolicited calls from someone pressuring you to do something or buy something? Those calls are usually annoying at best, downright rude at worst. Very often we feel that when we are talking to individuals about our situation, that there will be a loss of face for us and a fear that they will misinterpret our call and think that we are asking **them** for a job. We don't want to appear to be pushy or manipulative or lose face, either. Rather we want to be in a position where people come after **us** as opposed to us having to go after and uncover the right job for ourselves. The extent to which we have these concerns and considerations is the extent to which we are roadblocked from networking effectively. Notice how many assumptions and beliefs are involved in this perception of networking. As we saw earlier, networking isn't cold calling or pushy if done well.

Your Networking Strategy: A Road Map for Success

To help you overcome your natural reluctance to network, let's talk about your networking **strategy** or **road map,** about how you can effectively network and "break through" your concerns and considerations about networking. **The core of networking** involves three primary activities which, when you master them, **will significantly enhance and accelerate your positive exposure in the marketplace.** We recommend that you create pocket cards with these tips on them and carry them with you as reminders. You may wish to call and order the "Anatomy of Networking" chart from our office which graphically outlines networking. This chart will serve as an effective guide for you, and it will also help to keep you from getting lost as you work through this topic in depth. Now, some people use index cards, other people use banners, flip charts, it doesn't matter. The point is, use whatever is a good trigger for you to master networking. In general, personal networking **is** the most powerful job source and job avenue. Networking will produce the highest yield for you in terms of job leads and activity in your search. Invariably, networking will produce more activity than advertisements or direct contacts to companies combined. Now, people ask, "What's wrong with mailings?" Many individuals changing jobs have heard that they should spend lots of time and significant sums of money sending out thousands of letters and résumés to companies. One popular but misguided job-hunting book that appeals to senior executives suggests that you should mail your resume to all 3000+ search firms in the country. Ridiculous! There are many search firms that have no business receiving your credentials because of their local focus or specialty. This is not meant to be a game of pure chance. Narrow your field of mailings down to the major firms, to your field of expertise and/or to a geographic region. However, some searches can be conducted by firms literally anywhere in the world. The operative word here is *appropriateness*—be appropriate in your selection of firms. Choose target organizations and search firms which match your profile of job, company, product category, and career objectives.

The most important tools of a job search is access to a fax and a telephone. What's wrong with mailings? Well nothing, really. However, there is a real danger in mailing to "beaucoup" target companies or to search firms or even to advertisements. Why? What's the danger? The danger is that while you are depleting your economic and time resources, you feel that you are productive because you are active. You are actively writing letters, getting them typed, and sending out your résumé. (By the way, there is hardly any good news in your mailbox.) The good news comes over the phone through networking calls initiated by you or by returned telephone calls on the basis of target companies or search firms. What we're saying is that **personal networking,** perhaps seen or experienced as the toughest market channel, **can produce the biggest yield for you.** We'll let you in on a little secret. It doesn't have to be the toughest. Effective networking is really a very simple process. It's like playing par golf. Playing par golf is simple—stay out of the water, stay out of the sand, and stay in bounds. On a par-5 hole, get in on the green in 3 strokes and putt out in 2. With a par-4 hole, get in on 2 and putt out with 2. Continue to shoot like this for every hole, whether you are playing 9 or 18 or 36 or 72 holes, and we guarantee that you will play par golf. Playing golf is simple. Effective networking is simple. It's a function of picking up the phone, informing people of your status, confidently asking for their help, and then legitimizing the sending of your résumé. These are fundamentally the three networking steps. It's simple, right! Everyone should be able to make it work, right? Riigghhtt? Nooo! Well! So, while playing par golf or networking is a simple process, it's not always easy, and therein lies the rub. Because we link "networking" with ideas and feelings and beliefs such as "difficult" or "uncomfortable" or "imposing on other individuals," we have a lot of hesitancies about it, and so we do not network as well as we could. Our premise is—let's make it easy on ourselves and let's learn how to network confidently, boldly, *and* effectively.

You Are Not Networking to Get a Job ⎯⎯⎯⎯⎯⎯

"What!??!! You're crazy, Dave and Clyde!" No, really. Your networking goal is not to **get** a job. (We thought this point of view would capture your attention.) Let us explain. If your goal in every networking call is to produce a job, then you will be putting yourself and everyone you call under a lot of unnecessary pressure to perform and conform to your expectations. You will be, without a doubt, one disappointed person and, indeed, may create upset when there is absolutely no need to have done so. We recommend that you recontextualize how you view networking, that is, shift your perspective on how successful networking might look and how you can gain confidence in the process. Consider the perspective on networking of a highly successful sales representative friend of ours, Carol Rogers. Carol has excelled in opening new accounts all over the country for her company. Over the past three years, she has led her company in winning contracts with many new customers in a highly competitive marketplace. Although excellent at retaining old business, Carol Rogers is the "hands-down" resident expert in generating new business. How does she do it? Carol says, "I don't go in to sell! I go in to help!" Carol estimates that while she is developing a relationship with a target account over several months, she may make half a dozen calls or more, not one of which generates a sale. Are her sales calls failures? Not at all. During these visits, Carol builds confidences by helping analyze and solve problems which she learns about. She establishes an image of competence, quality, service, and caring. In emergencies, she gives willingly, offering to be a back-up supplier or to provide the needed services to prevent a catastrophe. One day a need arises. They call Carol, and she reports a new customer. Carol does not visit target accounts to make sales. Rather, she visits to establish relationships of value, out of which sales will arise.

In much the same way, **you do not network to get a job. You network to establish your presence, add value, and introduce your ability to contribute to an organization's growth and profitability.**

We believe that success is defined as learning something from everything. You **fail** only if you have **failed** to learn from your experiences. To that end, **lighten up.** Look for ways you can be successful and joyous in all that you do, especially networking. Looking for a job is tough enough, don't make it tougher by setting unrealistic standards for yourself. Your new context for networking should be no less demanding than your most demanding day at work. In fact, it should be much less strenuous. **Your goal in networking is to *create* widespread visibility and exposure.** You are not networking to "trick" people into telling you about job leads or open opportunities that they might know of. Trying to "pull" leads out of people is high pressure. It isn't really straight, and what's more, it doesn't work. If you are like most people, you may be as concerned about how you are coming across or how you are being seen as you may view this process as a real hassle. Minimally, you want to be seen as bold, self-assured, and able to add value—so that your contacts willingly offer you all kinds of information and leads. If you have been terminated, you certainly don't want to appear to be damaged, pushy, upset, or frightened. Rather, you want to be confident and enthusiastic. **When your only goal in networking is to support others and establish a strong "value-added" relationship, it isn't difficult to be confident and enthusiastic!**

One of our clients, let's call him Tom MacT, felt so awkward about being terminated twice within two years, due to his new company's closure, that he did virtually zero networking. He was embarrassed and concerned about what people would say. He felt that because of his dismissal—through no fault of his own—he would be viewed as less competent than he really was. Tom knew that the job with the second company was high risk, but he took it anyway. As the general manager, Tom believed he could turn the company around quickly enough to salvage his job and also the jobs of 150 other people employed at this specialty consumer products company. Unfortunately, the bottom continued to drop out of the market, and the parent company closed this division. Try as Tom might, he could not convince himself that his networking contacts would understand and be supportive. Since it was awkward for Tom, it was awkward for others when he tried to talk about it. Regardless of the language which we helped him script out, he would invariably sabotage the support from others by his words or body language which apologized for being "zapped" or blamed the company for his fate. It was only after one of his best friends soundly criticized him for this self-defeating behavior that he snapped out of it. Once he regained a proper perspective and his confidence, Tom MacT started to yield results with his network. If you find that **your** networking with your colleagues or acquaintances or even relatives, does not produce the kinds of results which you want, there is a normal tendency to become discouraged, put yourself down, or even blame others. We know from personal first-hand experience what it is like when you create a victim role when your networking isn't very effective. In our book, *In Search of the Perfect Job,* Clyde tells of a time in his career in which he got zapped for the first time a number of years ago. It was not only devastating, but in addition his networking did not produce the kind of yield he had expected. He was very disappointed and saddened by this. It was **very** uncomfortable; he reported that he felt less than whole, and, ironically, he found himself retreating from others at the very time when he needed them the most in his life. As Clyde indicated, since he did not know then what we are teaching you now, he unknowingly isolated himself. Clyde was isolated and didn't have the skills to pull out of an emotional tailspin. Clearly, things weren't working. If you are like most of us on the planet when things aren't working, you will probably begin a dialogue with yourself like, "You really know who you're friends are!", or "I'm not as good as I thought I was," or "Maybe I don't have all the needed education or experience," or "Maybe I don't have the kind of endorsement I need from others to be successful." What happens when you hear this kind of internal discussion is that your confidence can be significantly eroded.

Turning *No's* into *Go's:*
The Power of Recontextualizing

Recently, we were working with a good friend, Bruce, who had been zapped from his aerospace defense employer when its military defense contracts were slashed. As an Engineering Manager, Bruce was technically very skilled and could be best described as an extremely bright, somewhat shy, and talented person; he had a terrible time networking. For all of his intellectual horsepower and accomplishments (which he took for granted—doesn't everyone?), Bruce had difficulty breaking out of his disempowering beliefs about networking. Bruce is a very gracious person and did not want to impose upon others in his job search. One of his strengths is often that he is able to effectively operate autonomously from others. So looking for a job without anyone else's involvement and intervention seemed normal to him. As an engineer (not unlike others in an analytical or scientific profession), he is comfortable with and skilled at relying upon his experiences to generate the results he envisions. Since networking was outside of his set of experiences, it was uncomfortable, unnatural, and awkward for Bruce. He associated negative feelings with networking and clearly gravitated away from learning the skills necessary to do it effectively. Bruce went even further to justify **not** networking. He created a "belief" or notion that people who actively networked had no pride, took advantage of others, and besides—it didn't work! He tried it once, and yes, no job resulted. See? He got what he focused on and believed.

How effective do you think Bruce's networking and job search really was? How effective do you think he was in developing positive new job opportunities given these beliefs? Not very? That's right—not very. He approached networking with feelings that alternated among **apathy** ("I know this is not going to work"), **anger** ("I hate doing this! I'm no good at it and it makes me uncomfortable"), **guilt** ("I'm only doing this because Clyde is making me"), **fear** ("I don't want to be rejected again, so I won't network"), **defeat** ("There are no jobs out there for me"), and **vindication** ("See Dave, I told you networking did not work!").

At first blush, you would think that Bruce would be highly effective at networking. He was educated, bright, highly skilled, very likeable, gracious, results oriented, willing to work hard to help his company and team succeed, and committed to contributing to his organization's growth and profitability. It was obvious to us he would make an ideal employee for the right employer.

We were frustrated in our attempts to help him until we asked him two key questions which unlocked the solution. The first question, "When do you feel **most** confident and powerful?" Bruce revealed he felt most alive when he succeeded at something—either solving a difficult engineering challenge or winning at sailboat racing or iceboat racing—two newly acquired passions. To the second question, "when do you feel the **least** powerful or capable?" Bruce further revealed that he really beat himself up when he was not successful. Although Bruce had all of these tremendous positive attributes and skills, he was paralyzed by his fear of failing in networking. He hated the prospect of not being successful. Ah hah! The key was for Bruce to experience some networking successes. Our role was to positively reinforce all of Bruce's efforts in networking, however so rudimentary. Everyone, even a household pet, will tend to repeat a behavior if positively reinforced. Bruce needed some solid successes to demonstrate that he, too, could effectively network.

Upon further exploration, Bruce realized that he was too passive in expressing his worth and too vague in the way he directed others to help him. Bruce needed to more clearly focus and telegraph the specific industries which he was targeting and more deliberately communicate the value which he could add to others. When he began to do both of these, his networking started to pay off. People opened up more completely and pinpointed contacts for Bruce to zero in on. Bruce went from grudgingly making three calls a weeks to initiating 10 calls a day while generating an average of three additional leads per call. It is truly amazing what can be produced when people believe in themselves, know what they have to offer, and are clear about their desired outcome. As a footnote, we're happy to report that Bruce accepted a great job as an Engineering Manager in a manufacturing operation as a direct result of his recontextualized networking efforts. The job was created especially for Bruce even though the company had not been planning to hire anyone, because it saw how valuable Bruce could be to its long-term technical strategies.

Developing networking competencies is like developing muscles—only this time—we are developing "networking muscles." Any new exercise is uncomfortable, awkward, difficult, and, sometimes, painful, at first. We may avoid it—even invent excuses to get out of it. It takes a lot of courage to consider doing it; after all, muscles ache and complain as they take on new loads and "build new competencies." But if we persist, soon the discomfort disappears and the muscles willingly and capably take on the new task. Persist and soon you, like Bruce, will be wondering why you hesitated to acquire this valuable new ability.

Three Steps to Effective Networking _____

We've alluded to the major steps in networking before. Now we will explore them in more detail. The three steps to effective networking are:

Step 1 **Inform** people of your status.

Step 2 **Ask** for help.

Step 3 **Legitimize** sending your résumé and **follow up.**

OK, now that we have an overview, let's deal with each one of these steps, one at a time.

Step 1. Inform People of Your Status

When you make contact, it's recommended that you quickly get into your agenda, in other words, the reason for the call. Most people will appreciate your doing that, besides they know that you have some agenda for calling them in the first place, so just get on with it.

> **Marian—as you may or may not know, my company is currently going through some downsizing, centralizing its operations, and I've been impacted. I may have had the opportunity to remain in the company, but I didn't want to put my career on hold for three to five years while the company sorted itself out and the industry stabilized. So I am looking now with the full knowledge in support of the company.**

Pause. Allow Marian to give some sort of an appropriate response, which might sound like: "Yes, I understand. These must be frustrating times for you. I'm sure you will do just fine. It sounds like you are a talented professional and you appear to have an excellent record of success. How can I help?"

> **Marian, thank you for your encouragement and your support. I really appreciate it. Perhaps, it's appropriate for me to give you a little bit of background of just who I am from a career standpoint, because you and I have only known each other socially. Will that be alright?**

> **Marian, as you may know, I've been the National Sales Manager for my company, and in my capacity I was involved in new product introduction, field sales, account penetration, and dealer development. My strengths lie in creating distinctive promotional campaigns and training approaches which quickly produce results and have improved profits for the company. These are the kinds of things I've done in the past, as well as the kinds of things I'm looking for in the future.**

> **Marian, what I'd like to do is pick your brain, perhaps getting some leads from you on search firms, target organizations, and some of your personal leads.**

Pause now again, allow Marian the opportunity to volunteer some information. Marian knows intuitively that you're going to ask for some help. Which leads us to the next step.

Step 2. Ask for Help

Get the point? Don't "beat around the bush" delaying the reason for your networking call. Keep in mind that your contact is possibly a busy person with people waiting and calls piling up. Your contacts will take time willingly to speak with you only as long as you are purposeful and focused. Your purpose is simple: "inform people of your **status;** ask for **help.** The longer you wait to get into the main agenda with your networking contact, the more potentially awkward things may become. When you're talking with Marian or any other networking contact, it's appropriate to follow the same four traditional careering avenues that you've been exploring generally. Those are: search firms, target organizations, personal leads, advertisements or specific opportunities that might be available. So when you're talking to your personal contacts, it's appropriate to ask them for the names of people whom **they** know in search firms, target organizations or personal contacts. You should also ask them about specific opportunities they may be aware of, as well as ask them to review those companies which you may have on your target organization list for possible intelligence or internal contacts. Your target organization list is composed of the top 10, 20, or 50 companies which you deem to be high-priority firms based on your selection criteria.

Step 3. Legitimize Sending Your Résumé and Follow Up

It's surprising to us the number of people who do **not** think to forward their résumés to their networking contacts. Indeed, it's baffling because it is so obvious and so expected. We have asked, "Why wouldn't you send your résumé to your contacts and then follow up to see if they have any questions, comments, suggestions, or additional leads, at the very least?" While the answers vary, the responses usually fall into three camps: first, they do not want to bother their contacts any more than they already have; second, they reason that their contacts know them so well that, of course, they will call if they remember something else (talk about taking someone for granted); and third, they forget to ask if it would be OK to send their résumé.

Regardless of what you have done in the past or had plans to do (or not do) in the future, **please always send your résumé to the people with whom you are networking.** By the way, we are also referring to friends of friends of friends. We are not suggesting that you limit your résumé mailing to only the people you first knew. We encourage you to send your résumé to every single person you talk with, especially if the person is someone you just met and he or she is a friend of a friend.

Developing A Dynamite Networking Contact List _____

A good question with which to begin your network list is: "Who should be included in my list of personal contacts before I actually contact them?" That is a far reaching and challenging question. You probably have already identified a number of your personal contacts, either informally (by merely thinking about them) or formally (creating a list of names). The people whom **you know** personally are your **primary contacts.** Your coworkers (superiors, peers, subordinates) in all of your employers (both past and present) are excellent starting points in building your network. Add to this list your friends, neighbors, relatives, and your business contacts in the form of vendors, suppliers, or consultants. Remember, salespeople who call on you also call on a number of other companies and have access to some executive corridors which you might not have. Your pastor, priest, rabbi, and your church directory are excellent sources of job leads, as are the members of municipal groups (the Chamber of Commerce) or social clubs (the VFW, Lions, Jaycees, Elks, Rotary or Moose, for example). Do not forget the professional people with whom you deal—your doctor, dentist, merchants, or even your barber or hairdresser. We suggest that you pull out all the business cards which you have collected over the years. We also suggest that you contact some of the participants and instructors at conferences, conventions, or workshops which you've attended.

Simply put, the referrals that your primary contacts give to you are considered to be your **secondary contacts.** No matter how many succeeding generations of contacts you uncover, consider these new contacts to all be secondary contacts, linked to someone else. Your goal with your primary contacts is to secure 3 to 5 additional names per contact, either in the form of target companies, search firms, personal leads, or specific opportunities. Appropriately, your goal with secondary contacts is not quite as ambitious, but it really should be a minimum of 1 to 3 additional names or leads or contacts.

In a moment, we are going to have you complete Worksheet 13, "My Personal Networking Contacts" in developing your own list of personal contacts. Even if you've already developed a networking list, regardless of its length, it's valuable for you to go back and to add to it. Presumably, you are reading this book because you want to enhance your networking skills or advise others in this process. While you might be a master in networking, we'd like to address some fundamentals, then build on them. Vince Lombardi, legendary coach of the Green Bay Packers and well recognized as a tremendous motivator of people, used to start out each football season by holding up a football. With a twinkle in his eye and steel in his voice, he would boom—"**This is a football.** While many of you people know how to play football, we are going back to the basics, then build up your skills." Even though he was known for always delivering this preseason speech, it was still stirring. Coach Lombardi's point was, it's better to build on a foundation of skills that are solid than to assume that everyone knows all the fundamentals and needs no additional skill training. We don't mean to offend you or anyone by being too basic, rather our hope and goal is to provide the optimal context in which highly effective networking can occur. Everyone thinks they can network well, after all, we are not dealing with rocket science here, yet when we diagnose stalled career searches, the reason for the stalled search is invariably because some subtle but key networking nuance is overlooked.

So, please work with us as we go **back** and explore these fundamental building blocks to your networking success. We'll start you in on this process in a moment, and you'll have an opportunity to continue to expand your list of personal contacts, however short or long that list is now. Ultimately, your goal is to generate a list of 50 to 150 names or more! Now, if you already have a list of 150 names, here's an opportunity to expand that list even more. These contacts might very well be good business or personal friends, colleagues, or merely passing acquaintances. Consider this—you are managing four major relationships on a 360-degree basis, at all times. You're managing the relationships above you (your bosses and their bosses), beside you (your peers or coworkers), below you (your subordinates, or other people below you in the company), and you're also managing relationships outside your organization (with vendors, suppliers, consultants, professors, relatives, friends, neighbors, and people you've met at colleges, universities, seminars, trade shows or conferences—**wherever!**

As you can see, you have four major sources of networking contacts. And you ought to be opening up each of these sources at all times. Fifty to 150 names? Although that seems like a lot, it's not really. To develop your list of contacts, we recommend that you take a long, hard look at the individuals in your company. By the way, when we say "company," we are using the term rather loosely to encompass all forms of organizations: service or non-service organizations, manufacturing, assembly, distribution, for-profit and not-for-profit, large or small companies, privately held or publicly traded. Your current company list will vary with the size of your organization, but you probably will have **at least** 5 or 10 or 20 or 150 people in your company. Now, you will not contact every one of these people, but you **will** contact a number of them. If you think of a person, however so remote the contact, put him or her on your list.

Creative Networking Avenues _____

Creative personal networking gives you an opportunity to open up new channels that you might not have considered or examined before. Let's consider a couple of angles. Take a look at people who call on you—consultants or manufacturer's reps. They are usually great contacts because they know people that you don't and have a vested interest in keeping you happy and successful in the relationship. Evaluate your major competitors and ask people inside your company who they know in these corporations which represent their keenest competition. Your colleagues might very well know the names of these people and may be willing to share them with you. Please do not misunderstand us. We are not recommending for a moment that you go to a competitor and damage your current or former employer or reveal proprietary information. **Far from it.** If anything, you need to be more circumspect and "close-lipped" when you are with your competition. Obviously, your ability to connect with your competition will depend upon your employment arrangement with your corporation, because you may have a noncompete clause. What we are saying is that going to the competition may be a good networking strategy, as they may be "predisposed" to you since you are from the same industry.

Oftentimes, it pays to let relatives know of your situation, even though they may not be in the same profession as you. As we mentioned earlier, it is natural for us to prejudge whether someone will be a good networking source for us without giving them full consideration. Our best example of never underestimating a relative's ability (*or* neighbor, *or* friend) to contribute to our network illustrates this point.

A number of years ago, we had a client who had recently gotten zapped and was in the process of contacting his friends, neighbors, former business associates, and relatives. He had a strong desire to relocate to San Francisco, but after weeks of searching for contacts in San Francisco, declared that he knew absolutely no one in the Bay area with whom to network. He mentioned in passing that he did have an aunt, in her nineties, who lived in Menlo Park, outside of San Francisco, but that she would be no help. After some persuasion on our part and some deliberation on his part, he reluctantly mentioned his predicament to his great aunt. His great aunt, who had never worked outside the house, was saddened by the news of his termination and, to his surprise, was resolute in her desire to help. Slightly amused, our client didn't give this another thought although he sent her a résumé at her insistence. Lo and behold, she informed one of her bridge partners, Paul, a former executive, also in his nineties, how much companies needed the skills her nephew had to offer and gave Paul the résumé.

Convinced that he did, indeed, have an interesting background, Paul made some calls and opened up several doors for our client. You see, Paul was the retired founder and CEO of one of the premier executive search firms in the world. He was extremely well connected in the West Coast and San Francisco, in particular, and knew dozens of executives and industry and community leaders. As a result of this boost and subsequent introductions, our client generated 12 interviews with the presidents of a number of national companies and several local firms. The moral of the story is, **never, never** underestimate your friends and relatives, **especially** 90-year-old aunts!

Prejudging Your Leads

In networking, your objective is to develop a **long list** of contacts. Do not **prejudge** people at this stage. By **prejudging,** we're talking about the intuitive decision-making process which you and others go through when you are evaluating the value of your contacts as potential network sources. Instead of **not** writing people's names down because you don't feel they would be able to help, our suggestion is to write them down. After all, it's only paper, and, besides, this process will surprisingly yield other potential personal networking contacts which you would have invariably forgotten.

A good example of this occurred during one of our assignments for a major insurance company. A group of nonexempt clerical employees were displaced by the corporate office's relocation. Most of them were middle-aged, inner-city women. Many had minimal education, few were high school graduates, most were in routine data-entry jobs. Yet, during their job-hunting skills workshop, that group discovered that they were either the relatives or close personal friends with the vice president of Human Resources, the chief buyer, and the secretary to the president and CEO in three of their target organizations.

Don't prejudge the ability of people to know people and open up new ideas when you network with them. Be prepared for surprises, coincidences, and enjoyable "small world" experiences. Open up your list and be as inclusive as you can be at this point. Ask yourself the question, "Who do I know?" The ricochet effect of contacts may surprise you, as one person leads to another to another to another.

The **quality of your list** will be related to the **quality of the questions you ask** yourself and the programming you do with your brain. If you ask the question, "Who should I avoid contacting?" your brain will identify a number of people you should avoid like the plague, and the feelings you have through **this** process will be less than positive. To produce the results you seek, a much better question to ask is:

> **What people can I call who are well-connected, will support me, and provide me the names of search firms, target organizations, and leads?**

Networking through Professional Associations

Professional associations or societies have always been a great source for networking. If you are not affiliated with a professional group you may wish to consider joining, as you can link up with people, in a quasi-social setting, who you might never be able to meet quite as easily. If you are so inclined to join it is our recommendation that you do so with the notion of being active in the organization. If you join strictly on the basis of "getting" and not "giving" your ability to network will be thwarted and convoluted as you run the risk of manipulating others (and yourself), and you won't be in a particularly visible role where informal networking really pays off. As you know, many consultants, vendors, suppliers, and job seekers join professional societies strictly for the networking contacts that they might happen to generate. Believe us, we're not knocking this as a strategy. However, to gain the maximum benefit from an association, you should serve in a leadership or highly visible support capacity role. That way you will be giving back to the group, you will be focused on supporting others (and less concerned about your own needs), and your interactions will be more genuine and less manipulative. A great metaphor of association participation is that of tending a garden: If you plant the seeds of involvement and nurture your contacts with your support, these relationships will bear networking fruit. Granted, we had to stretch a little for that metaphor, but you get our meaning.

Let's shift back to active networking for a moment. One of the questions you might wish to ask your contacts is:

What additional directories, associations, organizations, and people will yield new networking sources and leads that I can utilize?

After developing an exhaustive list, prioritize these names according to "A, B, C" priorities. Cross off people who are clearly marginal and always keep fine-tuning your list. Take a look at the professional societies in which you happen to be a member or should be a member, be they local, regional, national or international. Invariably they will have executive directors, membership directories, or conferences, depending upon the size of the association. If you have any kind of professional affiliation at all, it may be very appropriate for you to become known to the executive director or other key people within that society so as to be able to network effectively with them. Get your résumé into the résumé books that they keep. And even if they don't have a résumé book, see if they would be willing to keep your résumé in their top desk drawer. Employers do contact the executive directors of trade groups to see whether they know of any highly qualified individuals in a particular niche. Clyde recounts that a number of years ago when he was looking to hire some chemists and chemical engineers with a particular R&D background, he contacted the American Chemical Society and those universities that would most likely know people that fit his specifications. As an employer, Clyde was networking to meet the most talented professionals he could, and, as it turned out, he filled about 30 percent of all his company's technical staffing needs through this avenue. According to Dave, there was often a "career corner" for conference attendees with the opportunity to sign up to interview with representatives from various member companies who might be looking to fill some role. These career corners will also have résumé books in which job seekers put their résumés in the hopes that a company decision maker would leaf through these books and be interested in them. If Dave was attending a society meeting specifically for recruiting purposes, he would pick up these résumé books and leaf through them. He hired many key people for his firm through such conferences. You might wish to attend the conference to interview one or more of your target organizations attending such a conference. Networking at trade shows and conferences does work! In both of our experiences, we were successful in getting leads this way and almost always conducted interviews in small conference rooms set aside for that purpose or back in our hotel rooms, if we were really interested. In terms of personal contact networking, you might think, "Gee, that seems to be more of a target organization market channel job source because you identified specific companies in this manner." We don't care what you call it, whatever avenue you utilize to make connections, the point is that there are numerous ways to gain exposure and you ought to be exploring all kinds of possibilities.

Enough of our ideas about networking for now. Let's develop your list of contacts. Please turn to Worksheet 13, "My Personal Networking Contacts" or, if you prefer, get a large pad of paper so you have plenty of room to write. Come on, this is not just a **reading** exercise. This is a **writing** exercise. No matter how skilled you are in networking right now, this will be a valuable exercise for you and can only enhance your skills.

Expanding Your Networking Contact List _____

If you are feeling that your list is complete and you don't need to "flesh out" your list any further, congratulations! You must have a lengthy, high-quality list indeed. However, we really encourage you to push just a little more. Why? Because you may be surprised at the additional names which you create and, more important, if you're not actively working through these exercises, you won't have the opportunity to open up new possibilities. You won't get quite the same level of benefit. If you actually write out some of these exercises and free up your brain to some additional possibilities, you will produce greater results than if you merely think through what you might have written down.

On Worksheet 13 or on your paper, you should have already quickly written down the names of people who would be **potential** contacts as they occur to you. Again, **do not be overly concerned about the quality of your list right now.** This first pass does not mean that you will be contacting each person—rather this is a "warm up." We want you to make a second pass through your list of contacts using the first set of names as a springboard for additional names. **Pull out your list or worksheet and refer to it now.** As quickly as names come to mind, write them down. Even

WORKSHEET 13
My Personal Networking Contacts

Write down the names of people you know from past or present employers, friends, neighbors, colleges or universities, vendors, suppliers, consultants, etc. Do not prejudge the quality of the relationship. Work quickly and write down every name that comes to mind. Your ultimate goal: 50 to 150 names. Assign A,B,C priorities with A contacts being the people you feel are your best contacts and C contacts being your weakest or remote relationships.

NAME	NAME	NAME
_____	_____	_____
_____	_____	_____
_____	_____	_____
_____	_____	_____
_____	_____	_____
_____	_____	_____
_____	_____	_____
_____	_____	_____
_____	_____	_____
_____	_____	_____
_____	_____	_____
_____	_____	_____
_____	_____	_____
_____	_____	_____
_____	_____	_____
_____	_____	_____
_____	_____	_____
_____	_____	_____

(Continued)

NAME	NAME	NAME
_____	_____	_____
_____	_____	_____
_____	_____	_____
_____	_____	_____
_____	_____	_____
_____	_____	_____
_____	_____	_____
_____	_____	_____
_____	_____	_____
_____	_____	_____
_____	_____	_____
_____	_____	_____
_____	_____	_____
_____	_____	_____
_____	_____	_____
_____	_____	_____
_____	_____	_____
_____	_____	_____
_____	_____	_____
_____	_____	_____
_____	_____	_____
_____	_____	_____
_____	_____	_____
_____	_____	_____
_____	_____	_____
_____	_____	_____

as you are reading and you think of a name, don't stop—write the name down. Even though you may feel that you have a large contact list now, you can still expand it.

"How do I expand my list?" you ask. Here's how. Command your mind to give you new names or names you already have but in a **new** context or in a way you've never looked at before. Ask your mind for new **linkages.** Even as you are reading, you're thinking of individuals as they come up. So write them down—write, write, write, write!! Additionally, ask your spouse or closest relative for ideas or people you know.

For those of you who are developing your list of names for the very first time, write down anyone or anything. "Anything?" Yes, anything—as your idea may be a school or a conference or a university or a company. Your mind will sort out these people in this category later, but first of all, get it down. Don't stop writing while you're reading; you can do two things at once! Faster, faster, faster. If you think of a name, write it down. Don't worry whether it's a person you'll contact later. Just get it down. You can cross out names later, if you like. A duplicate name, no problem. You will catch it later; don't stop now.

Keep in mind that you do not have to be in a close relationship or even one in which you've had recent contact. We recently had a former out-placement client who had graduated five years earlier stop by. Years ago, all of us had became very close friends as we helped him rediscover himself and manage an effective career search which landed him in a vice presidency role out of state. He was in town on business and it seemed like old times. "Boom!" Our reunion was marked by instant chemistry, great rapport, plenty of energy, lots of smiling and laughter followed by serious discussions and an in-depth strategy session as to his next career move. However distant the contact, write it down; friends, neighbors, relatives (yes, even your great aunt!), business colleagues (past or present), vendors suppliers, consultants, and even college or university contacts (which should include students, faculty, and staff).

OK, at the end of this paragraph, we want you to **stop reading** and write without interruption for about 5 minutes more. Then you can come back to the narrative. Even though you have been jotting names down all along, we still want you to brainstorm for 5 short minutes longer. Thanks. Now turn aside from the book and write. We'll be right here in 5 minutes. Good luck and have fun!

Developing and Expanding Your Networking List _____

Welcome back. OK, stop writing! However, keep your pencil or pen handy in case you get a flash of inspiration now that your brain is warmed up. We're going to capture the names of people you've developed and take it one step further. To be able to complete this exercise well, we are going to pretend that we are across the kitchen table from you and you have just shared the names of some of your personal contacts with us. Yolanda, Carolyn, Sam, Rhasid, Beth, George, Chris, Emily, Juan, and Patty. For illustrative purposes, let's take George.

One of the things that you're going to do with George is that you're going to call him, right?? And you're going to inform him of what? Your status. Good. So let's role-play a little bit. When you contact George, you might say something like the following:

> **George, as you may or may not know, there's been a reorganization and downsizing in my company and I've been impacted. I'm coming out of the organization with its full knowledge and support, and I have just begun to network. I wanted to tell you of my situation. You are one of the people that I trust and I respect, and you seem to be pretty well connected.**

Obviously, this aforementioned statement is relevant if there has truly been a reorganization. However, if you have left or are contemplating leaving given a significant shift in your company's direction, you may wish to consider something like this:

> **George, due to unforeseen economic conditions, the company has decided to reposition its priorities. This shift significantly limits my career options for the future. While I don't mind delaying some of my plans, I'm not interested in putting my career on hold for several years. To that end, I'm looking with the company's full knowledge and support, and I am actively networking. Can you share with me the names of the search firms you know of in the area, please?"**

Or, let's try another one.

> **George, as you may know my company has been restructuring over the past few years. In order to gain more control of the business during a growth time, they have been centralizing a number of functions. Over the past few months, I have helped centralize much of the control of my own function and position. It's a good idea and I support it, however, it leaves me with less managerial duties and in a sole contributor role. While I can do this, it's really moving me backward and I have had to reconsider my overall career strategy. I've talked this through with my company and we've come to a positive understanding which allows me to look for something which will move my career forward. So, I'm leaving the company with their full knowledge and support and I need some help. You are one of the people I trust and respect. You seem to know a lot of people, George. May I ask for your help?**

By the way, you have three agendas in your conversation with your friends, like George. You want to **inform** George of your situation, **sup-**

port him by acknowledging how much you value the relationship, and **ask for assistance** in providing leads into search firms, companies, and personal contacts. After all, George is well connected and a friend, isn't he? Right? Right!

Increase Your Personal Power— Take Responsibility

When you talk to George and all your other contacts, be straight-forward, confident, self-assured, and nonblaming. Most of all, *do not be a victim.* Volunteer why you are leaving. Look for ways to begin with the phrase, "The reason why I'm leaving my company may be of interest to you. It is because . . ." If you operate as a victim, talking about what has been "done to you," people will flee from you because victims are blame-oriented and generally emotionally damaged. They are certainly not much fun to be around; they are depressing. It doesn't work for you to be operating out of the context of being a victim. If you're a victim in your perspective and language, you will have very little personal power. People don't want to be around individuals who are whining and complaining about things. Have the tone of voice that says—

> **Actually, this might be the best thing for me. This fits in rather well with some of my personal and career plans that I haven't been able to implement to date. This move enables me to do something different. I appreciate your support; I'll be OK.**

If they volunteer or observe that, "Gee, I'm really sorry that you've been terminated after 22 years with the company. It must be pretty disappointing." Our recommendation is that you respond with something like,

> **Thanks for your concern. I'll be fine. It was initially a shock to me as well, however, I've found that it's actually operating in my interest. While I did have a chance to remain in the Company after its reorganization, I didn't want to put my career on hold for three to five years. On balance, I'm actually pretty excited about the possibilities that lie around the corner. I'm not exactly sure what is in store, but I know that things will work out just fine.**

However you say it, it's important that you acknowledge that while you were initially disappointed, that you will be fine. Indeed, you might even have been a little shocked by this situation, but you are in good shape and in good spirits, and you're managing this process well. It's well accepted that we sometimes get involved in situations where things are promised to us and then, for any number of reasons, they don't work out. People understand that life's not necessarily fair and that involuntary termination is, unfortunately, increasingly commonplace. **It's not so much what happens to you, it's how you react to things that counts.** And interestingly enough, people will take their cues from you. If you are incredibly upset, others will be, as well. However, if you are confident and self-assured, you will significantly minimize the upset in your family and friends.

W. Mitchell: A Study in Courage

Have you heard of W. Mitchell? His incredible story is a testimonial of the strength of the human spirit and a powerful metaphor of every person's ability to push through life's toughest adversities. Mitchell is a former San Francisco trolley car conductor who was involved in a life-changing motorcycle accident. As Mitchell tells the story, he was driving home from an airport, where he was a student pilot, and got distracted by something on the side of the roadway. When he turned back, to his horror, he noticed that a truck was stopped in front of him. Unable to stop at 65 miles an hour, Mitchell effectively dropped the bike on its side and skidded along with the bike. For a second or two of slow motion action, things were fine until the gas tank cap popped off and the sparks from the skidding bike ignited the gas spewing from its tank. Burned over 75 percent of his body, Mitchell endured months of searing pain and agonizing skin grafts and excruciating rehabilitation. His fingers which once gripped were now stubs, as the fire had burned them off to his knuckles. His features were unrecognizable. Mitchell recovered slowly and painfully through much determination and courage. Several years after his hospital stay, Mitchell became an entrepreneur and built a sizable business in, of all things, wood burning stoves and, indeed, became the leading entrepreneur in a small town in Vermont. Years later, Mitchell took up flying again and secured a multiengine rating. One day Mitchell was taking three of his friends flying. As he lifted off, life seemed almost perfect. Yet at 50 feet, suddenly without warning, the plane began to shudder and then plummeted to the runway and crashed. All passengers safely exited the plane, except Mitchell. He couldn't move. To his horror, he was paralyzed from the waist down. To be the victim of a disfiguring fire and now this! It was almost more than he could bear. But Mitchell also had the resolve that only a few of us ever dream about, let alone possess. Mitchell had a passion for living and was not about to give up. He tells of his rehabilitation time in the hospital when he met a young man who was an excellent athlete who loved mountain climbing. In fact, that was how the young man became paralyzed, he fell during a climb. He was angry, bitter, inconsolable. To this young man, life no longer had any meaning. He wanted to die. Mitchell recounted that he sympathetically, yet forcefully confronted the young man with the phrase for which Mitchell is now known:

It's not what *happens* to you that matters, it's what you *do about it* that counts!

Mitchell refused to give up. Clearly he had experienced a tremendous loss, certainly more than we'll ever want to know. For Mitchell, living to the best of his ability was the **only** option. He courageously focused on what he **could do** versus what he **couldn't do.** He assessed what he **still had** and refused to be defeated by what he had lost. For you see, Mitchell's belief in himself never wavered. The way that Mitchell viewed himself had not changed, though clearly his physical body had. A number of years ago, Clyde had the privilege of meeting Mitchell at the National Speakers Association annual convention in Dallas. Mitchell was a sight to behold, encouraging people, getting and giving hugs. A moment or two in his presence was all that you needed to be captivated by his sparkling eyes, sharp wit, and dazzling smile. Clyde indicated that he and thousands of others were emotionally touched by Mitchell's confidence and love for life.

W. Mitchell's story is a beautifully poignant example of how the quality of your life is in direct relationship to the quality of your communication to yourself and the beliefs that you hold. People responded genuinely to Mitchell because of his confidence, courage, and commitment to living life to the best of his ability. Likewise, **the extent to which your personal networking contacts will give you information will be in direct proportion to the extent that you genuinely communicate your confidence and well being.** The extent to which you appear beat-up, angry, and vindictive about your company, that's the extent to which your contacts will withhold information and endorsement from you. We can guarantee you that if you blame your boss or company, your personal contacts will not volunteer the names of companies, search firms, or people you need. And while you might feel that the people whom you contacted are really interested in knowing what's going on in your life, in actual fact, they may not be deeply interested. What they are probably interested in, however, is to what extent you're beat up. Please do not get "suckered" into providing more information than is required or information which may be construed as negative. If you have any doubts about how well you are responding, ask someone you trust to listen to your explanations and give you straight feedback.

For example, the question, "How are you doing?" is genuine, but it's also a normal societal response. It's like, "What's going on? What's the buzz?" People **really** don't want to know everything about your current state of affairs. Don't unload on them. So, although you might be down on your luck, you might be desperate, you might be destitute, you might really want a job, you should never communicate that level of desperation. Why? If you do, the opposite will most likely occur. What will happen is that brutal honesty will, in all likelihood, distance you from your contacts. Let us share with you an example of how desperation can unknowingly show through.

A number of years ago one of our clients, whom we will call Sam Gregarious, asked our advice on both his networking and interviewing approach. After observing and critiquing him, Sam asked us, "When do I need to worry about how I am coming across?" Our response was, "Sam, when you are worried about how you are coming across (or being seen), that **is** the time when you need to worry." Sam was so concerned about making the right impression, that he was always seen as trying too hard—trying too hard to be liked, trying too hard to get his ideas across—so much so that it turned employers and networking contacts off. He was **waaay** too intense. Our advice to Sam was to slow down, sell less, listen more, and concentrate on finding out the needs of the other person. When he focused on the other person he discovered he was much more credible and effective. He was able to simply and easily step out of the way of the networking process and be himself. Sam also discovered that the leads were being more readily volunteered without him having to force them out of his contacts. As it was in Sam's case, it is very important for you to speak calmly, coolly, rationally, to have a sense of positive expectancy, and be of good cheer. If you have conflicting emotions, it may be appropriate to acknowledge that fact with your contacts. **"While I'm a little disappointed that I have to look for a job, I'm enthused by the possibilities that I see out there."** It's really ironic that the time when you need a job the most, when you need the contacts the most, when you need the support the most, those are those times in which you are least likely to get them. The time when you're **most** desperate for a job is the time when that desperation will invariably show through. When times are getting tough, that's when you need to be even **more** "enthusiastic," more "excited," and more focused on your outcome. Remember the adage, "When the going gets tough, the tough get going"? To master networking, this needs to be more than platitudes or clichés, this needs to be your operating philosophy and approach to life.

MASTER THE FOUR AVENUES OF NETWORKING

The four major avenues for job hunting and networking are:

1. Executive retainer search firms or contingency recruitment firms
2. Target organizations
3. Employment opportunities
4. Personal contacts

Let's go back to our networking example that we started in Secret 5. When you call George, you're going to ask him for his help pursuing these major job-hunting avenues. So, if George immediately says to you, "Gee, I don't know anybody," what you've just done—albeit unintentionally—is perhaps communicated that you want a job or job lead from George or that you have very specifically asked, "George, do you know where a job that's perfect for me is?" Keep in mind that there may be some level of pain associated with your departure. And if George gives you a lead into a company, and you get connected, and then it doesn't work out, George may feel responsible for causing you additional pain. George may not want that responsibility. To that end, you may need to make it safe for George to help you.

Search Firms—Retainer and Contingency

George, what search firms have you worked with and who do you know in these search firms? Have you ever been contacted by a search firm?

If yes, "who are they, who are the account executives, what are their telephone numbers (both general numbers, direct dial, and quite possibly residence numbers)?" Now is the time to let George talk. You shouldn't continue to ask questions. Give him a chance to respond. If he responds, great. If he doesn't, then you should gently continue the questioning and probing:

George, I know it might have been a while since you last spoke with this person. Do you recall the name of this account executive? Might you have the phone number? When was the last time you talked to this person? Might you have the secretary's name and phone number, as well?

It's appropriate to gather this kind of information so as to be able to quickly establish rapport when you call these search firms. You're trying to make a distinction between yourself and dozens, maybe even hundreds, of other individuals calling. So from that standpoint, try to get as much information as you can.

Now if George has never connected through a search firm or has never been contacted by a search firm, then you want to ask,

George, do you know anyone that has ever been contacted or been hired through a search firm?

George will either say yes or no. If it's yes, follow the same procedure.

George, who is that? May I have his or her name, telephone number, company, etc.

George just gave you Regina's name, let's say, as he thinks she recently was hired through a search firm. It's our recommendation that you contact Regina and turn her into a networking source. By the way, we've included some specific language you may wish to adapt for your own use to initiate contact with a secondary contact. When you contact Regina, approach her in the same manner that you've contacted some of the other leads from George. Your contact with Regina could sound something like this:

Regina, George gave me your name as a person who could possibly help me with an introduction into area search firms. He thought that since you most recently connected through a search firm it would make sense to get this contact information. To give you some background on me, I am an experienced sales and marketing manager whose organization recently restructured, eliminating my position with many others. George respects you very much and suggested that I contact you, as I am interested in networking with search firms. What search firm did you recently connect through? _____ Thank you. May I have the name of the person you dealt with, please? Do you have their numbers?

Another wrinkle to the executive search firm lists is that if George has never been connected in a company via a search firm or employment agency, if he's never been contacted for a job by a search firm, or if he doesn't know anyone who has ever been contacted or hired through a search firm, then the next option is to see if you could contact a knowledgeable human resources professional in George's firm.

George, who is the head of Human Resources in your company who may know of high-quality search firms?

George responds, "It's Terry Thomas."

Great. What's Terry's extension or when we're done here, can you transfer me?

Why do you want Terry's telephone number? Quite simply, it is because you want to network with Terry about search firms. However, you may wish to prequalify Terry first.

George, tell me a little about Terry, what kind of a person is he? Is he approachable? How might he respond to a phone call from me? What do I need to be on guard against? What are some of his "hot buttons"? What's his secretary's name and telephone number?

Our best educated guess is that 80 percent of the people whom you call at first aren't going to be around; they're not going to be available to take your call. You will have to leave a message. To that end, you're going to need all the "hooks" that you can possibly get to have them call you back on a timely basis. Although we know we're speaking about some pretty obvious things here, the name of the secretary and the secretary's extension and direct telephone number, night lines, and all this "stuff" are important hinges for you to be able to leverage back into these companies in a powerful manner. If your network contact knows this information, it may be very helpful to you later. You're trying to establish rapport with your secondary contacts, and the more areas of commonality, the more pieces of information you've got, the more skilled in networking you will be. Now, let's just assume for the moment that you now have the name of the human resources head and you've already determined that George does, indeed, have a good relationship and he is not outplacement bound, insofar as George knows. When you call Terry Thomas, the Human Resource vice president, you say,

Terry, George recommended that I touch base with you, given that I'm conducting a job search, and he thought you would know the best search firms in the area. Could I ask you some questions about the search firms your company uses?

As you can see, we've quickly introduced the agenda to Terry. Don't beat around the bush, don't get into 25,000 well chosen words about your life's story or any of that sort of thing. This is not an autobiographical sketch, rather a brief introduction. Just get right into it.

Assuming Terry identifies some of the company's search firm contacts, be sure to get Terry's permission to use his name when you contact each search firm. If you turn back to the first part of this conversation, you'll notice how we started out with George as one of our contacts and we've expanded it. Although Terry doesn't know you, you're a friend and colleague of George's, so hopefully he will give you several names. It's really no skin off Terry's nose because the search firms will or won't have jobs for you and then correspondingly you'll get connected or you won't. In actual fact, Terry doesn't have any loss of face, per se. Nonetheless, always, always, always, **ask** Terry, "What is the best way to be introduced to these firms, Terry?" If you strike up a warm conversation and present yourself as confident and bold, Terry may even volunteer to call on your behalf.

Anyway, when you're chatting with Terry, your focus is on search firms. But in much the same way that you've informed George of your status, asked for help, and legitimized sending your résumé, you'll also want to do the same thing with Terry Thomas and all your other contacts: "Terry, thank you very much. You've been very helpful. I look forward to contacting these search firms. By the way, may I use your name?" (Yes or no.) If he says, "Well, I really don't know you," say

> **Terry, I can well appreciate that. You don't know me, and besides I'm really not looking for a job, *per se*. As you know, the goal of networking is to gain visibility and exposure. It's a little bit like the old adage about moving string. "There are two ways to move a string. You can either pull it or push it. I'm really more interested in pulling the string—gaining leads and contacts because I know that at the end of the string eventually is the right opportunity. It's all a matter of timing and luck. As you know, networking increases that probability. So Terry, I promise not to embarrass you or be inappropriate. May I have the names of the search firms you'd turn to?**

If you legitimize Terry's objection, add a little value, relate to Terry as a colleague, and operate in the same kind of results-oriented style as he does, chances are pretty good that Terry will allow you to use his name. Why? Because you've established rapport and you've conducted yourself in a way to make Terry feel confident in your ability to call these search firms and other people and not embarrass him. Executives don't want to get caught with their data down and don't want to be surprised. Now, we should note that George (and your other contacts) may have already given you the names of search firms to whom you've already sent a résumé. You may even know the people Terry gives you and have perhaps even called them. That's OK, as **your goal is broad-based networking.** It's OK to call them again and say, "Terry told me to call you." "Oh, you know Terry too." See, the more contacts, the more hooks that you've got, the greater the probability of a connection. Now, we're not suggesting that every three days you recontact the same search firm. We guarantee you that if you do, you will be seen as desperate and inappropriate; besides—you won't get any of your calls returned. There are two schools of thought about contacting search firms. The **Search Firm School of Thought** is don't contact them, they will contact you—if they are interested in your background. A highly visible national retainer search firm will receive up to 5000 unsolicited résumés a month. A friend of ours, Dan O'Hara of Lynch, Miller, Moore Partners, a well-known Chicago-based retainer search firm shared that they, like most search firms, clearly want to avoid getting unsolicited telephone calls because if they took every call, there would not be time left over to conduct bona fide searches. However, the **Job Searchers School of Thought** has as its premise active, assertive, and creative networking. Although you are certainly sympathetic to the search firm's plight, you want to be able to distinguish yourself from the hundreds and hundreds of other job candidates. Without a doubt, it **is** the relationship you are able to create with people that will make the difference. To that end, you have to become known to the retainer and contingency search firms, as that is where many searches are found.

You've heard our truism: "People hire people they like." Well, that's true. People hire people they like and that are like them. The way to build rapport and trust is to have areas of commonality, that is common interests or common friends. It stands to reason that the more points of commonality which you can identify, the greater will be the probability of personal chemistry and rapport. Have you ever noticed that when you make a connection with someone, the personal chemistry and the enthusiasm between the two of you seems to dramatically increase? Isn't that interesting? Having something in common tends to bond people together like glue. If we are networking or marketing ourselves to a potential client firm, we are always on the lookout for areas of commonality with the other person, be it family pictures, travel experiences, some hobby, or philanthropic interests that we both have in common. Let us illustrate the point with something Clyde is involved in. Again, in Clyde's words:

As part of my "midlife crisis," I earned my private pilot's license. Actually, learning to fly was something I have always wanted to do—since high school—but I never felt that I had the time or the money. Well, now I've got the money and I have considerably less time, but it has become a much higher priority for me. I really enjoy flying—it is such a kick. To be able to take off and see commonplace sights from an uncommon angle is beautiful, and to be able to master the art of flying is immensely rewarding. The thing that I really enjoy about flying is that I am continually learning and challenging myself to be more skilled and more observant as to what is going on around me. When you are flying a single-engine plane in controlled air space, you have to be constantly monitoring your environment— you cannot daydream. You have to be vigilant, as you get immediate feedback as to how you are performing. If you don't pay close attention you can easily stray off course, your landing will be an embarrassment as you bounce down the runway, and your flying will appear erratic and unsafe. If it sounds as if I like being challenged and being on the edge of the comfort zone, that's true. I personally like being on the edge of my competencies, although it can be pretty uncomfortable at times, as that is where the real

test of myself is. For the vast majority of pilots, flying is a tremendous oppor-
tunity for them to get in touch with themselves at a most profound level. So
when I discover another pilot, the jump in the personal chemistry and rap-
port is clearly visible. Both of us become visibly more enthused and excited
and we smile more freely and laugh more easily. There is a solid connec-
tion, and the discussions which follow become richer and warmer, as the
camaraderie which links us as air travellers now seems to bind us together
on the ground. A certain level of trust is implicit, for as a pilot you have to
be a person of discipline and integrity to be able to pass muster behind the
yoke of an airplane. Now, there are some pilots I personally wouldn't spend
5 minutes socializing with, but insofar as flying is concerned the height-
ened and instant chemistry is certainly there, nonetheless.

Our point is that making "chemistry connections" are important and valuable. However, please do not misunderstand us. Whereas highlighting areas
of commonality, like Clyde's flying, greatly assists him in establishing closer
rapport, there is no substitute for being competent in the techniques of networking. To that end, it's really quite important to take a look at critical
points where you might have similar background, interests, and experiences.

Just to set the record straight. **Neither the retainer firms nor the contingency firms work for you.** The retainer firms are clearly working for
the employer, they're not working for you. They have a job that is open,
and they have been retained to fill it. If your credentials and temperament
fit the specs of the position—great! You may be considered a viable candidate; if not, you won't be. Don't ever let down your guard down on the
basis of the relationship you have with the search firm account executive.
The good account executives are skilled in building excellent rapport and
creating disarming relationships. To that end, you need to exercise sound
judgment as to how much you reveal, and don't be misled by the warm,
supportive relationship which you appear to have with these search firms,
thinking you've got the job. You may not have it. The good search firms are
really selling two sides all the time. They're selling the company on your
credentials and they're also selling you on the company. So they're clearly
in a sales role. Keep in mind that even though you might be the better
skilled person for the job and have a great relationship with the search firm
recruiter, if another candidate is better liked by the company, you probably
won't be seen as a lead candidate. So, don't **ever** let your guard down.
Always remember: **You** are responsible for managing your campaign and
producing the kind of results you want. Do not turn over the management
of your campaign to a search firm believing that it has **your** best interest at
heart. The firm is interested in your success **and** it has the client's best interest in mind, way ahead of your own.

With contingency search firms, you might not represent the best fit, but if
you're close, your résumé will be sent to a company as soon as they can get
it in the mail. It may feel like a contingency firm is actively marketing you
to a company and they are. But they are probably more driven to **close the**

deal and **get their fee,** than by an altruistic desire to see you in the right career path. We are not being cruel—we are being realistic; it **is** a numbers game for contingency search firms. The greater the number of résumés sent out to companies, the greater the probability of a successful connection **and fee** for them. Lest we run the risk of painting all contingency search firms with the same brush stroke, let us point out that there are some very good contingency search firms or employment agencies who operate at the same high-quality level and performance standards as do the well-known retainer search firms.

Let's talk a little bit more about contingency search firms and how they might refer your résumé between affiliate offices. Depending upon how these contingency search firms are affiliated, they will refer your résumé and name to other affiliate firms twice, but probably not three times, as they have to split the commission if you get connected. It does not pay for these firms to split the commission check between more than two offices.

By way of example, we had one client whose résumé was referred from a contingency firm in Chicago to an affiliate firm in Los Angeles, who in turn referred it to a company contact in Cincinnati where the person was interviewed and subsequently hired. This leads us to another reality about networking through search firms (retainer or contingency): There can be a tremendous ricochet or pinball effect between firms. Even if you are committed to conducting a local search, you should broaden your search firm exposure, as many out-of-state firms have local connections which you're not aware of. Indeed, they will often conduct searches in your own backyard. We are clearly a global economy with multinational companies creating opportunities when you least expect them with out-of-the-area search firms having local assignments. As an aside, the *International Directory of Corporate Affiliations* is a good resource for you because the U.S. subsidiaries of these international firms are identified. This enables you to contact them about opportunities locally, regionally, nationally, or internationally. It's also appropriate to look at firms in your industry which may be headquartered overseas with state-side facilities.

In summary, you're asking the same thing from each and every one of your contacts with whom you are chatting:

Have you ever been connected through a search firm *or* do you know others who have been contacted by a search firm *or* who is the head of human resources who knows of quality search firms?

You get to turn these leads into additional networking contacts. As you do, you inform them of your **status** and you ask for **additional help** with leads into companies or other well-connected people.

Worksheet 14 has been created for you to identify those search firms which are known personally either by you or by your contacts. This exercise will no doubt evolve and expand as you uncover additional search firms. Use the worksheet or a pad of paper to collect your thoughts.

WORKSHEET 14
Search Firms and Employment Agencies

Identify all those search firms or employment agencies with whom you have previously had direct contact. Also, identify how you know them or the source, so you may refer to them later. In the examples below, you identified Heidrick & Struggles as a firm you have previously been in contact with and identified Dan O'Hara, Dave Robertson, and Clyde Lowstuter as people who possibly know other search firms.

Search Firms Employment Agencies	Source of Referral	Search Firms Employment Agencies	Source of Referral
Heidrick & Struggles	Self	Management Recruiters	Dave Robertson
Lynch, Miller, Moore	Dan O'Hara	Clarey & Andrews	Clyde Lowstuter

It's our recommendation that when you're talking with your contacts, you should also broaden your networking discussion by asking, "what **other** organizations should I turn to?"—which leads us to our second networking avenue, **Target organizations or target companies.**

Target Organizations _____

Target organizations are the second major market channel you should use to get connected. You should always be exploring that avenue when networking. In addition to your own list of target organizations, you want to tap into the people and organizations known by your contacts. Remember George? Let's go back to him for a moment. Ask George if he knows any organizations or companies which you should contact **locally** or in your **industry.** You might even wish to use language such as:

> **If *you* were to look George, which companies would *you* go after, regardless of whether they are actually hiring or whether you actually know any personal contacts there?**

Hopefully, George will identify some companies, because you're helping him focus on a specific path. Thank him for the company names which he gives you, then ask if he knows any **people** there. **Securing additional leads is done *one layer* at a time.** Not unlike when you slowly peel the layers back of an onion, you get into the heart of it—one layer at a time. Your goal is to get into the heart of these data. Just having a name of a contact is but one point of reference, as **you want to dig deeper and deeper and deeper into the core of your target organizations.**

As you know, the brain is a tremendous, remarkable instrument, and it has a lot more data stored in it than we often credit it for having. When you are networking, help your contacts move from the general to the specific. As you start out generally, help George zero in on increasingly more detailed contacts and information.

Let's use Smith's Industries as an example of a company with whom you want to interview. Although George might not have given you any names at Smith's Industries, you know Smith's Industries is a huge company. As you want to **network** into Smith's, try the following:

YOU: George, who do you know at Smith's?

GEORGE: I don't know anybody at Smith's.

YOU: Well George, do you know anyone who would know of **anyone** at Smith's?

This is called **branching out.** George doesn't know anyone who works directly at Smith's, but he thinks he might have an indirect contact for you to get into Smith's. He thinks of his friend, Russ. Russ is a new contact mentioned for the first time in your conversation with George. He thinks Russ knows someone at Smith's. Well, upon contacting Russ, you discover that he does, indeed, know someone at Smith's and he is willing to help you network into that company because of George. Russ gives you the name of Dave who works at Smith's which is your lead into that company. Beyond your contact into Smith's, you now have the opportunity to broaden your networking leads from Russ even further. You probably know the networking drill by now, don't you? Inform Russ of your **status,** ask Russ for additional **help,** . . . or leads into search firms, target companies or people that he might know, and **legitimize sending your résumé** to him. By the way, if it is at all possible, you should also turn Russ and Dave into "full-blown" networking sources for you, as well.

Don't be overly concerned if George or Dave or Russ are giving you duplicate names of companies or people. If you say to George, "Well, I got that one, got that one, got that one," what do you think is going to happen? You are right! We can guarantee you that after a while, George will clam up. He and all your other contacts will stop providing names if you cut them off prematurely, before they have exhausted their lists of contacts. They are likely to say, mentally or out loud to you, "Well, I guess you've got all the names that I have." Invariably, the next name would have been the perfect name for you, had you not shut the person down. So, please, do not shut off the flow of communications from these very important contacts. All of your networking calls and informational exchanges should feel like friendly conversations—not interrogations.

Be aware of your network contact's reaction during your conversation with him or her. If the person starts to get tense or appears upset, back off for a moment. Do not press on. If you are not careful you can inadvertently create the feeling for some people that they've been put under hot lights, and you can be seen like the late Sam Kennison, whose screaming networking technique probably would sound like **"Give me names now!—I want a job now!"** Unless you are particularly adept at interrogating people in a way that folks like and at mending broken relationships, **lighten up.** People don't like to be interrogated. They don't appreciate it; indeed, they resent it deeply. Besides, you certainly won't get the results you want.

The **second** dimension of target organizations is your **own** lists of organizations which you've identified either through your own extensive library research or windshield research. Windshield research—you know what that is, don't you? Driving past companies and looking at them through your windshield. Conducting windshield research is somewhat crude and time consuming, but it does provide a first-hand look at companies close to your home or in a specific area of your city or of the country. To help you develop and expand your own lists of target organizations, please turn to Worksheet 15 and follow the instructions in brainstorming additional companies that you might possibly target as viable employers, regardless of whether there are any employment opportunities available.

WORKSHEET 15
Developing Your List of Prime Target Organizations

Your list of prime target organizations will number 20 to 50 and represents the group of companies you want your networking contacts to provide leads into. Brainstorm specific high-priority A list companies in which you might have keen interest. In addition to specific companies, also write down company categories that you wish to target. Write quickly and spontaneously; your first response may be your best response. Fine-tune your list later.

_____

_____

_____

_____

_____

_____

_____

_____

_____

_____

_____

_____

_____

_____

_____

_____

_____

_____

_____

_____

With your list of target organizations in hand, it is appropriate to ask George (and all your other contacts) if he knows of anyone in your prime target companies. Let's go back to George.

George, you've been extremely helpful, and I have one last question for you.

Presumably, George is a pretty good friend. Look at all the value he's provided to you so far. His input has yielded Regina, Terry, Russ, David, and a score of other search firms, target organizations, and personal contacts. He has been very helpful. Remember the saying, "It's better to give than to receive"? It's true. Individuals do receive a lot of psychological and emotional payback when they give and add value to others. Now you're clearly getting a lot of value here from George, right? Hopefully, George is feeling great about this because you're responding positively. However, common sense dictates that you not be patronizing or overly solicitous in your gratitude. So when you ask him one more question, hopefully he'll respond with, "Hey, no problem." However, there's a judgment call here. **Don't be overbearing about continuing to press for networking leads.** Without meaning to, you **can** overstep your bounds—though most people stop far short of overstaying their welcome if they network **effectively.** People sincerely want to help. Acknowledge George's contribution and your gratitude. You may wish to say something like the following:

George, you have been extremely helpful and I sincerely appreciate it. I have a list of additional companies, and I need some help in getting my foot in the door. Might you have time to respond to *my* list of target companies and identify people you might know there, directly or indirectly?

If you're face to face with George or one of your other personal contacts, you can easily slide your list of target organizations across the table. It's been our experience that if you're face to face with your contact, you could probably get the person to respond to a larger list than if you are on the telephone. If you're on the phone, your list of 20 companies is about as large as you can reasonably ask people to respond to. But, if you're face to face, you **can,** in all likelihood, have your contacts effectively respond to a list of 30 or **maybe** even up to 40 target companies. After you ask for a reaction to your list, don't continue to prattle along. Fall silent and allow George time to think about these company names. George knows what you need at this point. Don't continue to press.

As George starts down your list of top organizations, you mention a company, George grunts, "Nothing." You identify another company. George grunts, "Nothing, I don't know anybody." About the third time when George responds with, "I don't know anyone," gently stop him. Back George up to the beginning of your list of organizations. Gently and supportively ask,

George, you might not know anyone there yourself, but do you know anyone who knows someone there, perhaps? Are you sure that you don't know anyone who knows anyone at, let's say, Allen & Bradley?

Then just stop and let George think about that company for a bit. If George is feeling tension because of his time schedule or he is not providing any names or he's feeling overloaded, then you just might wish to make a note of that and get back to George at a later time.

Keep in mind that your ability to press your contacts will directly relate to the kind of rapport which you've got with these individuals. If you have a very good rapport with George, you could say, "I **know** you know someone there." Now, you're obviously not going to do that when you have only a passing professional relationship with a senior executive (or if it's a secondary contact). **Do not** be that forward. Clearly, there's a balance to be struck. **If George draws a blank and can't think of anyone, do *not* continue to press. Rather, be supportive and positive.** If he's face to face with you, then give him your list of your top 10, 20, 30, or 40 organizations. If he's on the phone, you'll need to send your résumé to George as a courtesy, as well as you might wish to include your list of target organizations. The point is, you're looking forward to having George provide some additional names in this category of target organizations. Again, always peel back the layers—dig deeper into the data until you secure some additional data or until your contact begins to stiffen up—whichever comes first. Just because you had contact with George one time doesn't mean that's where you should stop. You should continue to get back with George on a periodic basis regarding the status of your search, as well as your list of target organizations, provided it's both convenient and that you're not wearing out your welcome. Make sense? Good.

Employment Opportunities

Let's shift gears a bit and look at a dimension related to both target organizations and personal contacts, dealing with **employment opportunities.** There will be times in which your friends and colleagues will be very helpful by revealing great opportunities to you. However, there may be other times in which your personal contacts are reluctant to reveal employment situations because they feel the job is inappropriate for you. In your networking, **ensure that your contacts know the *range* of jobs you are interested in *and* qualified for.** The last thing you want is to miss an opportunity because someone misunderstood what you would be willing to consider.

If you are employed in a job in which you have clients or your company utilizes the services or products of salespeople, distribution firms, consultants, vendors, or suppliers, you have a built-in source of network contacts. These people are constantly in contact with other individuals in a wide variety of companies potentially related to your own firm. However, lest you start calling these people with whom you have contacts and "put the arm on them" because they "owe you" some way, we recommend that you figure out the most comfortable and acceptable way to approach them without compromising either them or you.

Fundamentally, you approach all your contacts with the profound belief that you have a tremendous amount to offer and that there is an employer out there waiting for you to materialize, whether the employer knows of the need yet or not. Keep being in front of lots of people, letting them know of your intentions, background, and capabilities—always enthusiastically and confidently. The reality of dealing with vendors, suppliers, and consultants is that they know you've been in a recommending or decision-making role about vendors and suppliers previously and most likely will be again. So you can approach these contacts pretty assertively and straightforwardly. However, do not expect them to know of any immediate opportunities. Also, do not think for a moment that they will respond positively to implied threats of discontinued business if they don't help. Don't imply promises of future business if they do help you. Clearly, it's in their best interests to help you if they can, so lighten up about having to get really hot leads from your current or former vendors.

One of our clients got connected through this method of networking into a consulting firm. Gary, our client, leveraged an introduction through a network source to the partner in an equity management investment firm. This partner headed up the turnaround division of his firm. He bought troubled companies and put in the management team to rescue and turn around the company. Fortunately, the partner had an opportunity for a seasoned executive experienced in managing troubled companies to bring them back into profitability. As luck would have it, Gary interviewed well and demonstrated how his background, skills, and capabilities fit exactly what the partner's needs were. In summary, Gary was hired and has, indeed, turned the company around. Under his leadership, Gary has reorganized the company, strengthened the management team, installed more efficient systems, and revitalized the venture workforce. Gary found that contacting consultants was an excellent method in developing specific leads, which sometimes turn into jobs! Gary's success story is a perfect example of the adage "You can't control timing and luck." While you might not be able to control the timing, you can influence luck by being prepared. For if you are prepared, you will see situations as opportunities, not merely as events.

We personally don't believe that opportunities knock at our door—rather they merely lie there and go largely unnoticed, often disguised as problems to overcome or road blocks to circumvent. All too often, we are not "lucky" in our job searches because we do not expect the best, we are pessimistic in our approaches. We fail to view these problems as opportunities to learn or demonstrate how we might be the solution to an organization's dilemma. Keep looking at every opportunity as a different way in which you can be successful, and be prepared to cast aside your conventional ways of operating in favor of a different approach if it is a strategy that works. We should note that Gary shifted his career focus from his goal of a presidency of a well-known, financially stable company to a high-risk, entrepreneurial firm because the opportunity to really grow professionally and monetarily was right.

Risk Taking—Selling Yourself Into the Job

We would like to draw a parallel between selling "up" in networking to selling "up" when you respond to ads which are not a perfect match for your credentials but you want to be considered anyway. Although responding to ads doesn't seem to pose much of a difficulty for us, we sometimes hesitate when we are networking "up." **When responding to advertisements,** and the title might not be perfect, the job location might not be the greatest, and you suspect the money might not be the ideal, don't be overly concerned about that because organizations tend to shift roles, perhaps even locations. Regarding compensation, that whole issue is typically negotiable and flexible if the right individual comes along. Even when companies declare that compensation is not negotiable, that statement is a negotiating posture. **If the position is not perfect, send along your résumé in response to that ad anyway** because advertisements are written on an ideal basis describing the ideal job, longing for the ideal candidate. And although companies might wish to hire an individual with an M.B.A. or Ph.D. with 10 years of experience and pay only $30,000, they might very well be pleased with an individual with a background that looks different from their original picture if there is substantial value other than that defined. To that end, you might represent an ideal fit for them. Another point to keep in mind is that you have not left a job or you're not coming out of a job which was the same as when you went into it. Because of your own personality, your technical skills, and just the conditions in the company, you influenced the role and it changed. To that end, we are recommending that you respond to an ad and even interview for a job which on the surface may not appear to be a perfect fit. Close, but not perfect. In the interview you may even hear, "Well, your credentials are different than those which we're looking for, but I see you have some real interesting skills and capabilities, and we're willing to accommodate these."

Selling up in networking is similar to selling up in response to advertisements, in that you have to first believe that you have a lot to offer beyond your current organizational rank or function and that you are promoting your value-added capabilities at a level higher than originally thought. Remember Herman Mendez, in our lead-off story, who had trouble believing that he could operate effectively at a higher plane than he envisioned himself. In networking, as in most things in life, people take their behavioral cues from you. If you are nervous and hesitant, you will be communicating to a more senior person that you are "junior" to them. However, if you were able to envision yourself operating as a senior executive and capture the same level of confidence exhibited by these executives, you would be seen as operating at the same level.

When networking up, you want to make it **easy** for people with whom you are chatting—to give you data and to help you out. Certainly, you do not want to hamper your contacts' ability to network for you by stating too many careering demands which you have. Demonstrate your flexibility by opening up position parameters versus holding tightly to restrictive parameters. Indeed, you may even wish to use language similar to the following:

> **I'm pretty *open* with regard to this next career opportunity. As I mentioned, I'm looking for a challenging sales and marketing position, and although I've had a senior marketing management role, I'm open to the possibility of doing a wide number of things including taking perhaps one or two steps back to get into a company in which I could really contribute. I don't want you to think that I'm *only* looking at a particular level, in a particular industry, in a particular location, or perhaps even at a particular income level. The money and title are important, but the *opportunity* to contribute to the growth and profitability of a company is most important. That's what I'm really looking for—a place where I can make a difference.**

Having your networking contacts know of an ideal opportunity for you would be great. However, short of them revealing such a job to you, the next best thing would be for you to occasionally remind them of the activity that you are generating. It is appropriate for you to "telegraph" the kind of position you want your contacts to be alert to by periodically updating them on your progress, mentioning specific titles or industries. As we have discussed before, do not press your contacts to come up with leads for you. This is your job, not their job. If contacts are shared with you, even after a bit of gentle nudging, great! Do not create the impression that others are falling behind in doing your work.

Personal Contacts _____

The fourth avenue of networking is **personal contacts.** These are the contacts which George or others would call or visit if they were looking for a job. In much the same way that you know people George doesn't know, George knows people whom you don't know but want to know. By way of transition, you might wish to use some of the following words with George:

George, thank you so much for all your help. One of the things I'd like to do is tap into some of your contacts. Let me ask you, "Who would _you_ call if you were to look for a job? Hopefully, you would call me. So that's one. But other than myself, George, who else would you think of to call?

Now do you see the distinction we are making here? Instead of asking the question, "What people would be the best contacts for me, George?" you cut to the root of the real issue. You get George to **identify** with you, and you simply ask him for some of his contacts. The ones which he would use if he was really intent on exploring a job change.

What you are doing is shifting the emphasis _off_ of yourself and _onto_ George, as to the people with whom _he_ would network. Now remember how we began our contact. This is very important. We acknowledged George. We said,

Thank you so much for all your help. If the tables were reversed, you certainly could call on me to help out anytime. While you might not have someone immediately in mind that you feel would be helpful for me to call, let's think about whom _you_ would call first if you were to be looking for a job.

Hopefully George would respond, "Well, now that you put it that way, why I'd call Sam and Darlene and Fred. I'd call . . . well, you know I'd call Charley and Ann and Rosemary and Tom and Fred, and. . . ."

Great! Alright! Those are the people I'd like to get to know, George; those people that you would call. Thanks very much! Can we talk about them?

Look at what happened when you begin collecting a few names, as we have just done with George. You can see how quickly an initial networking contact with George has dramatically expanded.

By asking for the names of people in each networking category, you have greatly expanded your contacts to 11 individuals who were previously unknown to you. Hopefully, by using this technique you avoid pressuring George (and all your other contacts). Rather, you are "partnering up" with him in a way in which he is more than willing to volunteer information, certainly, of course, with your careful guidance.

The point is, that **when networking is done right, people are glad to help out and supply you with leads.** If for some reason you don't get at least three to five additional names from your primary contacts, then you may have asked something which they think may be out of the ordinary or you may have given the impression that you're asking the person for a job or a lead for a job. You don't want to do that. Asking people you know for the names of others to whom you can speak about your campaign is not out of the ordinary, but they may have heard it differently from what you intended. Sometimes there is a significant distinction between **what you intend** and **what people think they hear.** You might have the most honorable intentions in the world as you network and the last thing you would want people to feel is crowded, manipulated, or pressured. But they may have talked to other people who didn't understand networking, and these other people misused or abused the networking privilege. If you approach people awkwardly, or in a demanding manner, implying somehow that your personal contacts "owe you" in some subtle manner, you run the risk of really turning people off. If that happens, no matter what you **intended,** they will definitely **interpret** your request for help as a pushy, manipulative demand for personal data. They may feel violated and become irritated. Unbeknownst to you, if you haven't really gotten your networking approach polished before you start, your contacts may have heard you incorrectly based on their own interpretations of your hesitant behavior and what they think you need. They may have thought that you asked for a specific job and it sounded like, "Do you know anyone who is hiring? Do you know of any good job openings?" They may have thought that you were asking for the names of someone who could lead you right to a specific job opening. Or, you **may** simply have just caught them cold. So, when you ask an individual for the very first time for leads or information that would help you in your campaign, and he or she blanks out on short notice on you, help them save face by rephrasing your request.

> **I know it's difficult sometimes to come up with names, but let me clarify exactly *why* I would like these names and what I'm going to do with them. I promise not to embarrass you by asking them for job leads—I've got that covered. I really would appreciate the names of people who can help me think of good search firms and companies and be my "eyes and ears" for the next several months. Does that help suggest someone?**

If this approach doesn't work, you may wish to indicate that you will recontact them in about three days. You might say something like:

> **I know I may have caught you by surprise and can well appreciate that you can't think of anyone right now. I'll tell you what, I'll call you back in three days and see if there are any other search firms or companies, or people who have come to mind. Perhaps in the interim, some additional contacts may have surfaced. Would that be OK?**

Here's an idea which you can use immediately. Jim, one of our clients was developing a network contact with a business colleague who, like George, was having serious trouble coming up with names of mutual friends, acquaintances, business leaders, and companies. Jim's networking contact said to him, "Let me go through my Rolodex file here with you and see if I get an idea." Well, he did just that. He generated 16 excellent contacts within 20 minutes. People enjoy going through their address and phone files. It's low threat and it produces results. Try recounting this story with a network contact having trouble getting started and ask if she or he would be willing to look through the address or phone file for ideas for you.

Keep in mind that when you begin a networking conversation with someone, they may feel uncomfortable at first until you reassure them that it's OK that they drew a blank. **Your goal is to keep all your networking contacts comfortable.** If George does become a bit uncomfortable, it may be because he hasn't been able to help you out, though he'd like to. He's in a tough spot as he really doesn't understand why he can't think of anyone, for he knows a lot of people. You don't want to press him too much, at this time. George may just want to extricate himself from the conversation and get back to work. If that's the case, thank George for his help and support. What you're trying to do is establish a relationship. Relationships develop over time. In addition, you are doing one more thing. You are programming a request, with George's full knowledge, that within three days, he will generate some names for you.

Have you ever programmed your mind at night before you've gone to sleep with a particularly difficult problem? You say to your brain—"OK, I don't have clarity on this problem, but when I wake up, I want the answer or I want some possibilities!" Your mind never really sleeps. It will continue to work on this problem even while you rest. It's been our experience that your mind will generate some very interesting options or ideas. Now these ideas may go off in a completely different tangent than that which you might have otherwise wanted or have been comfortable with and it may get you up at three in the morning. But the point is that your brain will always work on a problem or an opportunity if you focus on it. Create for George an opportunity to provide some valuable information for you.

In George's case, you have now placed that problem-solving challenge in his head to help him create some helpful data within that time frame. When you call him back on that third day, if he hasn't been able to think of a friend or business acquaintance or colleague, you might ask him if he is uncomfortable supplying names to you. If he says, "Well, yes," or if he hesitates, be gracious and understanding. Indicate,

I understand perfectly, George. I tell you what, let me keep you posted on my progress on a periodic basis, but in the mean time, I'll get back to you within three days to see if you have thought of anyone. George, I sincerely appreciate your help and your support. I'll talk to you soon.

You want to keep your network person comfortable. It is entirely possible that next week that very same person may just happen to come upon a great name or even a lead which you can use. Keep the door open by being warm and supportive, yourself. Tell everyone, all the time, that you are very successful and encouraged in your search efforts. Success breeds success. If

George understands that you are being successful, then he may, in all likelihood, also get enthusiastic about you and respond in a positive manner, willing to help you out. Here's another idea which you can use. You may wish to identify the career path or direction which you are pursuing and mention the various industries which would most likely yield the jobs you are looking for. Ask George if he happens to know anyone at a specific search firm or target organization you want to know. This approach helps because you aren't asking open-ended questions, which may be intimidating to George. Rather, you are guiding George to give you some information, and he is also starting to experience some genuine success in networking.

Although you will be striving to make it easy and safe for your network resource people to respond, one or more of your friends may not provide any support to you at all. We suspect that you'll probably know that fairly quickly into the conversation. If that's the case, don't keep pressing the person for information. Rather, just solidify the relationship that you have and share your enthusiasm about the successful results you are getting in your search efforts. Never talk about negative things or how tough the marketplace might be or how difficult it is to network. Speak only in a positive, upbeat, and enthusiastic manner. Perhaps, at some point in time, your contact might come up with something. That is exactly the person who might even surprise you by calling you back with leads. Who knows!

Prequalifying Your Leads

Not all the leads and linkages provided to you are ones you want to use. Some of your primary contacts will be both well connected **and** also may have a spotty reputation. For any number of reasons, these contacts may not have the best relationship with the people whose names they recommended to you. Although you want to call the secondary leads which these primary contacts gave you, you would be wise to exercise proper caution about being unknowingly tarnished by association with someone whose reputation or image may not be entirely positive. What to do? Our advice is to prequalify those contacts which are given to you. Prequalify? Absolutely! You don't want to be "blind-sided." You want to ensure that the names which your contact gives you are solid and that he or she has a good relationship. Now most of the people you contact will be terrific and their reputations solid. They will be well respected. They will be the kind of people you'd be proud to know. But you don't always know what has happened in other times and in other circumstances. With other individuals, they may not have quite the same endorsement and support. They may well be great people, but because of some event or eccentricity, there may be a mixed reception when you call them or use their name to open doors. Since we know that George is well respected and has a great reputation, let's use him as an example. Your goal is to clarify with George his relationship with the people whom he suggested you contact. This is especially important if it is with one of your target organizations, search firms, or other very important contact. It could be that one of George's contacts is in an organization which you want to get into, but you suspect the connection with George may **not** be the most influential. Here's a case of "What you don't know **could** hurt you." Let's say that you suspect that there might be a problem, but you are not certain. So you might ask,

George, how do you know Fred?

George may respond, "Well, I know Fred because he and I used to work together." Pursue the thought,

When was that and what did you do together? Tell me, George, when I call Fred how would you suggest that I approach him? What would create the best first impression?

Now hopefully, George is probably thinking that you're asking about Fred from the standpoint that if you know more about him it would be easier to establish rapport. That's true. But you also have a second mission; you are also qualifying the relationship which George has with Fred. Continuing on,

George, do you know Fred's direct telephone number or his office's night line. How does he feel about calls on his direct line? Would you know his secretary's name and extension? Does he or she have a night line? Are there particular hours when she or he comes into work? When's the best time to get Fred? When do you suspect he'll be least busy and most receptive to a phone call?

This is very valuable data and is important to capture. Write the information down on an index card or enter it into your computer system. Build a file of information which is easy to access. We have found that index cards work best for some people as the cards can be shuffled alphabetically and information easily retrieved. Regardless of the system which you use, you should capture the following information: the name of the individual, the title, the company, the address, telephone number, the secretary's name, and his or her telephone numbers.

Don't forget to include the best time to reach Fred. Does he get in at 7:00 am and his secretary, at 8:00 am? If so, conceivably between 7:00 am and 8:00 am might be an ideal time for you to call and to get Fred before his meetings start and before he gets caught up in the day's events. It really is amazing the number of decision makers you can reach before 8:00 am or after 6:00 pm or during the lunch break. The night lines are often picked up by the executives themselves in the early and late hours because the administrative staff isn't there. Also, during the noon hour the regular secretary may be at lunch and the substitute may be willing to put your call through. It may be appropriate, when you're talking with George to ask how busy Fred is and how much travel Fred does. See if you can get George to call Fred for you to alert him to your call—either at the office or at home. To that end, you might wish to get Fred's residence number. And you obviously want to legitimize from George that it's OK to call Fred at home. Ask George if Fred receives calls at home and how does he feel about that? If you do plan to call Fred at home, you might wish to determine if Fred is married, and if so, learn his wife's name in case she answers the phone. While you are clearly networking, when you call someone at home, you're trying to establish a rapport and make contact on the basis of a colleague and friend, not purely a business contact.

Does all this seem like a lot? Would you qualify every lead on every single call? Of course not. If you did, you'd probably spend three days on the phone with George alone getting everyone's personal history. Keep in mind that this is not background research for "This is Your Life." It's only to get enough information to prequalify individuals so that you are comfortable that you're going to be warmly received and you will be appropriate in your conversations. Only go to this trouble of prequalification if you have a concern about your primary contact's ability to establish good relationships with others and if you really want to increase the probability of a successful connection.

Turn to Worksheet 16 to ensure that you are creating the most supportive approach for your contacts. Here is something else you may wish to consider: If George or your other primary contacts **don't have any** of this information (they don't know his contact's company, or direct dial, or night line, doesn't know Fred's secretary's name, hasn't talked to Fred in about six years), you might begin to ask George some questions:

George, when did you chat with Fred last?

Just because George doesn't have much of the expected contact information is no cause for alarm, necessarily. (George may not be into collecting this kind of data on all his acquaintances.) However, George may respond, "Oh well, he was really ticked at me, because I didn't do that project the way he wanted it." Here might be a good place to ask,

So let me ask you, George, if I use your name, is that going to help me or hurt me?

Oh, I see what you mean. Well, it might hurt you.

Great. Look, I appreciate your candor. Is there someone else I should probably contact first to get to Fred?

It may be that there is nothing at all wrong with the relationship. It may simply be that the relationship is too sensitive. For example, George and Fred

WORKSHEET 16
Prequalify Your Leads

If you are concerned about the quality of the relationships your primary networking contacts have with people you want to reach, ask some of the following questions. As you think of additional questions that would qualify this relationship, fill in the blanks provided below.

"How do you know _____ ?"

"What is _____'s telephone number? Night line or direct dial?"

"What is _____'s secretary's name? That telephone number?"

"When does _____ generally get in to work?"

"What is the best time to reach _____ ?"

"How would you describe _____ ?"

"Can I call _____ at home? Residence number?"

"What is spouse's name?" _____

Now you write some of your own prequalifying questions:

_____

_____

_____

_____

_____

_____

_____

_____

_____

_____

_____

_____

may be competitors, and that fact may work against you. Your task is to pre-qualify the wisdom of utilizing the contact person's name, or choosing another person who may be better able to help you establish linkage prior to your call. Watch for hesitancy on George's part when you ask if there is someone else whom you should contact. You are getting into an area that conceivably could be a bit threatening to George. In effect, you want to slide into it—nice and easy. You don't want to just say, "Alright George, since I don't really trust that contact, who else should I talk to?" That's a bit too harsh. You want to help both George and all your other contacts to save face whether they are primary contacts or secondary contacts. Obviously, you want to make sure that you express your deep appreciation and thanks for whatever level of support which George and your other contacts are providing. After all, they're being kind, so it behooves you to be gracious as well. In every case, you want to positively reinforce their support and interest. You want to encourage them to get back to you. Keep in mind the Law of Reciprocity. It goes by any number of names and has any number of catch phrases that are appropriate. We're certain they are familiar to you and that you have heard many of them:

- "One hand washes the other."
- "What goes around comes around."
- "You help push me into a promotion, and I'll pull you along."
- "You give to people one time, then it's their turn to give to you."
- "You give, I get. I give, you get."
- "What you give away returns to you tenfold."

It is well accepted that when individuals provide value to others, they receive many positive emotional benefits in return. So if you are very positive in your response to George, because he's given you some leads, then he's going to feel good about that. As human beings, we gravitate toward those things which bring us pleasure. Make this a fun process for George and for all of your network people. Share your enthusiasm with them and let them experience some of your excitement and confidence. We want to experience pleasure, and we want to avoid pain even more. Make absolutely certain that you only provide positive reinforcement, and **never** cause pain by inferring that someone failed or did poorly by not doing enough for you. If there is pain or discomfort associated with networking with you, we can guarantee that the person will try to avoid you the next time you call for help. Why should people extend themselves when all you do is cause discomfort and pain, not pleasure.

Let us come back to a situation to which we briefly referred earlier, that there might be a problem between George and his contact Fred. Because there might be a problem lurking there, we said that you might want to identify another person who can form a linkage to this valuable contact.

The question is, how might you do that? How might you uncover other opportunities or channels to get in touch with Fred? What other methods will you employ? Because this issue is so common and potentially damaging, we provided Worksheet 17 on alternative networking contact approaches. Please turn to this worksheet now and review it.

How difficult did you find Worksheet 17? Remember what we said earlier about programming your mind? Program your brain to provide three solid avenues or approaches that could lead to an introduction which we haven't mentioned here. These approaches can be variations on what we proposed earlier. It's OK for you to say "this is difficult" as long as you add "**and** what are three more ways I can do this?" Your brain will search for the answer.

Let us help you out. We'll provide an assist with some other approaches to connect with Fred:

- See who else George knows in Fred's company. Maybe that person knows Fred quite well and would be an ideal referral
- Find out what sports Fred is into; maybe you will find a sports friend who knows him.
- Determine if Fred is into any professional associations and attend as a prospective member or go as a guest of someone who knows Fred.

You may be wondering why we are taking the extra time and space here to demonstrate how to get unstuck and break through your mental roadblocks when it seems that your trail to a key contact has "hit the wall." The simple reason is its criticalness. This is the point in networking when you feel your network has dried up. No, your network has not dried up, rather you have run smack into your own considerations and road blocks. At this very juncture, you may lose tremendous potential opportunities. We really do not want that to happen to you. The vast majority of us get stuck at some point in our search and we are presenting a practical remedy—so hang in there with us. You'll be glad you did as these exercises will keep you going in tough times.

Here is another way in which you can look at moving on to get unconventional new ideas. Think of an individual whom you would envision to be extremely good at networking—very creative, very powerful, very effective. Think of someone who would be very good at coming up with bright, innovative ideas to solve perplexing problems. Let's say that you think of someone who fits this description—Karen. Now Karen has really mastered networking. She is a superb model of this skill, and she is an excellent teacher. Karen always seems to know exactly what to do, and what to say. It is really easy to follow her techniques. So, ask yourself the question, "What would Karen do? How would Karen go about uncovering these leads?" A networking dilemma? Take it out of the realm of **you** having to do it, and put it in Karen's lap to solve. Because after all, Karen can do this, and all you will have to do now, figuratively, is look over Karen's shoulder as

WORKSHEET 17
Alternative Approaches to Making Contact

Fantasize some alternative methods or avenues to initiate contact with your network sources. Use the five examples outlined below as a way of starting your brainstorming:

1. Ask other contacts if they know Fred or might know someone who would know Fred.
2. If Fred has published something or was referenced in a recent article, perhaps you could call Fred directly.
3. Fred was recently appointed to a new position or to a highly visible task force in his company. You read about it or heard about it through mutual friends, and you are calling to congratulate him.
4. You know of him through his general reputation and you always wanted to meet him. Ask some penetrating questions about a specific issue of interest to you both.
5. Contact the executive director of your trade association of which Fred is a member. Establish sufficient rapport with the director to generate an introduction through him.

Now, it's your turn. Identify three more ways in which you could make Fred's acquaintance other than through George or the linkage of a friend or acquaintance:

1.

2.

3.

she thinks through the strategies and she says them out loud to you and to herself. We do this all the time with each other if we happen to be stuck on an issue. Dave will ask, "Hummmmm, what would Clyde do in this case?" And Clyde would ask, "Hummmmm, how would Dave handle this?" And although we might be stuck in our own considerations or fears or concerns, as soon as we shift over and ask, "What would Clyde do?" or "What would Dave do?" or "What would Karen do?" we immediately free up a whole new set of data because we have a pretty good sense as to how each other would operate, what we would do, what we would say, and how we would be. It's terrific, it really works! And you know what? It works **every single time!** Why? Because we take the best the other has to offer and we modify it to our personalities and situation. Now there might be some time that one of us asks the question, "What would Clyde (or Dave) do?" and we'll come back, "I don't know what to do." Then we'll have to visualize someone else addressing these challenges. Maybe we'll be James Bond for a day. But in the interim, we're asking you to shift out of your own frame of reference of what you know to be true and shift into this new perspective and see what kind of new ideas, approaches, and results it will produce for you.

A Referral Which Blew Up

Let us share with you a story about communicating personal names before we move on to the next section. This experience may help you learn from another person's oversights in being too open while networking. A number of years ago a friend of ours blew up a major new business consulting assignment with an organization which he had literally locked in.

It was a good engagement. His firm was perfect for the job, and the fee was great. The relationship seemed both solid and intact. Our friend, Stan, was dealing with the president of an advertising agency who was representing his client who had an immediate consulting need at an executive level, and yet they had no idea what Stan's firm really did or how he functioned. This advertising agency president had a working familiarity with Stan and his firm and performed the preliminary screen. The president called Stan up, interviewed him along with a number of firms and selected Stan's firm for this very special engagement. After he had already decided on Stan's firm and had actually agreed to the fee, Stan let slip, "By the way, I know so and so." The executive's response was, "Oh." And he said it in a flat tone of voice. Stan missed the signals entirely in his enthusiasm to establish the relationship. "Oh yes, this fellow and I used to work together at the same company. Very bright guy, little difficult to work with, but an extremely straight shooter." "Oh? Yes, I suppose that's the way you'd describe him" said the agency president in a dull monotone. From that point on, Stan didn't hear diddly from the agency president ever again. Wrote him, called him, wrote him, called him, and after 30 days, Stan just gave up. When Stan finally hooked up with his former colleague/friend three months after the line went dead, Stan asked his old friend, "Tell me, what was your relationship with this executive (the ad agency president)?" His verbal response and body language answered, "Oh yes, I know him quite well." Stan revealed that he was discussing the particulars about some consulting work that he might have possibly done with the executive's firm. As he was midstream into the explanation, Stan's friend stopped him abruptly and said, "You didn't use my name did you?" At which point Stan said, "I'm afraid I did." He said, "Well, two things. Number one, you should have checked with me first, and second, this executive and I have a love/hate relationship, and it looks more like hate than love. He only loves me when I make him lots of money, so you probably ran into a buzz saw if you used my name."

Stan, and all of us with whom he shared this experience learned a very valuable lesson. Never let your guard down, and be very careful how you reveal the names of people whom you know and that are also known to others unless and until you have prequalified them. When in doubt, it is best not to reveal that you know the other person. Especially when you're talking with a potential employer or contact, don't reveal that you know, (in our example George), without getting some clearance from George first and learning that it would be OK to use his name. Stan lost a big piece of business as a result of this networking error. Mark our words, if you want to link up with other people, you need to be very clear about (1) how they are perceived in the marketplace, (2) how and who you're linking up with, and (3) to whom you refer. If you say, "I know these people, they're really great," you had better have checked out the relationship with all these parties before talking about how great the person is and thereby portraying yourself as a similar person so as not to put a bullet in your foot or stick your foot in your mouth.

Having Others Send Out Your Résumé

We would like to share some additional thoughts about what happens when you network. It's not uncommon for your contacts to ask for multiple copies of your résumé. Although we recommend that you might wish to provide one or two additional résumés to contacts who ask for them, your friends often volunteer to help beyond your expectations, "Tell you what, why don't you give me 10 of your résumés and I'll pass them out." Now, your most likely response would be—what do you think? "Thanks very much. I really appreciate your willingness to contact ten people on my behalf. That's fantastic."

But remember, people sometimes get busy and they may not be able to send out your résumé in a timely manner. To that end, you need to legitimize taking control. After all, whose campaign is it? You need to manage it, it's your campaign. Not their's, yours. If someone is really insistent about sending out your résumés, that's fine! Don't turn them off, but be sure to get copies of the letters being sent out. Intentions notwithstanding, people get busy and don't follow through on those kinds of things regardless of how much they want to help. Remember how it is at work. Think about how many things you really intend to do, but then the phone rings and the boss steps in and the first thing you know, the day is gone and the high-priority project falls lower on the pile of things to do. What you want to do is allow people to be part of the solution, not be part of the problem. You also want to control where your résumés are sent. Always try to be in control of **your** job search. You really don't want to have people just send out your résumé hoping that it will connect with a specific employment opportunity without having some way of retrieving that data. So, one of the things that you might wish to do is consider saying something along the lines of,

> **George, thanks very much. I really appreciate the fact you're going to be sending out these résumés on my behalf. It makes me feel really good that you are willing to extend yourself in that regard. Since you're so busy, let me suggest an option, if I might. Rather than impose upon your gracious hospitality to do this networking on my behalf, give me the names of the people you were going to send my résumé to and I'll contact them directly using your name. Would that be OK?**

"Well, I wanted to mail these out myself as a favor to you, besides its time I touch base with them myself."

> **That's very nice of you, George. I sincerely appreciate your volunteering to help out to this extent. Let me ask, when would you fit all these calls in with your busy schedule and when would you have them completed? Let me take a more active role George. I'll tell you what, give me the names. I can write the letter and send it out straight-away, I can write the letter and pass it by for your approval, or I can call and use your name. What is the best and easiest approach for you, George?**

In this way you have volunteered several very strong options. Clearly one option is that George can go ahead and call on your behalf. He might say something like, "Don, this is George. I'm calling for a friend of mine. He is a qualified sales and marketing executive, and he's looking for a challenging career opportunity." That's nice and you **do** appreciate George extending himself, however, you do not know how powerfully George is representing you to this other person. The question you might have is, "Will George create a better first impression than you would, if you were to call this person using George's name as a door opener?" If you are in doubt as to the answer, you might ask George if you could use his name to make the network introductions yourself.

Maintaining Your Network _____

An individual once remarked to us, "OK, I've contacted everyone on my network. Now what do I do?" Clearly he did not understand that networking isn't just something you do once. It is an ongoing process. As a metaphor, you need to operate like a commercial fisherman who is the consummate professional. The conscientious captain of a fishing vessel will visit his nets regularly, keeping them always in good repair and diligently harvesting the good things which they may have caught since the captain's last visit. This is a critical dimension you must know and engage in. You must nurture and take care of your network. The following is a list of tasks to help you build and maintain an effective network:

How to Build and Maintain a Results-Producing Network

1. Positively reinforce your network people for the support and the leads which they've provided.

2. Say, "I appreciate your help very much." Say it genuinely and say it every time you talk to them. Every time you talk to your network contacts, be positive, enthusiastic, and confident.

3. Make copious notes of what your network contacts tell you, especially as it relates to action which you or they commit to taking, including dates and "next step" strategies.

4. Always remain in charge of your campaign. Always have the ability to recontact people and to retrieve information. Legitimize call-backs to your contacts:

   Thank you for your willingness to get back to me in a couple of weeks. I'll make a note of it and if I don't hear back from you then, I'll follow up to see if you have reached your friends.

5. Get permission to periodically keep them posted on your campaign, then do so. Always keep these calls brief, informative, and to the point.

6. Inform your network people of the progress which you have made with the contacts they provided to you.

7. By all means, send them a copy of your résumé so they can more fully know your background in case they have inspiration flashes or get any calls asking for people with your credentials.

8. Ask your network contacts for advice about some relevant decisions which you are facing in your career search. They'll appreciate having an opportunity to contribute beyond purely providing leads.

9. Inform them when you are connected. Call them and send them a **personalized** letter of appreciation. Include a business card and possibly an annual report.

10. Call them 120 days after you start, express your enthusiasm for your new job and express your appreciation once again for the help and support they provided.

11. Once a month, take a network contact to lunch. Once every two months, meet someone noteworthy. Once every three months, take a search firm account executive to lunch.

Networking—Is It Worth the Investment? _____

That's a darned good question, and only you can answer it. Are you worth the investment? Are you willing to invest in **you?** If you aren't committed to your success, how successful will your networking be?

When we network effectively we start with the basics. We develop solid credentials and prepare ourselves to interview well. To use our commercial fisherman's metaphor, we bait the area and cast out our nets into the marketplace. As networkers, we work our nets. We do all the right things. We work the nets in an orderly manner, paying attention to the currents and all the signs. We go back again and again to spots that are likely to produce results—patiently, patiently, patiently. All too often people look for quick and easy ways to get a job. They haphazardly try contacting people, asking them for leads into jobs again and again. They engage in what we consider to be a passive campaign, that is a mail campaign to the exclusion of active, effective networking. Networking requires a constant vigilance—maintaining ongoing contact with your networking sources.

Notwithstanding that you might have some reservations about making or receiving telephone calls at your home at night or on the weekends, the point is that you will need to make (and receive) them to sustain your search momentum. So, it is very important to maintain some level of contact and an ability to close the communication loop on a regular basis. Think of it this way. If George gives the names of personal contacts, he is going to want to know what's happened with those folks. Invariably, the personal contacts George gives you may very well get back to George before talking to you. They may want to ask about you, your background, and your skills. They may want to verify that George really knows you. After these contacts chat with you, its not uncommon for them call George back and inform him about what you said and how you handled yourself. Why might they call George ahead of contacting you? Well, they don't know you yet, and they might not want to spend time or reveal important contacts to a time waster or to a lightweight. So, you always need to be getting back and closing the loop with your contacts, like George. If you call one of George's contacts two or three times and you can't get a hold of this person, then you may wish to go back to George to get his address to write him. You may even wish to acknowledge,

George, I haven't been able to get a hold of this person. Do you have any recommendations on how I might reach him? Should I continue to try?

Come to think of it, that's a great question, isn't it? How **do** you reach someone who is either ducking your calls or just doesn't seem to return them. All too often what we'll do is make up a bunch of stuff about an individual in terms of: "Well, they are just arrogant, they've heard negative things about me, they're rejecting me, they're too busy, something's wrong or they're probably not the kind of people I want to be associated with in the first place." These are the tricks your mind will sometimes play on you unless you are able to stop this destructive cycle. Until you know for sure, **don't make up this disempowering internal dialogue, because it *will* defeat you every time. Most important, none of it is true for sure.** If you don't get a return telephone call, the only thing that you **know** for certain is that you haven't gotten a return call. That's it. Period. Nothing more. Don't start to fantasize beyond this point, it probably is not in your best interest; just dismiss this type of imaginative thinking and get back to the facts. If you are going to make up stuff, make up good stuff since you are making it up anyway. Why not say,

Business must be really good at this network contact's place because he is always busy. I'm sure he will have a lot of good ideas when we finally make contact.

How Often Do You Attempt Contact Before Giving Up?

It depends. Let us answer that question through an example. Recently, we gave a secondary network contact name to one of our clients. After some time, he reported that he hadn't been able to reach the person. He had tried and tried and tried and tried and tried. There were times when he would leave his message, and there would be times when he wouldn't. He tried in the night, in the morning, in the day time, using all the techniques that we were talking about. What should he do? He had overlooked one item that is a good rule of thumb. **Don't make more than three or four telephone calls without writing a letter.** Don't make the mistake of making five or more calls. Call and leave your name and also your referral contact's name and telephone number once, twice, three times. If it's over an extended period of time, and you're traveling, then maybe three, four, or five times at the **max.** Our premise is that after about the third call, you should write a short letter introducing yourself, leading off with a reference to your mutual friend. Why keep calling? You depreciate yourself. Why do that? If you continue to call, you demonstrate to the person you are trying to reach that he or she has all the power and you have none. Keep the power base on equal terms, don't get out of balance with regard to this. If after your letter, you call three more times and there's no call back or pick up, then you can do either one of two things. You can just move on—"next!" You've got better things to do. **Or,** you might get back to your original contact and inform him of the situation. If your original contact for this person was George, go back and involve him in this process:

Can you help me out here? Would you get in touch with this person and see if you might be able to introduce me or find out when would be a convenient time to call? I'm just about at the end of my rope. Would a breakfast or luncheon meeting make sense? I would really like to get in touch with this person, but I have not been successful in doing so. I really appreciate your help, George. Thanks.

Create a Large "No" List As a Goal _____

If George can't get a call back or can't get a response to the letter, then just move on. Think of it this way: **Your goal is to create a large *No list,*** not a bunch of yeses, but a large *No* list. "A large *No* list, why?" Because it takes the pressure off of you. It takes about 10 *no's* to generate a *yes*. So, there's a greater probability of a *yes* if you've gotten a lot of *no's*. People hang up on you? Great, no problem; that's one *no*. **Next!** People are real brusque with you? Hey, no problem; that's another *no*. **Next!** Write thank you letters back to the senior executives in your key target companies who couldn't wait to get you off the phone. Very often the people who were the most curt with you are the people with whom you want to work because they're the busiest. They're "rocking and rolling," not in every case of course, but often that's the case. Just think of your own schedule when you have a particularly hectic and busy day and you had 20 phone messages waiting for you and you had back-to-back meetings. It's tough to get back to many of these people on that kind of day. And it's particularly tough to get back to people who you don't know. If your call is merely a referral, it becomes C priority. If, on the other hand, you were the president of their company, you would get a call right back. So you see, it's a matter of priorities.

Don't let yourself become upset about getting a no. Just keep track and move on. There is a great phrase which you might wish to put on an index card next to your desk or by your phone: **lighten up. Be appropriate, but lighten up.** Work toward being professional and making the contacts to be as solid and as valuable as is possible. But lighten up. It's not the end of the world when you get a no. They didn't reject you. They don't even know you. They are just busy. Lighten up and go on. Have fun with your network and really rejoice every time someone says. "Sure. How can I help?" Those are the times that make networking worthwhile!

Secondary Network Contacts—a Strategy _____

If you recall, the people you know are your primary network contacts and the names your primary contacts share with you (provided you didn't know them previously) are your secondary network contacts.

Let's get back to George. If you are calling George and if you leave a message with George's secretary, George will recognize your name. OK, so George, in all likelihood, will call you back pretty expeditiously since you are a good friend. But if you're calling George's friend, Darlene, she won't recognize your name so there is only a moderate probability of a call back. Right? But if you say to Darlene's secretary, "I'm calling on a personal matter concerning George," chances are pretty good that you'll get a much better response. Although your name wasn't recognized, George's was. Curiosity is often the trigger to get a call back from a secondary contact. Why is that? This is a world of possibilities. Maybe you're an executive search firm recruiter and George told you to call Darlene for this $200,000 a year job. Or maybe George just won the lottery and he wanted to share it with his friends. Or whatever. From a curiosity standpoint, Darlene will probably call you back if she has a decent relationship with George.

If you call and say, "I'm calling on a personal matter concerning George Farley," you'll probably get call backs about 85 to 100 percent of the time. If you call Darlene and say to her secretary, "I'm calling as a result of a conversation I had with George regarding my career search efforts, and he suggested that I call Darlene." If that's the message she receives from her secretary you'll probably get call backs much less than 50 percent of the time. Mentioning your career search is too threatening, because Darlene doesn't have any definite answers for you and, besides, all such inquires are handled by Human Resources, anyway. She may make an assumption that you will be asking about job openings. She knows of none, so why should she call you? She may even acknowledge that recruiting is all done in personnel and recommend you call them instead. So, our suggestion is to keep your introduction tight and personal while being confident, bold, and informal. You might even wish to sound like a busy executive yourself: "Is Darlene there? Right, Darlene Hopkins." Now if you say Darlene in an informal manner, Darlene's secretary may just put you through or certainly say that you're going to get a call back. Now, if Darlene gets back to you on the phone and says, "Well, what's this personal matter concerning George?" You need to respond confidently,

> **I'm conducting a discreet, confidential career search. As you may or may not know, Acme Company recently had a reorganization and I have been impacted. George suggested I call you as he felt you had an excellent knowledge of several of the good search firms in the area. He also said that you might be willing to share them with me. If so, I would certainly appreciate it, Darlene.**

Does this make sense? This approach addresses how to get past some of the secretarial screens. What is the risk of this approach? Well, you could run the risk of generating some resentment when Darlene says, "Hey, this isn't a personal matter. This is a foot-in-the-door technique." If that occurs, respond with

> **Darlene, George said that if I indicated to you that it was a personal matter that you wouldn't mind. I'm sorry, I didn't mean to miscommunicate that this was George's personal matter. Darlene, let me share with you my situation. It's a personal matter *and* a business issue as well.**

Legitimize her reactions, add value, refer to George in the conversation, and keep moving forward. That'll make the difference. If you get stuck and start to apologize tremendously, you'll really depreciate your position. It's a little bit like the line from Hamlet, Act 3, "The lady doth protest too much, methinks." If you protest too much, if you apologize too much, you will totally undermine your effectiveness with the other person and then he or she will have the upper hand. Being in that position, you can't press forward with them very well.

How to Press On When It's Easier to Fold Up Your Tent

Some people upon receiving some pressure when they call a second-tier contact, get flustered and say, "I'm sorry" and sign off with no additional data. They just close the door to further networking. Or they don't keep pressing. This whole technique is about saying, "who do you know or what organizations do you know, what search firms do you know, what opportunities do you know about?" effectively in a warm, personable, and professional manner. Our whole approach in networking is to keep moving ahead. If you run into an objection, legitimize the objection, add more value, and ask for more data. Press for closure and for more information on search firms, target organizations, or personal leads.

Remember earlier when we talked about George drawing a blank and not being able to think of any contacts to share with you? Well, it can happen here too! If a person can't think of anyone, say,

I can well appreciate that you can't think of anyone right now. I probably caught you cold and you are probably in the middle of a number of things. Let me call you back after I send you a résumé. I will follow up to see if you have thought of any search firms, organizations, or personal contacts. Will that be alright?

When you do follow up with a phone call to your contacts who did not give you much data, follow up within about a three-day period. Don't wait three weeks to call. If you call someone and he or she doesn't give you any data or doesn't give you much at all, you may have caught the person cold. Consider the first contact to be more of an "alert call." Tell this person that you will get back later, in several days, to pick his or her brain and commit to doing that. Keep your word! Don't let more than a week lapse or the contact will have forgotten you. The next time you call, let's say you call on a Monday and then you wait a whole week, you must reeducate the person all over again as to why you're calling. But if your initial call is Monday and your follow-up call is on Wednesday morning, the contact is still somewhat fresh. "Oh, yes, you called me. That's right, you're in sales and marketing, right?" "Right." The individual is instantly back into the context of your initial call, hopefully. If you wait more than three days between calls, the second call actually becomes another first call and it will probably not yield much, which means you need to call a third time. Understand that you just keep compounding the problem, elongating your search, and, quite possibly, irritating your contacts.

So, when you call your contacts and you don't get any information, or very little information, and they acknowledge they haven't been as supportive to you as they like, then call them back no later than three days after the initial call. Legitimize the call back:

I'll get back to you in three days because I know that if I wait a week, we will both get busy. I want to revisit this when it's fresh. Would that be OK with you?

Again, get them involved in the process. If you involve people in the process of networking with you, there is a higher likelihood of them helping you out. One technique is to ask questions, then wait for a response—hopefully an affirmative response. Involved people are committed people. **Create networking partners by involving others.** If you don't get them involved, if you just say you're going to do this or you just call back in three days, or if you haven't asked, "will that be alright?" you haven't involved them. You run the risk of mere compliance and, at some level, creating resistance or hostility and rejection. So please do not trigger that negative reaction. Always be vigilant and look for ways to solidify relationships which you have with everyone. Besides which, if you say "Would that be alright?" and they say, "no it would not be alright!" it gives you an opportunity to find out what the problem is. It might be that they're going to be going away for a few days and it's not going to be appropriate to call them back in three days but rather three weeks or the next day. Or they might also have a real strong negative feeling about networking and so what you get to do is defuse their negative biases. If they are unwilling to support you at even the most basic level, thank them and move on. You certainly don't want to keep pestering someone if they are not going to be responsive to you. So, ask the question, "Would that be alright?"

A "Personal Matter"

Let's revisit for a moment, the whole issue of referencing a personal matter when you are leaving a phone message. Sometimes there is a misunderstanding, and we want to clarify what we mean. If you get in the habit of calling somebody up and telling the secretary it's a personal matter without linking the call to George (or another personal contact), you may get an immediate call back, but it may be that the person will have interrupted an important business meeting out of a sense of urgency. Your potential networking contact does not want to be disturbed by this type of call. Always link the call with your contact so the secretary or target contact **does not** think it is a family-related emergency, i.e., a **personal matter.**

If the response on the part of the executive is bold, confident, and immediate, then you need to be equally confident and bold and get quickly into your agenda. Now, after you have quickly established rapport and at the very least identified your agenda, then you can open it up a bit. However, remember that if you are networking properly, **you never, never ask for a job lead or who might be hiring.** You don't ask if the company has any plans to hire someone with your background in the near future. That's just too much; it feels like pushy, hard selling. Believe us, it doesn't work, and it erodes your ability to genuinely network.

When you reach a secondary contact, you probably would say something like,

> **George suggested that I call you. My company went through a reorganization recently, and I've been impacted as V.P. of Sales. While I've survived a number of reorganizations, I didn't survive this one. I, along with a number of senior executives and midlevel managers, had our functions consolidated. At any rate, our mutual friend, George suggested that it might be very beneficial if we could spend a few moments together personally. He felt that some of your ideas might be helpful and that because you have excellent contacts with**

people, that you might be willing to share the names of some of them who might also have some good ideas about my campaign. When do you think we might be able to meet briefly?

Make it safe for this contact to talk with you. Hopefully, through this process you will have also peaked the contact's interest because you are beginning to demonstrate that you are a competent professional and that you are not going to be a threat, because you're looking for contacts and leads **not** for a **job** in that company or any other company. And in those times in which you find you are not gaining any headway, you get to be creative by developing ways in which you can get back to your valuable primary and secondary contacts and encourage them to help you by giving you additional information, all the while making them **comfortable** with who you are and with your request.

Stand Up and Gesture When You Network on the Phone

Networking **is a very simple process.** However, although it's simple, it is not always easy. And therein lies the rub. It is, however, merely a function of always being up in front of people. As soon as you hang up from one call, quick make your notes, pick up the phone again and make the next call, make your notes, the next call, make your notes, the next call, make your notes, the next call. Boom, boom, boom, keep moving. **Stand up** when you make these telephone calls, **gesture, and project your voice.** Work at speaking from your diaphragm as opposed to the upper registers of your voice, because if you speak real high, you may sound whiny and not very effective or powerful. Speak conversationally and straightforwardly. Talk to the people on the phone as if they're right in front of you. Maintain eye contact. Yes, maintain eye contact. Pretend that they're there and engage them in the conversation. Smile, gesture, be enthusiastic, be confident, be bold. **Use the good feelings and personal power that you have from one conversation to create positive momentum over to the next call.** You may wish to start your networking day with those people who would be easy to reach and be a great boost for your morale. Think of these calls as **warm-up calls** to ready you for the real thing.

Let us share with you an experience one of our clients had in turning his networking fear into networking power. A few years ago, we were working with a director of Engineering who had tremendous difficulty networking. Tom had many contacts and he had a good story to tell. He was an extremely competent individual and was fun to be with once you got to know him. But the telephone just absolutely freaked him out. As a result, he was not very effective in making networking calls. In fact, he was terrible! So he asked us to help him out and we did. We sat in on some of the conversations that he was initiating. And he was right! He was totally ineffective. He froze up at every turn of the conversation and didn't project himself very well. It was as if he was auditioning and the audition didn't even begin to reflect his true talent. So, one of the first things we did with Tom was to take a look at some areas in his life in which he felt really powerful. We zeroed in on both personal and business areas in which he felt in charge. We looked at how he felt about things, how he visualized the world around him, how he carried himself, how he moved, how he gestured, how he was with other individuals in which he was particularly bold, powerful, and confident. Interestingly enough, he revealed that he physically stood and moved differently when he was with individuals with whom he had a good, close, comfortable relationship.

We highlighted for Tom the differences between operating and speaking in a fairly uncomfortable, nonpowerful manner from being interpersonally grounded and powerful. How did we accentuate these distinctions for Tom? Simple. We had him **stand up** and **replicate** previous conversations in which he was feeling great—feeling bold, confident, and well grounded. Once he visualized and recaptured those times in which he knew he could not fail, we had him **gesture** and **smile** and **move** like he had done previously. Guess what? Tom produced the same desired outcome in his body, and he felt **unstoppable.** We also sat him down behind a desk and had him recreate poor performance on the telephone. Interestingly enough, by putting Tom in and out of these powerful and unpowerful states, he discovered something pretty unique about his own physiology. What he discovered was that the more he **moved** and the more he **gestured,** the more **powerful** he became. For us, this was old stuff, but for Tom, it was a new revelation, as he had never "objectified" how he operated. No one had ever shown him how he gained and lost personal power before. Tom discovered something else that was really interesting. If he stood with his foot on the radiator, it was if he was talking with one of his old buddies on the phone and he was able to generate the kind of rapport that he never experienced before while networking. In this relaxed, powerful, and confident state, Tom was transformed from a timid networker into a powerful and effective job seeker. When he made this shift, his campaign took off like a rocket. Previously, he wasn't producing the results he wanted; he would set up maybe one or two interviews a month. Now he was generating three to five interviews a week! As such, his confidence soared and his interviewing abilities enhanced tremendously. Within a short period, Tom successfully connected in a company of his choice, in a career move that represented a great opportunity for him. He shifted out of engineering into technical sales, selling in the niche industry from whence he came! For a guy who hated to pick up the phone, his transformation was nothing short of miraculous!

Think of Your Secondary Contacts as Your Colleagues _____

To gain a little more confidence in networking with your secondary contacts, the people you don't know, think of them as colleagues in your company, perhaps in another division you just haven't met yet. These are people about whom you've heard a lot, you may have even talked to them on the phone, and they are excited about meeting you. You just know it's going to be a good meeting. With that mindset, you're not going to a meeting with them dreading rejection or feeling that you're going to have to do battle. No. Rather, you come into meetings with your colleagues with tremendous positive expectancy that you're going to create the kind of results you want. Tell your brain that it is going to be a great meeting. Your brain doesn't know any different. **Focus on your desired outcome;** don't focus on your greatest fear, because **you always get what you focus on.** It takes as much energy to visualize disaster as it does to visualize beauty. Why not turn your thoughts to the things that uplift you versus tear you down. When you network, **affirm for yourself out loud that this will be a great call or a great meeting.** Tell yourself that it will be a **win-win** experience with everyone benefiting.

When you are contacting individuals whom you have **not** met or talked to previously, we want you to **recontextualize** how you're operating and **see people as friends, not strangers.** The warm and personable Will Rogers was fond of saying, "I never met a man I didn't like. A stranger is a friend I haven't met yet."

One of our former clients and dear friends, Roger Brown, is an excellent networker, and we want to share with you how he recontextualized how he networked. Roger is bright, creative, energetic, enthusiastic, supportive, and committed to making the extra effort that keeps him in the forefront of people's minds. As a human resource vice president, Roger was conducting a career search during a time in which there was a glut of human resource professionals on the market and the competition for really good jobs was extremely stiff. However, Roger operated differently than did most other people. **Roger heard there was a recession and he decided not to participate.** Even though the job search was tough, very tough at times, Roger chose to operate out of abundance rather than lack. Roger was always willing to lend a hand, even to those who might, conceivably, be construed as directly competing with him on a given position opening. Interestingly, Roger never saw others as competitors, even though they might be directly interviewing for the same job he was. He saw others as colleagues who might benefit from some of the leads for positions for which he was not interested. His mindset was one of always providing more value than he receives. His style of extending himself to others created a more relaxed and confident Roger, for he took the pressure of having to win every time off of himself. By doing so, he discovered that he totally eliminated the adversarial relationship that is sometimes inadvertently created while networking and interviewing.

When we were talking with Roger about this networking book, he wanted us to relate two experiences which he recently had. The first experience is entitled, "The Eighteen-Car Pile-Up." If you have ever seen or been involved in a major highway pile-up, you know that there can be a significant chain reaction when one car smashes into another into another into another, and so on. That was Roger's metaphor for one of his networking experiences, with one name leading to another to another to another. Since Roger was interested in securing a lead into a particular health care company, we gave him the name of Jim who was very experienced in that field. He gave Roger the lead into another health care professional named Debbie. Debbie seemed to know everyone worth knowing, and she gave Roger several leads including the name of Rick who referred Roger to a search firm and then to Sam G. who was ironically an old friend whom he had forgotten to call. Sam encouraged Roger to call Kyle, senior vice president of human resources in his targeted health care company. And he did!

Isn't that a great example of networking at its finest! Clyde to Jim to Debbie to Rick to a search firm to Sam to Kyle and to the interview! Seven connections! Roger rightfully concluded that once you get a lead, continue to follow up on all the other leads generated. If you stop short, you never know what you would have missed—or gotten.

Roger's second networking example he entitled "Going. Going. Not entirely gone!" A division president of one of his target organizations had received Roger's résumé early in December. Because there was no need in his division which was downsizing, the president sent Roger's credentials to the parent company which contacted him in mid-March for an interview. Although Roger knew this type of connection didn't always happen, he was nonetheless delighted that his early efforts produced something for him several months later. "After all," observed Roger, "it only takes one connection to lead to the perfect job."

We want to ask you a question which has been popularized by Dr. Reverend Schuller in his church services and in his books. The question is, "**If you knew you could not fail, how would you act? If you knew that you were going to be successful, how would you feel?**" **If you knew you could not fail before you picked up the telephone to network, how would you act?** That's right! You'd probably act more confidently and more boldly. So, operate in that context. Use the excitement of the positive responses that you've created for yourself from previous calls as **leverages** for the next calls. View these people that you're calling as your **friends** waiting for your call so they can help. If you're having difficulty making some networking calls, then we suggest that you visualize the call that you're about to make as one to an old friend—or to the same person you previously called with whom you made a great connection. **Recapture the**

positive feelings you enjoyed when you had a really tremendous conversation with one of your primary or secondary contacts. Just take the feelings and your image of that person and plug them right into the conversation you're now having—or are about to have. **Speak with the same level of confidence to the stranger as you have with the people with whom you enjoy a solid relationship.** Recreate that emotional state in which you were most powerful, most confident, most relaxed. Sound too good to be true? Let's see if we can continue to crank up your confidence and skill in networking a bit.

FOCUS ON YOUR OUTCOME AND YOU'LL PRODUCE RESULTS

—————————————— SECRET 7

*The key to success in life is having a definite purpose,
backed by a definitive plan and immediate action
executed with unswerving belief and confidence.*

Studies over the years of people who had accumulated fortunes well beyond the multimillion-dollar mark revealed that every person had the habit of reaching decisions promptly and of changing decisions slowly, if and when they changed. The essence of success is: Know what you want and you'll generally get it!

The key to effective networking is sixfold:

1. Have a definite outcome in mind before you call or meet.
2. Become confident and work at increasing your confidence on an ongoing basis.
3. Keep making those calls, keep moving forward through your list of contacts, regardless of how you feel.
4. Understand that people **are** interested in you and they're willing to give you a hand, even though they haven't met you yet.
5. Always look at ways you can expand your networking sources. Every time you begin to limit yourself or you feel it's difficult, ask yourself the question, "Granted that it's difficult, what are the five solutions?"
6. Follow the secrets of networking success outlined throughout these chapters.

To succeed in networking, indeed in all aspects of your life, you have to have a goal and also realize, without a shadow of a doubt, that you are completely in charge. You are the person who can create your career or your life, anyway you want. You're responsible for your career, your life, and your campaign. If you don't like what's happening, look at ways to change it. If you are overweight, don't blame your parents or your environment, or your heredity—change it. If you don't like the image that you create, get help on your dress and personal presentation. If you are not as successful as you would like, get around successful people and learn what they think, feel, and do to be successful. Work at being bold, confident, and credible.

Networking _is_ a simple process and it will yield significant results for you if you're prepared to work at it and believe in yourself. If you believe you've got a valuable background, have good strong talents, skills, and abilities, and can significantly contribute to the growth and profitability of an organization, others will take their cues from you and respond positively. The world has a habit of making room for the confident people whose words and behavior demonstrate that they know where they are headed.

To help you achieve focus and produce results in both your life and career, we recommend that you study and apply the following _Self-Confidence Formula_SM. Thousands of our clients have produced some remarkable results by following these five steps. People who took these steps seriously have generated breakthrough accomplishments and enhanced their self-esteem, self-confidence, and self-control. We know that if you, too, incorporate these steps into your daily life, you will significantly enhance your ability to operate more effectively, both on and off the job.

Step 1. Develop Superior Credentials and Model Success

During your career, it is imperative that you seek out opportunities to broaden your skills and experiences. Create a burning desire to be the best you can be, for this is the starting point from which dreams are realized and careers take off. Dreams are not born out of indifference or satisfaction, rather impatience—impatience with the status quo. Operate with the philosophy that you will always give more value than that which you receive and that you are willing to do more than expected. Do not look for extra compensation each time you enhance your skills or when you contribute beyond your peer group. Nonetheless, it is wise to communicate your results achieved, not in the form of bragging or attention getting, rather merely reporting an activity. The development and strengthening of your capabilities should be seen as an investment that will never be wasted and one from which you will reap rewards in due time.

During your job search, it's vital that you communicate both what you **have done,** as well as what you **can do.** Create a powerful résumé and attention-getting marketing letters which clearly distinguish you from others and reveal how you can contribute to another organization. Presumably, at this stage of your career search you already have a résumé. But if you don't have a powerful, results-oriented résumé you certainly need to develop one. We have found that most résumés fall way short of fully portraying a person's ability to contribute, operate effectively, persuade others, conceptualize a project and execute its plan, or get along with others. Most résumés limit the person's options versus expanding them, and the résumé is too product-line-specific, company-specific, or industry-specific. When in doubt about the clarity or the power of your credentials, have people read and react to your résumé—people *not* necessarily from your company or industry. Ask them if they understand it and ask them to share with you the image, profile, or impression your résumé created for them. If the "mosaic" of your skills and accomplishments is not as powerful as you would like, then work on your résumé some more.

Success breeds success. Successful people have learned to manage life's difficulties and follow certain strategies which have worked for them. If you are desirous of acquiring any skill or achieving high-performance results, you need a "success coach" or a "success model." A model is more than a good example, much more. In terms of modeling success, you need to identify people that you deem to be successful in, let's say networking or any other particular skill area which you want to master. Go to them, ask what specific behavior they engage in or thoughts they hold to be successful. Write them down. Verify with these people what they do and then model or replicate their successful behavior. Think of it as following their proven recipe or strategy of success. If they are successful and you are not, then you are probably not following *exactly* what they are doing, thinking, or feeling. If they're doing things that you're not, even subtle things, then you need to be doing things that they're doing to replicate their success. Do what they do. Think the affirming thoughts they think and feel what they feel.

If you're not producing the kind of results you want in your life, you may not be modeling or replicating successful behavior or thoughts closely enough. Try this modeling process again. Write down and verify a successful person's strategy until you begin to produce the kinds of positive results you want and can generate positive, powerful, affirming feelings any time you desire. Be alert to the fact that you might struggle with this new behavior initially. That's OK, as awkwardness is all part of learning. Don't struggle against the newness of your learning, rather, embrace it as something exciting and an affirmation that this is an area which you are in the process of mastering. Let us give you an example out of the ultimate in being on the jagged edge of a learning experience. In Clyde's words:

As I previously mentioned, I recently secured my private pilot's license. One of the maneuvers that every student pilot has to be able to do well is recover from stalls. A stall is that condition in which the plane no longer has any lift and it starts to fall. I'll never forget the first time I experienced a stall. My good friend Jim Schneiter was teaching me how to fly and stall. Jim has been flying for more than 25 years and is an incredible pilot. So, I felt safe and secure with him in the cockpit. With Jim at the controls we pointed the plane up in a near vertical position until the stall horn sounded. With a minimum amount of fuss, Jim adjusted the controls and we leveled off quite nicely, notwithstanding that my heart was pounding like a jack hammer. Now it was my turn. With a big grin, Jim asked me if I was ready. As I took the controls and pointed the plane's nose straight up, Jim cut the power and added flaps to effectuate the stall. As we approached stalling speed, the stall horn went off sounding like a Civil Defense siren going off in my ear. Intellectually, I knew what to do, point the nose down, add power and return to straight and level flight. While I had rehearsed the stall recovery perfectly in my mind, when the plane "broke"—that is the term used when the stall occurs—I did everything I was supposed to do, only with exaggerated motions. Instead of merely pointing the nose down gently, I felt like I had us in a power dive from which there was no recovery. I never knew the body had so many sweat pores nor your heart could beat so hard—and loud. Wheww! I will never forget my first stall. What a learning experience. Not only was everything brand new, it was also incredibly awkward and uncomfortable. While I was shaking from the adrenaline rush and perspiring in waves, Jim was calmly looking out the window and yawning. How he could be so relaxed in that near-death experience was beyond me. After several deep breaths, I got focused, and we did it again and again and again. Instead of losing 200 feet, as in the first stall, I confidently was able to regain control and create level flight with virtually no loss of altitude. What a difference! I learned very graphically how important it is to have competent instruction and a successful model! I am happy to report that getting in and out of stalls is now no problem, though I still have a twinge of nervousness whenever I do the first stall in a series. Learning this new skill of effectively controlling airplane stalls may be a little more nerve racking than picking up the phone and networking for the majority of people. However, we recognize that for some people the prospect of networking is terrifying. The tenseness, the pounding heart, the dry mouth, and the sweaty palms may accurately describe how you feel. I'm here to tell you that if I can learn how to successfully recover from stalls, I know you can learn how to successfully network.

The following is a personal inventory—use it to assess your credentials and role models:

Personal Inventory—Credentials and Success Models

1. How would others describe to what extent you communicate accurately and fully reflect both what you can do as well as what you have done?

2. How results-oriented and quantifiable are your statements about yourself?

3. Why would someone be interested in your background? How do your summaries of your experiences and accomplishments demonstrate this?

4. Are you more powerful or less powerful than your résumé? Why?

5. What are the five main things that employers are looking for? Are these reflected in your networking statements and your résumé?

6. What persons have accomplished what you hope to accomplish?

7. What about them makes them a "success model"?

8. How do they operate differently than you do?

9. What are you willing to change to operate like your "success models"?

10. What do they **believe** about networking? When they network, what do they think?

11. What do they **feel** about networking? When they network, what feelings are they experiencing?

12. When they are networking, how do they **act?** How do they physically gesture, move about, and create their physical "presence"?

Step 2. Manage Your Emotions _____

Whether you have recently been "let go" or are merely beginning to contemplate a career change, you may have a number of conflicting feelings: fear, anger, shock, disbelief, self-doubt, denial, betrayal, guilt, depression, shame, or maybe even a feeling of freedom or excitement. Relief is an emotion people experience, as well. People often report to us that they feel as if a "50-pound weight has been lifted off" of their shoulders.

Millions of people experience and feel that which you are feeling (and have felt) when they find themselves in your situation. What you feel is normal and common to all of us.* Do not worry about being discouraged or anxious about feeling out of control emotionally; most people experience a wide range of emotions. These emotional swings are normal, and they do shift. It is like being on an "emotional roller coaster"—many ups and downs. But letting these emotional "moods" control you for an extended period or becoming paralyzed by them can defeat you when you most need your courage and determination to come out of this situation as a winner.

If you were zapped, the moment you became aware of your changed status your first and natural reaction may have been, "This can't be true. This isn't happening!" (**denial,** quickly followed by numbness). When the reality of your job loss began to sink in, you may have become mad (**anger**). "How dare they do this to me! It's not fair! I'm going to get even!" Once your

---

* A respected psychologist, Dr. Elisabeth Kubler-Ross, found that people living through periods of uncertainty or trauma, such as job loss, usually go through a series of emotional stages (see Fig. 7-1).

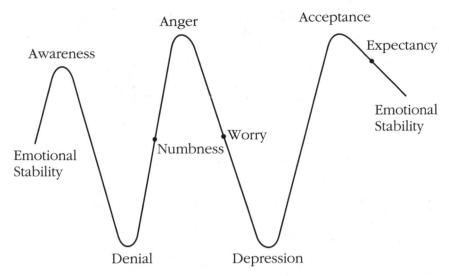

Figure 7-1. Your emotional stages. (*Adapted from Kubler-Ross,* On Death and Dying, *MacMillan, New York, 1969, Used with permission.*)

anger subsided, you might have become even deeply worried, saddened, or depressed. It is not uncommon for you to raise questions about your self-worth and technical competence **(depression).** "What do I do now? Perhaps I did deserve this. Obviously, I'm not as good as I thought I was."

While these emotional states are normal and can be pretty intense, most individuals can push through their emotional ups and downs and reach **acceptance,** albeit the healing process may take a while—perhaps even several months. When you are in an accepting state, you can face your personal trauma squarely as a problem to be solved or a hurdle to be overcome. When you accept that your situation is not unusual and that you are not alone (even though you may feel lost right now), you are beginning to get on top of the situation. It sometimes helps to have the perspective that your termination was a business decision, not a personal one. Granted, it may certainly feel deeply personal.

Our personal experience in dealing with hundreds of clients over the years is that you can move through all of these emotional states to **acceptance** or **positive expectancy** in the blink of an eye—or you may get stuck in **denial, anger,** or **depression** for a long period. **Whatever emotional state you happen to find yourself in is ok.** We ask that you work hard at not being concerned if you are in an emotional upset, now or even later in your job search. Being upset and having emotions is a natural part of life. To deny that you are upset is to deny a large part of who you are, of your uniqueness. Practice getting in touch with your feelings and your "inner voices"—the thoughts that rattle around in your head at night or in stressful times. Strive to create and manage those emotions that you desire, from being energized to being joyful, resourceful, confident, open, dynamic, bold, creative, innovative, and perhaps even wise!

You've probably heard more than one time that "repetition is the mother of skill." That's what practice is. Read and reread the following short exercise until you have a good handle on this so you can do this yourself or have your coach guide you through it. Before we walk you through this experience, we want you to rate your personal power, right now, on a scale of 1 to 10, with 10 being high. OK? What is your rating right now of your personal power? Thanks. To help you enhance your ability to get in and out of powerful states of minds, let's have you get into a positive emotional state.

*With your eyes closed and in a relaxed position, please take four deep cleansing breaths . . . slowly blowing out through pursed lips. Nice and slow. That's right. Deep breaths. Visualize an event or time in your life which captures that emotion you want to recreate easily. Let's say, feeling very confident. Concentrate on that specific scene in which you're feeling particularly confident and zoom in on it, not unlike a camera with a telephoto lens. Note what you are doing. Observe how you are moving, talking, gesturing, laughing, smiling, interacting with people. Note who else is with you in this scene. Open your mind up and imagine yourself in this scene **first** as an observer. Notice how crisp and bright everything seems to be. While keeping the energy and confidence high, "pop" yourself into the scene. Just open your mind up, just like opening your eyes up, and "pop" yourself into the scene. Actually **experience** what you only observed earlier. Feel the excitement and the power of being highly confident . . . incredibly bold. Notice how you are standing, if you were indeed standing. While remaining standing (or sitting) and feeling particularly high and confident, make a fist, flex your bicep, hold for a moment—1, 2, 3—then release. Squeeze your fist again and as you do, raise your confidence level even higher each time you squeeze your fist. Squeeze your fist again and allow your confidence to soar. Repeat this process often to recapture these empowered feelings so you can feel confident and we mean really confident any time you choose, just by squeezing your fist and gesturing. OK. Do you remember that? Alright. After four deep cleansing breaths, we want you to open your eyes and come back to us. Breathe in and out—nice and slow. Don't rush the process. That's nice. Big breaths. 2, 3, 4, Nice job. Please slowly open your eyes and come back to us.*

On a scale of 1 to 10, with 10 representing high personal power, what ranking would you give yourself now? If your evaluation is less than 7 then you may wish to experience this exercise again and see what changes you could experiment with to generate heightened personal power. You might try breathing deeper or sitting on the edge of your chair or leaning forward or gesturing more vigorously, so you might replicate this at will.

Use the following list to take a personal inventory of how you manage your emotions:

1. How would others describe your emotional state, generally? Why would they say that?

2. Under what conditions do you experience emotional swings? How do you behave?

3. What gets you "up"? How might you create that "up" feeling? How easy is it?

4. How do you think, feel, and act when you are "up"?

5. To what extent are things easier or more difficult to accomplish when "up"?

6. What gets you "down"? How might you create that "down" feeling? How easy is it?

7. How do you think, feel, and act when you are "down"?

8. To what extent are things easier or more difficult to accomplish when "down"?

9. What happens to your personal power after you have been trying to get an answer to "why" something bad has occurred?

Step 3. Recontextualize Disempowering Beliefs

If you **think** you are beaten, you are.
    If you **think** you dare not, you don't.
If you like to win, but you **think** you can't,
    It is almost certain you won't.

If you **think** you'll lose, you're lost
    For out in the world we find,
Success begins with a fellow's will
    It's all in the **state of mind.**

If you **think** you are outclassed, you are,
    You've got to **think** high to rise,
You've got to be **sure of yourself** before
    You can ever win a prize.

Life's battles don't always go to the
    Stronger or faster man,
But sooner or later the man who wins
    Is the man WHO THINKS HE CAN!

AUTHOR UNKNOWN

Change how you think about things which get in the way of you being fully effective. The intensity of the meanings that you attach to things will significantly influence how you feel about them. In other words, if you've viewed something as the **worst** thing that's ever happened to you and it is incredibly **unfair,** then you'll probably feel victimized, maybe even violated and betrayed. You may even be righteously indignant about it. Conversely, if you feel that the identical event is mildly disappointing, appropriate, and fair, you'll probably view this as a normal part of living and move on. For some people, not receiving a promised promotion is a tremendous loss of face, prompting an immediate job search. For others, a promotion loss is a sign that perhaps they didn't build the kind of organizational endorsement they needed for the promotion. So instead of failure, the lack of promotion really is viewed as a learning experience and opportunity which really energizes them to seek out new ways to gain the endorsement, the visibility, and the kinds of skills they need to be ready for a promotion the next time. See the difference in how accountability and responsibility show up? Refer to Figure 2-1, "Recontextualizing Your Road Blocks" in Secret 2, for a review of how to shift your perspective when stuck.

Use Worksheet 18 to recontextualize your disempowering beliefs.

Step 4. Learn, Understand, and Apply Behavioral Models of Success

Behavioral models help us take a complex topic, such as how we behave, and simplify it through a representation or model. Models make real the abstract, not unlike the clay model of a car that is the designer's concept put in physical form so we can see what previously only she or he saw. If you incorporate the positive behavioral models identified in this discussion and other models that you know are productive, you will make significant shifts in the way you think, feel, and act. If you make these adaptive changes, you might significantly alter the way you run your life. Who knows? Maybe you can significantly increase your contribution to others and make even more of a difference in your life. Take a look at how things come together for you. Identify how successful people behave similarly to and different from yourself. Become curious; become an investigator, and of these successful people, ask:

- "How did you become successful?"
- "What do you do to create success in your life?"
- "What beliefs about how you should operate do you have?"
- "What do you personally seek out?"
- "What do you personally avoid?"
- "What are your strengths? What are your weaknesses?"
- "You seem to really enjoy being with others. Why is that?"
- "What do you think, feel, and how do you operate differently than the way others do?"

WORKSHEET 18
Recontextualizing Your Upset
and Disempowering Beliefs

If there is something in your life which isn't working well or isn't working as well as it could, rather than looking at this as a major failure or as a major disappointment, focus your thoughts on what you can **gain** from this condition. If you've lost your job, certainly there's been a loss. But there's also the opportunity for significant learning.

Identify your biggest fear, upset, obstacle, hurdle, belief, or roadblock which prevents you from realizing your potential and gets in the way of you being fully effective:

To recontextualize your upset, defuse your emotions, and to shift your perspective, write your answer to the following questions:

1. What is most upsetting me about this situation right now?

2. How would I like this situation to look?

Now

In the future

3. What is good and right and perfect about this, just the way it is?

(Continued)

4. What are all the positive things can I learn from this experience?

5. How can I turn this around, **right now,** and enjoy the process?

6. What should I do differently in the future?

7. What didn't I do previously that I can do right now?

8. What are my options now?

9. Who do I need to see and what positive things do I need to do or say to really "unlock" my upset?

Note: If you can look at job hunting as an exciting learning opportunity as opposed to a major setback or failure, you will have significantly increased the likelihood of creating greater confidence and personal power.

You might need to legitimize these successful people being straight with you, so as to understand the distinctions between how they operate and how you operate. We're typically not very straight with people. In most cultures, we help people save face. We don't want to confront people. We don't think it's polite, we generally don't know how to do it well and people become uncomfortable and defensive around us if we are too straightforward. So we choose to avoid being open and vulnerable with others which means we are engaged in "withholds" which tend to distance ourselves from others. Therefore, if you really are serious about receiving honest reaction to, let's say, your plans to launch an entrepreneurial venture, you need to legitimize people giving you straight feedback. We have a friend who cannot receive any constructive criticism. He becomes incredibly defensive, fully displaying his stubborn streak by shutting down his listening skills whenever he is criticized. Interestingly enough, he still asks us for our opinion on things. Why he continues to do so is an interesting study in his high need for recognition. Rather than continually get sucked into a raging emotional battle of wills, we have learned to warmly and very positively affirm his best efforts and his hard work. We have abandoned almost all attempts of constructive criticism, except in those cases where we have stepped in and prevented obvious disasters. Like parents who make perfect their young children's drawings and support them, so have we supported our friend even when his best efforts fall way short of the mark, though it is moving in the right direction. If you are not getting any constructive criticism, you might try saying:

Please be straight with me because I'm really interested in shifting how I operate and I do want to grow both personally and professionally.

When people give you some feedback, consider it to be a rare and precious gift. If you deem the criticism to be unfair or totally accurate, look long and hard at the data provided *and* positively reinforce the other person nonetheless.

Thank you for feedback. I sincerely appreciate it. I must say, I never looked at it quite that way before. What do you see that I don't?

If you are truly appreciative, then you have significantly increased the probability of ongoing feedback and reinforcement. *Guard against the tendency to discount or disregard the other person's opinion when it disagrees with your own. Becoming defensive and upset is an indication that you have lost some control of your emotions, in that you let someone's perception of you rattle you. Usually when a person becomes defensive, there is some element of truth in the information.* We know that asking someone for feedback poses a bit of a risk; however, you might garner some data that will significantly help you operate more effectively. Keep in mind this truism: a person's perception is her or his reality. If one person sees you in a given light, then there is a strong probability that others do as well.

Step 5. Identify and Focus on Your Outcome

In his enormously successful book, *Think & Grow Rich,* Napoleon Hill coined the following operative phrase which captures the essence of goal setting and the power which comes from concentrated and sustained focus:

> # Whatever the mind of man can conceive and believe, it can achieve!

Determine what you **want** and **need** in your life and in your career in specific terms, not just in generalities. Goals such as wanting a better job, more money, less hassles, better relationships, or reduced stress are too general. Besides, you may **want** more money but what you really **need** is better control over your finances. You may **need** transportation, but what you **want** is a 1965 Corvette Stingray. (Now, that's transportation!) Specific goals enable you to focus on the outcome you desire with greater clarity and determination. A metaphor that comes to mind is taking a picture with a high-quality 35mm camera. In the hands of a fumbling amateur, you might be able to distinguish that the out-of-focus picture is indeed a house, not a dog, but not much beyond that. Conversely, if you were to put the same camera in the hands of Dan Robertson, Dave's son, who is a highly skilled professional photographer and president of Framework Video and Sound, he could create an incredibly crisp and powerful photograph by precise balancing, lighting, and focusing. Likewise, once finely focused, your goals have the power to bring clarity to your purpose, mobilize you into action, and help you achieve your desired outcome. We had another client who was having great difficulty in networking. Although he was a well-known and well-liked person, he did not generate the kinds of leads we thought he should. We coached, we counseled, we poked, we prodded. Nothing seemed to work. Only after tape recording his side of the conversation did we realize that he had zero focus. Surprisingly, all the focus work we had done earlier was lost when he started talking about all the different things he wanted to do in his life and his career. Once we refocused him, John was able to speak clearly and convincingly of his career goals. Correspondingly, his networking improved 1000 percent.

Use the following list to take a personal inventory of how you focus on your outcomes:

1. What is your goal in networking?
2. How do you plan to achieve this goal?
3. What are you willing to do, and commit to, to accomplish this outcome?
4. Who else will be involved in your efforts?
5. What do these people get in return from helping you network?
6. What can you do to enhance this reward and recognition?
7. How will you personally benefit by attaining this goal?
8. What will happen if you do not attain this goal?
9. What is your time frame, by when you will have achieved this goal?
10. How will you know when you have obtained your desired outcome?

EFFECTIVELY CONDUCT AN INDUSTRYWIDE OR A GEOGRAPHY-SPECIFIC SEARCH

_____ SECRET 8

Two Geography-Specific Search Success Stories _____

A modified form of networking is to geographically target a part of the country and leverage whatever contacts you might happen to have in that area. Obviously, it's more difficult if you don't know anyone locally, but you can, nonetheless, make significant inroads if you are committed to doing so. Assertiveness, ingenuity, and persistence seem to be the three main ingredients especially needed for area networking. A couple of examples spring to mind.

A senior management client of ours, we'll call Pam Jacobs, wanted to relocate back to New York City. Her strategy was to identify 36 recruiters in the greater New York City area, many with Chicago offices. She networked through her local personal contacts into these Chicago affiliates, who in turn gave her the opportunity to leverage into the New York firms. Her story is as follows: She did some networking locally and opened up some doors but not enough to justify flying out at her own expense. However, she went anyway. Her first full day in New York she sat in her hotel and chased people down from 7:00 a.m. to 7:00 p.m. and set up appointments for the balance of the week. For three days she interviewed at a break-neck pace from early morning to late afternoon. At the end of her fourth day in New York, she had conducted 13 interviews and generated requests for 4 second-round interviews. In the two months that followed, she was extended three offers, one of which she accepted. It was a pretty remarkable performance against any performance standard. Pam acknowledged that the key to doors opening up was twofold: First, she indicated that she was in the area on a *series* of interview trips and her search was extremely active. Nothing creates excitement around your search efforts like being in demand—which you can create the illusion of quite nicely. The second dimension is leveraging the search firm contacts from a "sister" office in another city to open up network discussions or interviews in your target city.

Another client of ours, Pat Maxwell, always liked Phoenix, Arizona. In fact, he loved everything about it. The people, the weather, the culture, the business climate, and most important, no snow. Besides, he said he was tired of being pale 10 months out of the year and wanted a place in the sun to work on his tan. Pat, likewise, devoured Phoenix. He contacted the Chamber of Commerce, local associations, trade groups, search firms, asked everyone he knew if they knew anyone in Phoenix. He networked into companies in his industry, he networked outside his industry. He contacted everyone!! His enthusiasm for all things Arizona and Phoenix was contagious. The word got around town to area employers—if Pat Maxwell hasn't seen you, hold on, he will—and you'll enjoy the visit!

Pat became a master at networking in a "strange" city. He excelled in opening up doors that would normally be closed. While Pat worked hard in his *blitzkrieg* of Phoenix, he networked strategically, starting first with industry contacts, then personal acquaintances, then professional association members, then long-time, well-connected area residents. At his peak, Pat interviewed 14 companies in five days and developed relationships with most of the key players in Phoenix. Pat was eventually hired as vice president of sales and marketing by his top choice company in short order.

Note that Figure 8-1 graphically illustrates how you can generate networking leads, regardless if it is an industrywide or geography-specific focus. You'll note that the geography-specific search and the industrywide search look very similar, as the networking approaches parallel each other closely. Figure 8-2 explores the activity Pat Maxwell might have engaged in during his Phoenix search. Figure 8-3 outlines steps necessary to a geographic search.

Differences between Geography-Specific and Industrywide Searches _____

The main distinction between a geographic search and a national search is more one of focus and the parameters used to identify your target companies. Let us explain:

- With a geographic search, your goal is to identify firms which fall both within your SIC Code experience base and outside your industry experience. In effect, you are looking for opportunities geographically, regardless of industry. Now granted, you will delete some companies because

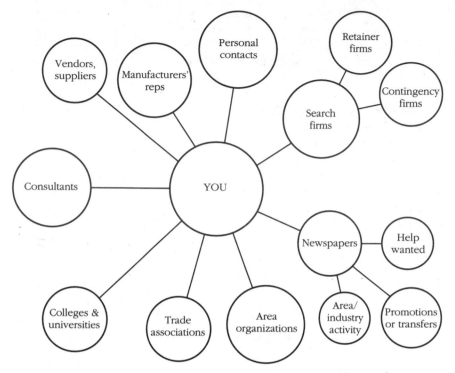

Figure 8-1. Generating networking leads.

of the industries they are in or the products they create or the customers they serve or your particular work environment preferences, needs, and biases. Common sense would dictate that if you are antismoking, you wouldn't include a tobacco company or if you are an animal rights activist, you wouldn't gravitate to a tanning or furrier company. If your entire work history has been in pristine sterile labs or consulting offices, you might feel out of place in a foundry or some other "smoke stack" industry environment.

- With a geographic search, you are open to the possibility not only of working outside of your industry but of networking into organizations much smaller as well as much larger. The organizational "size" relates not only to the number of employees but also to sales size, the number of facilities, and the extent to which a firm conducts business domestically or internationally.

- With national or industry searches, you will be focusing more on some specific parameters, such as "all international chemical manufacturers with sales in excess of $500 million, regardless of location, worldwide."

In addition, the following are some of the myriad number of parameters that job searchers establish for themselves:

Figure 8-2. Geography-specific searches: Phoenix, Arizona.

    Products manufactured

    Technologies employed

    Customers or industries served

    Sales size or employee size

    International markets served

    World class profile and reputation

- Whatever your search parameters, you might wish to justify your list to a trusted friend as a means of conducting a "reality check." Legitimize your friend asking you the following tough questions to help you evaluate

Steps in a Geographic Search

1. Identify the Standard Industrial Classification (SIC) Codes relevant to your current or former industries. Even though you are conducting a geography-specific search, contacting these companies represents the path of least resistance, in that you know the industry, you speak the lingo, and presumably you know the nuances of how to quickly and effectively contribute. In times of a buyers' market you can more easily demonstrate that you can "walk the talk."

2. Identify all organizations in your targeted SIC Codes in your geographic area. It's our recommendation that you not exclude too many firms by setting too tight parameters initially; rather, be more inclusive. You can always tighten the parameters of your search later to reduce the number of targeted firms, if you have too many. Part of your strategy will be to select your top 35 to 50 firms and **really** go after them, aggressively pursuing them with multiple value-added contacts.

3. If you know specific individuals in those targeted firms, great! You are clearly ahead of the game. However, let's operate on the assumption that you do not know anyone there. Ask yourself the following questions (which parallel the inquiry process that our networking friend, George, went through in Secret 6).

   - Who do I know in these companies?
   - Who might know someone in these companies?
   - What vendors, suppliers, or consultants do I know who might have a contact in these companies?
   - Who do I know in a professional association who might know someone in these companies?
   - Who is the executive director of the trade associations that serve these industries represented and might he or she know someone in my target companies?
   - What high-profile community leaders or well-connected professionals might there be and who might know someone at my target companies?

4. Identify all retainer executive search firms and employment agencies in your geographic target area. If your geographic target is Phoenix, then your objective is to meet with every single retainer and contingency firm to become known. It's a common practice for search firm colleagues to share leads about potential candidates or possible firms a person like Pat Maxwell might wish to contact. In the case of Pam Jacobs's networking in New York City, there would be too many retainer and contingency firms for her to reasonably contact, so she had to narrow the focus of her search

   (Continued)

firm contacts. Another wrinkle to contacting search firms is to identify those search firms and employment agencies that specialize in your industry or function. Your goal is, then, to contact these "specialized" firms (regardless of their location) and indicate your commitment to relocate to your targeted geographic region. Why would you contact search firms out of state for area opportunities? If you recall, many of these out-of-state firms will know of opportunities or have contacts locally. So, do not bypass this source of leads.

5. Develop your networking script, like we talked about previously, practicing it until you can deliver it without sounding stilted, stiff, nervous, or unsure of yourself. Keep in mind, you have a tremendous amount to offer an organization, you need to believe in yourself first before someone else will.

6. Lastly, prioritize these contacts and points of leverage, pick up the phone, and make the calls. Make your notes and then make the next call. You will soon discover that many of the names provided to you will cause you to shift your previously established networking priorities, as doors increasingly open up.

Figure 8-3.

your thinking and the extent to which your focus might be too limiting (you want to walk to work) or too broad (you'll work for any company regardless of size, industry, location, or the salary paid):

_____ 1. What is the employment market like within these parameters?

_____ 2. To what extent are these parameters too restrictive and what impact does this have on your ability to conduct an effective search?

_____ 3. To what extent are these parameters too broad, and what impact does this have on your ability to conduct an effective search?

_____ 4. How were these parameters established? To what extent were you influenced by family members' considerations?

_____ 5. To what extent will these parameters help or hinder your professional career moves, either now or in the future?

_____ 6. Do these parameters make sense and do they reflect sound judgement on your part? How will this impact your image in the marketplace and position you for additional opportunities as they become available?

WRITE POWERFUL NETWORKING LETTERS

————————————————————— **SECRET 9**

Each time you talk to someone on the phone or meet with them in person, **legitimize sending to them or giving to them your résumé.** The only exception to putting your résumé in their hands is that they have beat you off with a stick. Short of that level of rejection, we contend that you haven't really asked yet. Occasionally, we hear of situations where people got caught up in the conversation and simply forgot to get the commitment or forgot to pass their résumé over to the person sitting across from them. Forgot!!!!!! If you do happen to forget, just assume that you've got the OK to mail it along and do so with your thank-you note for the help and support. You'll note that we are recommending personalizing your "core" letter while keeping it fairly results-oriented so as to communicate your accomplishments, capabilities, and career focus. Or if you have a solid relationship with your networking contact, a brief hand-written note will suffice. The extent to which you are informal in your letters will depend, obviously, on how comfortable you feel. If you have any doubt, it is better to err on the side of being more formal.

Elements of Effective Networking Letters ————————

The following lists recommendations or guidelines for writing effective letters:

1. Make your letter brief, crisp, succinct, and punchy, and reference your conversation or visit.
2. Your comments are personalized and directed to specific instances.
3. Provide both an overview of your career focus as well as contain specific information about your credentials, responsibilities, accomplishments, and potential benefits to the organization who hires you.
4. Reference the specific assistance that your contact provided and additional action you'd like this person to take.

5. State the action you plan to take with the contacts provided and that you will be keeping your contact periodically posted on the progress of your search.

6. Be professional yet warm and inviting.

7. Mention your commitment to follow up with a telephone call.

The following outlines the key points to be made in a cover letter to a contact with whom you have already had a conversation:

1. Introduction and thanks for the support

2. Career focus and plans

3. Qualifications and accomplishments

4. Requesting additional assistance, as appropriate

Network contact letters look something like this:

Dear (First Name) _____:

It was great to talk with you recently and get caught up. Thank you for your care and concern, support and assistance. I sincerely appreciate the names of your search firm contacts and your personal leads. I am still in the early days of my search, but there seems to be a lot happening, and I am enthused about the opportunities out there. To recap, I am positioning myself as an experienced _____ skilled in _____. My strengths lie in _____. My credentials should be of interest and benefit to _____ organizations with a profile of _____.

My experiences and accomplishments include:

- (List key attention getting points that relate you closely to the job being sought. Items from résumé may apply if reworded.)
-
-

(Name), as promised my résumé is enclosed. After reviewing it, if additional names of search firms, target organizations, or personal leads come to mind, please call. I would certainly appreciate hearing about those, as well as any comments you might have about my résumé. Thanks again, and, as promised, I'll keep you periodically posted on the progress of my search.

Best regards,

J. Michael Commons

Enclosure: Résumé

The following is a sample **thank-you letter** to a personal contact at the **managerial level:**

Dear (Name):

It was great to touch base with you recently and get caught up. Thank you for your care and concern, support and assistance. I sincerely appreciate the names of your search firm contacts and personal leads. I am still in the early days of my search, but there seems to be a lot happening, and I am enthused about the opportunities out there.

To recap, I am an experienced sales and marketing manager skilled in new product introduction, field sales, account penetration, and dealer service. My strengths lie in developing distinctive promotional campaigns and training approaches which quickly produce results, improving sales, and profits. My credentials should be of interest and benefit to consumer product organizations with a profile of high brand awareness and superior customer service.

Highlights of my accomplishments include:

- Developing and managing a 500-dealer/distributor network, selling diverse product lines
- Reorganizing two major divisions and streamlining territories, nationally, which enabled greater account penetration and increased sales
- Creating and managing impactful promotional campaigns, dealer meetings, and sales training programs for the sales force

(Name), as promised, my résumé is enclosed. After reviewing it, if additional names of search firms, target organizations, or personal leads come to mind, please call. I would certainly appreciate hearing about those, as well as comments about my résumé. Thanks again, and, as promised, I'll keep you periodically posted on the progress of my search.

Best regards,

J. Michael Commons

Enclosure: Résumé

The next sample is a **thank-you letter** to a personal contact at the **administrative level:**

Dear (Name):

It was great to talk with you recently. I really appreciate your support, the leads into employment agencies and organizations, and your personal contacts. I am still in the early days of my search, but there seems to be a lot happening, and I am enthused about the opportunities out there.

To recap our discussion, I am an experienced administrative support professional with a strong background in facilities management, customer service, and meeting planning. My strengths lie in my creative problem-solving skills and my ability to exercise sound business judgment, evaluate priorities, and direct special projects.

Highlights of my background include:

- Protecting a $200,000 project for a major client by locating misdirected product and expediting its delivery to meet a critical installation
- Coordinating five major renovations of a 5000-sq. ft. showroom involving a total capital budget of $900,000
- Directing administrative and project support for regional manager, area sales operation manager, and sales representative of a leading furniture manufacturer

(Name), as promised, enclosed is my résumé for your review. Hopefully, it will trigger some additional names of employment agencies, target organizations, and personal leads. If you have any comments about my résumé, I would appreciate hearing those, as well. Thanks again for your help, care, and support. I look forward to hearing from you soon.

Warm personal regards,

Jennifer M. Heinz

Enclosure: Résumé

Interim Networking Letters

Although we have repeatedly maintained that it is important for you to initiate and sustain your networking contacts through phone calls or face-to-face visits, it may be appropriate for you to send out a brief "status report" versus a call. We strongly caution you to use this approach only in the most limited of circumstances—such as your contacts are out of the country or have a "back-breaking" travel schedule and the only reasonable way to reach them is through a brief note or letter. Creating and sending an interim status letter may also be appropriate when you have tried, unsuccessfully, to reach your contact and you have left three or four telephone messages. If you recall, we mentioned that you should not make more than four calls as you run the risk of depreciating your power base and position. You lose face, and perceived power, if you make call after call.

However, **do not** write letters when you can possibly be in personal contact. A quick 3-minute phone call from you informing your contacts of your status in an enthusiastic, upbeat tone will both boost your spirits and possibly trigger additional thoughts from your contacts. Letters are a nice touch if you just talked with your contacts, but should not be a substitute for them. If you are currently using letters as a means of a second contact (or you might have a tendency to use them), ask yourself:

1. To what extent am I using letter writing as a means of escaping making my calls or visits?
2. What am I avoiding if I do **not** make my networking calls, rather I send a letter? What pain do I avoid if I write versus call or visit?
3. Will I be able to generate more meaningful action in my campaign if I **write** versus **call** my contacts? Why or why not?
4. Have I exhausted the conventional ways to reach my contacts, or might there be some additional creative avenues I haven't yet attempted? What might be some of those ways of reaching my contacts? To what extent have I involved my contact's secretary to help get a call back?

Networking Letters as a "Fall-Back" Strategy

Use network letters only as a "fallback" strategy and not as a prime means of communicating with your contacts. "Wait a minute, Dave and Clyde! You are being way too restrictive, and you are assuming I will avoid making calls or visits in favor of writing letters. Don't you trust me to use a little judgment here?"

Of course, we do. Trust is not the issue. Rather, it is human tendency. It has certainly been our experience that most job seekers want to be in front of as many people as they can, in a high-quality manner, in the shortest time frame as possible. Hence, most people want to launch a large number of mailings to many, many search firms, target organizations, and even personal contacts. If you are somewhat uncomfortable picking up the phone and initiating networking calls, you will probably have a tendency to mail out something like these interim status letters rather than take the time to learn how to effectively make networking calls powerfully and confidently. Hey, we're not saying that you are "wrong" to want to create a mailing, we are merely saying that it's natural to avoid discomfort if you aren't as skilled in networking as you'd like *and* you haven't been able to easily generate additional leads.

Now, with all these cautions and provisos out of the way, let's turn to a sample **interim status letter** to a contact at the managerial level that will illustrate our point:

Dear (Name):

Thank you for all your help and support. It's meant a lot to me and has been invaluable in helping me sustain my focus and personal enthusiasm. Because of our very hectic travel schedules, respectively, I wanted to keep you in the loop versus leaving you "yet one more voice mail message." So, I apologize for the note, but it is the next best means of communicating directly.

The search has been active, and there are a number of things in the pipeline, but nothing has materialized yet into the kind of offer I'm serious about. (Name), it seems that I have become an informational resource and a "conduit" for search firms as they are looking for qualified people to fill opportunities that are inappropriate for me.

The senior sales and marketing role with the start-up company, A.C.C.E, in Cleveland still holds some promise, however the venture capital arrangements need to be finalized. I should know by the end of next month. In addition, the opportunity to shift careers and dabble in the consulting arena continues to perk along, though I suspect that I might miss the rough and tumble of being inside of a company. I still have the four other consumer product company situations that I am currently pursuing, at various levels of progress, notwithstanding my ongoing conversations with the search firms.

As I shared with you the last time we spoke, these are the hottest situations, but as you know from your own search efforts a while ago, it's critical to keep things always coming in far beyond that which you think you'll ever need. To that end, I am still trying to locate a lead into the following companies. Please review in light of the contacts you know there, as well as others who may have contacts there.

Proctor & Gamble   Quaker Oats
Toys "Я" Us   PepsiCo
Shakey's Pizza   Boston Chicken

Thanks again for all your help. Please call me at your earliest convenience so we can get caught up in person. Might we be able to take a quick spin through your Rolodex file at that time? All the best.

Best regards,

J. Michael Commons

New Position Accepted! _____

Once you have accepted a new position, it is most important to get back to your personal contacts as quickly as you logistically can and inform them of your good fortune and express appreciation for their support and help. It is recommended that you get back to your key primary and secondary contacts first by phone, then by letter enclosing your business card and perhaps even an annual report to some select people. As some people will have been very helpful—much more than others—you may wish to create two styles of letters: your "personal" letter should be warm and highly appreciative geared for those who helped you. Your second letter would be considered to be "professional" in that its function is to merely inform search firms, companies, or those personal contacts who helped very little yet you want to inform them, nonetheless. Although not totally businesslike, it is moderately appreciative. Examples of both styles follow. The first sample letter is a "personal" letter that goes to a contact at the managerial level:

Dear (Name):

I wanted to get back to you and say, "Thank you!" for all your help, care, and support over these last few months. As you know, I conducted a selective campaign of existing job opportunities, during which time I explored not only the private sector but consulting and equity situations, as well. I felt this was a critical time in my career, especially in terms of future growth and job satisfaction.

With these priorities in mind, I have recently accepted an exciting new position with Acme Corporation, a rapidly growing $150 million consumer products company, as its National Sales Director. I will be personally responsible for national account sales, as well as providing the strategic direction for an extensive field sales organization, product development and management, and merchandising. In addition, I have responsibility for the ongoing relationship with licensees throughout North America.

As of January 15, my new contact information is:

> J. Michael Commons
> National Sales Director
> Acme Corporation
> 1216 Any Street
> Plainview, PA 55500
> (713) 555-1212

I genuinely have appreciated your friendship and help during this time. It made a difference knowing you were there. If there is anything I can do for you, please do not hesitate to call. Thanks again.

Personal regards,

J. Michael Commons

This sample letter goes to a "professional" contact at the managerial level:

Dear (Name):

This is to inform you that I successfully concluded my career search recently, and I wanted to get back to you and let you know so you might update your records. If you recall, I conducted a selective campaign of existing job opportunities, during which time I explored not only the private sector but consulting and equity situations, as well. I felt this was a critical time in my career, especially in terms of future growth and job satisfaction.

With these priorities in mind, I have recently accepted an exciting new position with Acme Corporation, a rapidly growing $150 million consumer products company, as its National Sales Director. I will be personally responsible for national account sales, as well as providing the strategic direction for an extensive field sales organization, product development and management, and merchandising. In addition, I have responsibility for the ongoing relationship with licensees throughout North America.

As of January 15, my new contact information is:

> J. Michael Commons
> National Sales Director
> Acme Corporation
> 1216 Any Street
> Plainview, PA 55500
> (713) 555-1212

If there is anyway I might be of service, please do not hesitate to call. Thanks again.

Sincerely,

J. Michael Commons

Key Questions Asked about Announcing Your New Job

We are often asked a number of questions following a person's acceptance of an offer.

The following is representative of these questions and our response.

1. Who should receive the announcement of my acceptance?

Send an announcement letter to everyone who may feel they have played a part in you getting connected or those with whom you want to stay connected. Obviously, this requires a judgment call, as you do not want to send out another "mass" mailing. Rather, mail your "personal" letter to those that clearly helped and send your "professional" letter to those who may be in a position of influence and visibility and should know of your changed status.

2. Should I mail my acceptance letter to every search firm that previously received my résumé?

We don't think so; however, it depends. At a minimum, contact those search firms who considered you for engagements they had. If you only sent your résumé to 20 highly selected firms, then go ahead and contact all of them. However, there are over 3000 active retainer and contingency search firms in the United States, alone. Hopefully, you did not contact all of them, as it is inappropriate to contact every single one and besides, you could go broke informing everyone of your availability (and acceptance). The cost of this effort, notwithstanding, not everyone wants an update. Our rule of thumb: Recontact those who talked to you and all the major firms who either have a national presence or who represent a niche in your industry or function or management level.

3. How many people should get my acceptance letters?

Again, it depends. If part of your careering strategy is to launch a management consulting firm that might potentially solicit business from the people on your high-priority acceptance letter list, then you might wish to consider a broader mailing than if you accepted a position as controller in a mid-sized manufacturing company. We use a rather loose guideline that says "80 to 150 people should be contacted" about your new job. Since the bulk of your careering efforts will have been spent in networking, you will probably find that your acceptance letter mailings will fall roughly into the following categories: 70 percent to primary and secondary personal contacts, 20 percent to search firms or employment agencies, depending on your compensation and organizational level, and about 10 percent to the decision makers in those companies you interviewed (where you still want to be considered for something if things change).

4. How soon after I accept the offer should I inform my personal contacts and/or search firms?

With regard to this timing, there are a number of important factors to consider. Issues that impact when and how you inform others include:

- **To what extent is this a high risk role?**   If it is, indeed, high, you might wish to wait 30 days before launching a broad mailing until you get settled in place and determine "where the mines are buried"! It might be better to make a few select calls and inform these close friends that you have knowingly accepted a challenging, high-risk career opportunity that may have a short life span. To that end, you commit to keeping them informed *and* you plan to keep looking.

- **To what extent will your pending move be covered in the media soon after your acceptance?** The greater the press coverage, the less you should wait before informing your contacts of your new home. Granted, you might not be able to get back to every single person you'd like to within the first week of the *Wall Street Journal*'s announcement. However, people will appreciate you trying to do so, nonetheless.

- **If there are no complications with your accepting your new role, then we recommend the following.** Inform your key personal contacts within a week of accepting a position. These are the people who have really extended themselves for you, and courtesy dictates that you inform all your close friends or key contacts as soon as is practically possible. If you wait four weeks to call these people, you have clearly communicated that they are not very important.

5. How much should I "sell" my new organization?

Unless there are some major complications and risks inherent in your new role (or organization) and you want to maintain a low profile, then sell away! This new opportunity hopefully represents a good career move for you. As such, be enthusiastic, as your energy will be exciting and contagious. Be proud of your new situation and be wary of consciously apologizing if the search was elongated or if something wasn't quite perfect, like the compensation, title, location, etc.

TURN AROUND AND BEAT REJECTION

SECRET 10

Turnaround Strategies: How to Get Unstuck and Get on Top of Rejection

You will get rejected for a lot of reasons—some valid, many for no rhyme nor reason. The challenge is to sort out the valid rejects from the invalid ones and turn them into your advantage. To a good salesperson, a no is almost the same as a yes; it just requires a different strategy to win. In this process of job changing, you may get stuck. You may feel as if you are off track or are not moving forward like you should. Don't worry, that is a normal part of your network campaign. All is not lost; there are remedies to handle rejection and to get going again. Consider these ideas as part of your "turnaround strategies."

Some of your **personal contacts** may not support you as much as you would like because they may not honestly have any contacts or leads to pass on. Even though they may genuinely want to help, they get busy and do not follow through with information for you. The following are some remedies for this situation:

- Always be sure you know precisely what you want your personal contacts to do **before** you approach them.

- Give your contacts a typed list of your top 20 to 40 target organizations and ask whether they know anyone employed there or if they know of someone **else** who would know an employee.

- Prepare and practice your responses to some basic questions to demonstrate that you are composed and confident. Even with personal friends be prepared to answer such things as, "Why are you leaving? What are you looking for? What are your short- and long-range objectives? What are three of the most significant things you have accomplished in your career?"

- Refer to "Personal Networking" in Step Six of *In Search of the Perfect Job,* to refresh your memory. Remember to:

  1. Inform people of your status.

2. Ask for help and information concerning:
   - Leads or opportunities
   - Executive search firm contact
   - Target organizations

3. Gain commitment to send your résumé *and* follow-up periodically to see if your contact has any additional leads or information for you.

How Do You Know When You're Stuck: Recognizing the Signs

When you are stuck, your well-being is interrupted, and you experience discord in all parts of your life. When you are deeply stuck, do not expect to be fully aware of it. Although you may try to deny it consciously, your subconscious mind knows you are stuck big time and your body may start to manifest stress quickly.

You may divert your responsibility from how your career and life looks by blaming others or by making excuses for everything that has happened to you. It was not **your** fault that your network contacts haven't produced any decent leads or the first mailing did not hit the way you thought. It was not **your** fault that the interview did not produce an offer. And it **certainly** was not **your** fault that the ad you answered did not come through with anything.

At the same time, you may experience yourself finding fault with everything that others are doing (or not doing) on your behalf. The typographical error in a letter becomes extremely important. Your friend was supposed to get back to you with the key name from a major target company, and she has not. The executive recruiter has not called back yet. Things do not seem to be working.

These **are** important and should be corrected, but if you become obsessed with them, then it is a sign that you may be stuck. Your stress will consume a tremendous amount of energy that could more profitably be channeled into being optimistic, enthusiastic, and committed to a defined action plan. Let's look at how stress reveals itself.

Common Physical Sensations When under Stress

Drained	Insomnia
Lifeless	Fatigued
Empty	Cold extremities
Out-of-body	Shaken

Drifting
Falling
Tight
Muscles clenched
Teeth or jaw ache
Headache
Joints or muscles ache
Diminished
Uneasy
Nauseated
Weak
Energyless
Roaring in head
Slow motion
Fast motion
Clumsy
Under- overeating
Over smoking
Over drinking
Over medication
Overly loud talking
Overly soft talking
Load on back

Tunnel vision
Jittery, fidgeting
Clammy skin
Slurred, interrupted speech
Inappropriate behavior
Low tolerance for noise
Reddened complexion
Pale complexion
Tight clothing
Suffocating
Frequent need to urinate
Spastic colon
Dilated pupils
Tingling scalp and skin
Light-headed
Difficulty swallowing
Lump in throat
Cannot breathe
Hyperventilating
Biting nails
Spots in vision
Not hearing words said
Crowded

Common Feelings or Emotions When under Stress

Unloved
Discarded
Worthless
Unclean
Impotent
Emotionless
Alone
Disjointed
Withdrawn
Depressed
Attacking others
Need to be neat
Afraid to trust people

Apathetic
Used
Unappreciated
Sexless
Lost
Scolded
Forgetful
Sudden attack of doubt
Giddy
Hair-trigger temper
Indecisive
Blaming others
Ignoring differences

Attacked, threatened

Denying being terminated

Low self-respect

"Replaying" events

Low self-worth

Name calling

Sadness

Powerless, incapable

Unable to disassociate with firm

Common Thoughts, Attitudes, and Beliefs
When under Stress

It's not my fault!

I need to defend my position.

Effective people do not get stressed!

I am not stressed!

Others are biased and prejudiced; not me!

Broken promises are the rule of the day.

There is only one way to learn—the hard way!

I will now manipulate others for my gain; that's the way.

Oh, no—not another problem! I can't cope!

If I ignore this problem, it will go away.

I have been taking on problems which aren't primarily mine.

I can't seem to say no.

Most situations are impossible!

Can't anyone do anything right anymore?

It is not fair! How come? Why me?

Stress Comes from Change
and Irrational Beliefs _____

Stress comes from the somewhat idealistic view that "life should be the way we want it to be." However, we also know that "wishing makes it so" only works in the world according to Walt Disney.

Whereas your eyes may be the window to your soul, your language (the words you use) is reflective of how you think, feel, believe, and behave. Upset will emerge when you find yourself living in the context of your expectations versus reality, the way life really is. Even the trials and tribulations of everyday life can set us reeling and cause upset. **See if you use any of the words under the following Expectations column. You might wish to circle those words and add any other words that you use.**

Expectations of Life

Must be	Should be
Ought to be	Needs to be
Has to be	Want it to be
Wish it were	Could be
Got to be	Will be

The greater the difference between your expectations and life's reality, the greater the potential for . . .

1. Anxiousness
2. Frustration
3. Disappointment
4. Anger
5. Sadness
6. Fear

Life's Reality: The Way It Really Is—Here and Now

Note: Carried to an extreme, the end result is **failure.** Reality has failed to live up to your expectation of it. The only thing constant about life is change. If you find yourself frustrated or upset, the reason is probably because something has occurred differently than you imagined.

Remedy: So, lighten up and examine both how realistic your expectations are and how you might effectively close the gap between where you are now and where you want to be.

The greater the difference between our expectations of how life should look and how it *really* is, the greater the potential for stress.

Commitment—the True Difference _____

Individuals involved in the search process come in all different sizes and shapes, temperament, and make-up. Why is it that some career searchers are really on fire for themselves and others seem to be limp?

The difference is commitment. **Committed people cannot be stopped.** Committed people exhibit a special kind of motivation that keeps them moving unerringly toward their goal, regardless of obstacles or issues of personal convenience. Certainly, your personality will play an important part in the level of outward display of enthusiasm, but it will not necessarily influence your commitment to your success.

The military has a simple phrase to express commitment to a task at hand which we would like you to make operational in your life:

Hunker down and move forward.

Are you really committed to your success? Do you:

1. Create challenging personal career goals and develop realistic and viable action plans to obtain them?

2. Keep in balance the things you would **like to do** against the things you **have to do?**

3. Maintain positive expectancy about your life and search efforts? Do you have the feeling you cannot fail? Do you create the same level of enthusiasm in others?

4. Distinguish between being patient and being stuck?

5. Take responsibility for those things you have control over and not feel guilty about life's circumstances over which you have little or no control?

6. Continue to work when it is easier to quit? Is your operating philosophy, "It's OK to be down, just never give up?"

7. Critically assess the status of your campaign and have the discipline to put it back on track?

8. Commit to being the best you can be?

Here are 13 things you can do to get unstuck:

1. Observe and then verbalize where you are on your emotional roller coaster of **awareness, denial, anger, depression, acceptance.** Be honest with yourself; this is for your benefit—no one else's. Make a copy of the five emotional stages, post it in a highly visible spot and refer to it often.

2. Allow yourself permission to be angry or depressed and still have the capability to conduct an aggressive campaign. In other words, it is okay to be in whatever emotional state you find yourself. Having emotions and getting stuck is a normal part of life.

3. Focus your attention on the emotional state that you are in and determine what is making you angry or depressed.

4. Make the distinction between yourself and your behavior. While you certainly are responsible for your behavior, **you** are not your behavior.

Just because . . .	Does not mean that . . .
Your campaign fails . . .	You are a failure
Your campaign succeeds . . .	You are a success

5. Ask yourself:
   - Where am I stuck?
   - How do I know when I am stuck?

- When do I get most stuck?
- What do I gain or lose from **me** when I am stuck?
- What do I gain or lose from **others** when I am stuck?

If you draw a blank, ask:

- What is it that I am afraid to admit—the one thing I will never reveal?

6. Recognize that you gain tremendous personal power when you control your circumstances rather than allowing your circumstances to control you. When you assume responsibility for your life, you generally will experience a sense of freedom—freedom to be yourself.

7. Concentrate on the successes you have had. While it is far easier to zero in on failures, continue to focus on campaign **successes** and **progress.** This continued push will encourage additional successes.

8. **Focus** on target areas (personal contacts, for example). Identify goals that are measurable and represent a challenge. Try to make 40 quality contacts per week.

9. When faced with a seemingly impossible challenge, shift the intensity of the language. This might look impossible, but it is just a large and complex project. What are the five best actions to take right now?"

10. Identify the smaller bits of work that could move the larger task forward and start to accomplish them.

11. Ask for support from others in being successful in your career search. The support could range from asking someone to be a willing listener during tough times to critically evaluating a business strategy you have developed. **Caution:** Most people do not know how to ask for or receive honest feedback from others. Generally, we see it as too embarrassing, too brutally honest, or as an imposition on the person's time. If you are fortunate enough to receive honest data upon asking for it, graciously profit from it.

12. Commit yourself to the task.

13. Hang on and keep doing what you know is right and needs to be done—even when it is uncomfortable, not showing immediate returns, or easier to quit. Anything worth doing requires effort.

Success comes before work only in the dictionary!!

The Next Steps

PART 3

61 PROVEN STRATEGIES FOR SUCCESSFUL NETWORKING

Your success in networking will be directly related to the level of your commitment and the extent to which you follow a road map or strategy. The following are 61 strategies which have proven successful for thousands of our clients. Follow these strategies with a high level of passion and energy for 30 days and you'll notice a significant difference in your careering results.

1. Develop a long list of potential networking contacts and sources. Do not worry whether your list is too short or too long or if you will contact every single person on your list. These names are written on paper, not carved in granite, so don't worry about having lower-priority names on your list. If you think of a name, write it down; you can always cross it off later if you want.

2. Be enthusiastic and visualize success. Picture yourself being successful in your contact with others, gaining information, and securing solid leads. Remember, enthusiasm and confidence is contagious and is the core to rapport building. W. Mitchell once said, "Boldness has power, genius, and magic in it. If you can dream it, begin it!"

3. Always warmly and positively reinforce your contacts regardless of the information they give you or the efforts expended. Smile and gesture with your contacts while on the phone. Your genuineness will be felt and responded to, even if you are not face to face with the other person. Enjoy yourself, lighten up, and be straight with your contacts.

4. Become knowledgeable regarding your empowering beliefs as distinct from your disempowering beliefs. Focus on success-producing thoughts and actions and commit to discontinuing those activities which get in the way of your being successful.

5. Remember, you have as much to give an organization as it has to give to you. In fact, you will probably earn more and save more for the company—much more—than your total compensation.

6. Do **not** use your networking meetings or calls as a thinly veiled attempt at job interviewing. Networking meetings are low-threat, no-obligation discussions which succeed best on trust, respect, and rapport.

7. Learn the nuances of networking and actively explore every aspect of networking, modeling the excellent networking behavior of others who are highly skilled in it. If you do not personally know of a superb networker, ask people to name a person who would fit the bill.

8. Reassure your contacts that you are not calling them for a job, rather some information on their industries, the competition, related fields, and the like. Communicate that you are in the data-gathering phase of your search and you are trying also to generate greater marketplace visibility.

9. Learn how to ask relevant, penetrating questions that demonstrate you have prepared for this meeting and that guide your networking contacts into certain industries or functions. By asking detailed questions, you are able to "telegraph" a specific course of action or direction you want to take.

10. Never mail your résumé to your networking contacts when you could possibly call or meet them in person first. People resent it when they receive "network notices" in the mail. If you are guilty of this, you run the risk of communicating that you didn't think enough of the person to contact her or him personally. Granted, your rationale and intention is to contact as many people as is possible, and mailing "network notices" seemed like a good idea at the time. Trust us, you wasted a stamp and damaged a potentially good source in your haste to contact everyone immediately.

11. Ask for an appropriate amount of time so that you may network fully and completely. Requesting 5 minutes (or even 20 minutes) is probably too short a time frame and 60 minutes is much too long, except if you have a close relationship.

12. Keep peeling back the layers. If you run into an objection, respectfully legitimize the objection, add more value, and ask for more data pressing for closure and more information on search firms, target organizations, or personal leads.

13. Maintain control of potential contacts, especially if your friends have graciously volunteered to initiate a number of contacts on your behalf, including mailing out your résumé for you. Ascertain if your contacts would phone first, rather than mailing out your résumé, as the personal touch would no doubt open the doors more effectively. If your contacts are insistent on mailing, either ask for a copy of the list of names so you may quickly follow up or volunteer to mail out the résumés for your friend.

14. Be courageous in networking. Learn to network with people who you feel are much higher than you in organizations, be they in your own

company or in other firms. If you approach people effectively, they will help you, regardless of their stature or title.

15. If people draw a blank, say, "I can well appreciate that you can't think of anyone right now. I probably caught you cold and you might be in the middle of a number of things. Let me call you back after I send you my résumé. I will follow-up in several days to see if you thought of any search firms, organizations, or personal contacts. Will that be alright?"

16. Don't oversell when you network. Confidently and matter-of-factly communicate your situation and desire to connect in "X" role, industry, or area and your sincere appreciation of their help in identifying others who are fairly well connected in the industry or who would be knowledgeable in the trade.

17. Your networking contacts are more willing to provide leads, information, and answers than you thought possible. It's a function of how you approach them. Think through the strategy of both how to approach a contact, as well as answer the question, **"What does this person *need* and *want?*"** now in order that he or she may feel safe and comfortable in providing assistance.

18. There is no one right way to network. What might work splendidly for us may not work for you, and vice-versa. If you feel confident in your ability to contact a person or organization in a certain way, don't hesitate. Make the call, initiate the contact, create the connection. In the majority of cases, when a contact's name "bubbles to the surface," if you hesitate you may lose the fluidness, spontaneity, and personal power of the moment.

19. Develop a "short list" of 15 to 30 good friends and professional colleagues who are now (or would be) your advocates willing to advance your cause. You might wish to tell your "short list" contacts that you consider them to be your partners in this process and that you respect their judgment and look forward to getting their guidance and input as you network. Think of "partner" as a person who has a strong vested interest in your success—likewise, you are interested in their success.

20. Keep your networking contacts posted on the progress of your search. Do this on a periodic basis, either through a brief note or, preferably a phone call. For your short list of high-priority contacts, you will want to be in regular contact (let's say every two weeks) even if it is just a two-minute update. People **not** on your short list are all others and should be notified less frequently (every six weeks or so) but still provided value (in the form of an idea, article, observation, or question) which demonstrates that you are truly interested in them.

21. After a particularly good networking lead from a given contact, you may wish to circle back and express your sincere thanks for the opportunity to network with this person. Tell your contact specifically how

this other person was so helpful and that it made a big difference and that you look forward to the opportunity to secure additional names like the one previously provided.

22. Develop and regularly contact a rich cross-section of contacts in the form of search firms or employment agencies, personal friends, professional colleagues, current and former peers, supervisors or subordinates, vendors, consultants, trade association contacts, university professors and students, community leaders, etc.

23. Utilize what we call the **"law of recency"** to your advantage. The "law of recency" implies that people remember people who have most recently been in front of them, either in person, by phone or by mail, or fax. For your core group of contacts or target organization, commit to a strategy that has you up in front of these people at least once every two weeks.

24. Utilize the **law of reciprocity** to your advantage. The law of reciprocity has as its premise a stimulus-response relationship in which one response creates another—"one hand washes the other." It is providing value to others, not in a manipulating way so as to get what you need, rather it is like priming the pump to stimulate a sense of mutualness. This "law" is present in your everyday vocabulary already: "yin/yang, up/down, right/left, in/out, black/white, yes/no, push/pull." Compliment someone and notice how your compliment created a felt response on their part to compliment you back. Look for ways you can help someone else first, and you will have more networking contacts than you can handle.

25. Mail or fax articles of interest to your network contacts on a periodic basis. Get in the habit of reading articles from a wide variety of sources, even outside of your field. Develop a file of articles that cover diverse topics from leadership, manufacturing or service management, emerging technologies, new products, competitor's issues, pending legislation that may impact your contacts, and interesting sociodemographic trends. Follow up your fax with a brief "thought you might be interested in this" phone call. It builds wonderful rapport.

26. If you are attempting to shift out of your industry, develop a list of penetrating questions to ask your well-connected contacts so you might get some keen insights on this field's major issues, trends, pros and cons, prominent professionals, and resources to study. Questions will stimulate their thinking and will invariably lead to them saying, "You know, the person who you should also talk to is. . . ." This technique is a low-threat way to expand your list of contacts *and* gain valuable insights.

27. When you are talking to people who are having some difficulty thinking of names of account executives in search firms or their personal contacts, try to keep them on the line a bit. Watch your tendency to be

embarrassed and your desire to rush off the phone. Share with them some of your positive career search results. Also, ask them if they know specific search firms, organizations, or individuals you are targeting. Why? You will often catch people "cold" or in the middle of something, and they find it difficult to concentrate on your request immediately, so a little progress report helps stimulate their creative juices. It is common to have the most creative ideas and most productive leads come in the latter part of the conversation.

28. Open to relocation? Be prepared to spend some of your own money stimulating interest in another part of the country by launching a mailing and then spending your own money on an out-of-town trip. Create some deliberate visibility and network "interviews" by sending a mailing to select search firms, organizations, and key professionals in your target cities. This strategy is generally successful if you contact and then confidently follow up on these 20 to 30 firms or consultants in each target city, indicating that **"you will be interviewing in their area during the week of _____ and would appreciate an opportunity to meet for purposes of introduction as you have some exciting ideas to stimulate sales growth and company profitability."** You might be pleasantly surprised at how well you can leverage out-of-town meetings using this approach.

29. Watch your entry point into an organization. If your networking contact is at a considerably lower level than you are comfortable with, you may wish to consider delaying your contact until you have a stronger introduction if you have any suspicion that you may not be well represented by this person. However, keep in mind that just because a person occupies a lessor role does not diminish his or her stature in a company.

30. Networking will not always be fun, easy, enjoyable, or quick. There will be times when the only thing that keeps you going is your commitment, your word that you were going to conscientiously pursue networking to the best of your ability, with the most up-beat, confident spirit.

31. After you complete one networking call, hang up the phone and quick make your notes. Pick up the phone, make another call, hang up, make your notes. Pick up the phone, make another call, hang up, and make your notes. If you get blown off by someone—no big deal, maintain the perspective that you just caught them cold. Ask if it is OK to recontact them as you have something exciting to provide them. Make your toughest calls when you are the freshest and most confident. Most people prefer to make and receive these calls early in the morning rather than late in the day after being run over a number times. Also, try alternating "easy" calls with your more difficult calls. Use the momentum from one positive call as leverage into the next, more difficult call.

32. If you are uncertain as to why you are not creating the impact you desire or getting the leads you know others have, you may be uncon-

sciously sabotaging your efforts. You may wish to record your conversation, then erase it later after you have taken notes on your presentation style and personal power. Some may feel tape recording is an invasion of privacy, but you will be erasing it immediately after learning what you did (and didn't do) well. If you do not erase these conversations, then this violates the spirit of our recommendation—that this taping is for learning purposes only.

33. Even though you may be actively looking for a job, get your name and your ideas published in the leading trade magazines and journals which are read by your colleagues. Quote one of your well-known contacts, repackage an idea, mention an interesting trend which impacts your industry, publish the results of a survey you conducted. The more often your name and ideas show up, the more legitimate and attractive you appear. When you get something published, either through the popular press or through self-published means, hand-write a personal note to your contacts and send them a copy of the article. They will appreciate you thinking of them and keeping them posted on your progress.

34. Do not invite marginal contacts to breakfast, luncheon, or dinner meetings. Save your money and large blocks of time, such as meal meetings, for those senior executive meetings. You can reach many more people through telephone contacts, as opposed to meal discussions.

35. You are responsible for your career and life, no one else. You, alone, are in charge of how you feel and the extent to which you are successful in networking, no one else. When your networking contacts indicate to you that they will be getting back to you or will be sending information to you or will contact others on your behalf, don't turn over complete control to them. Always maintain the ability to recontact your colleagues. You might consider the following language: "Thanks for your vote of confidence and assurance. I appreciate your willingness to contact these people for me. In addition to me waiting for you to call me back, I will make a note on my calendar to touch base with you in two weeks to see how you are faring on these calls. Would that be alright?"

36. Avoid prejudging when it would be convenient for you to call a person. Acknowledge that there will never be a convenient time for each person you contact. Let them tell you if the timing is inconvenient. There are two schools of thought on asking if it is convenient. If you ask them if it is convenient, you run the risk of them saying no as a means of simply blowing you off. We recommend that you briefly state your purpose and ask when it would be more convenient to meet with them or call them back when they might have more time.

37. Networking is good for your ego, but don't lose sight of the fact that networking is a means to an end and not the end. The purpose of net-

working is to ultimately get you interviews for opportunities which lead you to your perfect job. Don't spend all your time on unproductive networking merely meeting people, as if you have no sense of urgency. Clearly, there's a balance to be struck, and one of the best ways we know to maintain it is to continually ask the question, **"What's the best use of my time right now?"**

38. Make sure your contacts realize your time is as valuable or more valuable than theirs. People have greater respect for and are more willing to do business with those people whom they regard as busy and important. One way to create this powerful image is to have the mindset of a busy consultant interviewing a client. A good consultant is fairly assertive, proactive, probing, and challenging while providing value.

39. Don't beg for a networking meeting or appear too easy! No one wants to do business with a person who is needy, desperate, or not in demand. Ironically, the time when you need help the most is often the time when you are least likely to get it as your desperation will show through. When setting a meeting time don't let them see your open calendar or say, "Anytime next week is fine" or "Since I'm unemployed and looking for a job my schedule is wide open." If you say these things, you give the impression that you have nothing to do and are not in demand. Instead, indicate "I am free to meet Tuesday from 1:00 p.m. to 3:00 p.m. or Friday between 9:00 a.m. to 11:45 a.m. Which of those times would be good for you?"

40. When first meeting with your prospective network contacts, clearly state your agenda and then stick with it! Make sure that they understand that your intention is **not** to ask them for a job, rather to gain either leads (into search firms or target organizations) or information about a different industry, as you are interested in exploring the viability of an alternative career path.

41. When networking, don't talk too much. You should be speaking about 40 percent of the time or less. God gave us two ears and one mouth— we should all use them in that proportion. While we understand rapport is developed through sharing of ideas and backgrounds, when **you** talk you learn very little. The more you are able to get the other person to talk and to respond to your thoughtful questions, the greater the probability of gaining additional information and leads.

42. Don't continue to relentlessly pursue people with repeated phone calls just because you have them listed. Our rule of thumb is that after the third call, drop them a note, either in the mail or fax it to them, indicating your desire to talk with them and your previous attempts to reach them. Indicate in your note that you will be following up on this letter with a phone call to see if you could either meet or, minimally, talk on the phone. Do **not** make 5, 10, 15, or 20 calls. If you do, you appear desperate, and we guarantee that you will create the exact

opposite impression of what you intended. You have good skills and will make a great employee for the right organization soon. Don't continue to beat your head against this unyielding wall of resistance if some people don't value you. As one of our clients used to say, "Next!" Move on—you have better things to do with your time.

43. On bona fide out-of-town interview trips in which more than pocket change might be spent, you may wish to ask, **"How shall we handle the expenses for this trip? Will you have your travel agency arrange for this trip and bill you back directly or shall I consolidate my expenses and then get them back to you after our visit together?"** When in doubt, it's far better to have complete understanding on the trip reimbursement policy than to incur the expense unknowingly.

44. When networking with your peers, be alert to the fact that you may appear as a threat to them, as you may take the job they would dearly love to have. Reduce the degree of threat by clarifying your agenda and by supporting them in their role. You may also wish to indicate that if you meet someone they might like to meet or if you uncover something they might be interested in, you will most certainly pass it on.

45. Do not, in the spirit of group networking, share your hot, breaking leads until you have had the opportunity to fully explore them and assess whether you are interested in pursuing them further. If you prematurely share a situation that you are qualified for, you may inadvertently create unwanted competition. Use good judgment, sound logic, and caution about joining job clubs in which every single job lead is supposedly shared and discussed. Although well-intended, many networking groups turn into negative gripe sessions in which the latest networking travesty and job-hunting war story is told and retold until the attitude of the group is self-defeating and self-fulfilling—"there are no jobs out there!"

46. Reject offers to interview for (or accept) positions that offer no "next step" or that are significantly below your capabilities because of the "exposure" and "potentially beneficial contacts" you might receive. You can't pay your mortgage with potentials, and you will gain additional exposure as you continue to look for the appropriate position. Exceptions to accepting a significantly lesser job would be financial—you have to accept something, anything, to keep bread on the table. By the way, a sound next-step strategy would be that you consult for an employer for several months with the commitment that you'll be hired at the project's conclusion. Another strategy would be that you deliberately take a significant salary cut to learn a new industry or a technology with the understanding from the employer that you will receive an increase after the training. Your strategy might be that you will launch out on your own business after you learn the business and build up a sufficient customer base after this mentoring phase.

47. If a personal contact is hesitant about providing a particular lead that you know she or he has, you probably will be well served to acknowledge and clarify his or her fears. Granted, it takes some effort and there is usually some risk involved in raising the issue, but if done well your rapport can significantly be strengthened. Besides, what have you got to lose? Your contact is already reluctant to volunteer the contact, and, by ignoring the issue, you maintain a position of less power as you are found lacking in credibility. You might wish to use language like the following: **"You seem hesitant about sharing the name of your contact at this company. Let me assure you that I will not embarrass either one of us by asking your contact for a job nor will I strong arm your contact in any way. Are these your concerns?"**

48. Respond to all high-priority leads received from your network as promptly as possible, certainly within three days. If you are travelling, check in regularly for messages (with your answering machine, answering service, spouse, secretary, neighbor—whomever). If you are not able to respond on a timely basis, at least communicate that you are travelling and you will set up an appointment later to talk.

49. Develop several crisp "commercials" on yourself that are no more than 3 minutes and quite succinctly present topics, such as your life story, work history, reason for leaving, management and personality style, strengths and weaknesses, the ideal job. These commercials are filled with "sound bites" which are pithy statements that highlight how you operate and what you believe. **Caution:** Don't be too flowery, too philosophical, way out, or too abstract.

50. Don't bad-mouth your current or former companies, bosses, peers, subordinates, competitors, or industry, as it only hurts you. Tell the truth, but not the whole truth if asked about why you left your companies or are interested in leaving. It is safer to posture your departure with something general like, **"the opportunity to grow in advertising support will be limited because my recently promoted boss has declared that we would be drastically cutting back on marketing expenditures."** If you throw dirt, all you lose is ground.

51. Become intimately familiar with the business reference directories in your municipal and university libraries. Get to know the Library Checklist in our book *In Search of the Perfect Job*. Ask the reference librarian what other innovative information could be drawn out of the directories. Browse through the business section of a well-stocked library and examine what new and exciting theories and management models are being presented. Take notes and pull up information on companies you might be interviewing, as well as their competition, and the industry. When you are networking, you then have the opportunity to "name drop" as a means of standing out from your competition.

52. Prequalify your networking prospects by asking them if they would spend some time with you if you could demonstrate a viable and cost-effective method for solving their problem (in human resources, for example) or helping them take advantage of an opportunity.

53. Make it easy for your contacts to be successful in the relationship with you. Ask them to provide information, advice, or leads in those areas in which they already have some degree of knowledge and experience. Thank your contacts and positively reinforce their efforts or intentions, even if they didn't supply any real assistance. Ensure that each contact knows what you want them to do and the agreed-upon timetable.

54. Your language skills, your dress, your mannerisms, and personal presentation should all fit the image you are trying to portray and should match the environment and people with whom you are interacting. If you are in doubt of your style or language skills, videotape a speech you would like to give. Have someone whom you respect to be brutally honest and straightforward, critique the presentation. Identify your skill set deficiencies and seek out cost-effective solutions.

55. Dress the way your network contacts or prospective contacts might dress, within reason. Don't be overly formal or informal. If you don't know, it is better to be more formal than informal. Increasingly you will discover companies have "casual dress," which does not exempt you from coming to a networking meeting in a business suit or handsome sports jacket and tie or dress.

56. When networking, always be on time. Being late is the height of discourtesy, so if it looks as if you are going to be caught short get a message to your contact. When in doubt as to the meeting place's location, it may make sense to make a dry run to verify your route and the travel time required. Shoot to be at your location 10 minutes early; if you are not there early, you're late!

57. Develop your interpersonal skills to such an extent that you are able to quickly and effectively "read" the operating styles of your networking contacts so as to flex and adapt your approach to fit the persons in front of you. You may find that being able to shift from a facts-driven rationale to a more values-driven, emotional style will enable rapport to be more easily developed and leads more forthrightly expressed.

58. Enhance your credibility by volunteering other people for opportunities for which you feel they might be more qualified. By turning aside a potential situation, you are communicating that you are confident in your abilities and are more than willing to help people in need. Hopefully, your network contacts will pick up on this subtlety and reciprocate by providing leads into search firms, target organizations, or other personal contacts.

59. Acknowledge the difficulties and occasional problems associated with networking. Ask your networking sources "how, when, how often, and under what conditions" they prefer to be contacted. Your contacts will appreciate it, and you will be demonstrating that you know what it is like to sit on the other side of the desk, where they are.

60. Have an offer? Ask for advice. You may wish to ask some of your contacts for some counsel after you get a job offer and definitely after you **accept** a position. People like to know that their efforts have been helpful.

61. Keep your network alive and well by informing your networking contacts of your new position with a brief description of the job and your contact information. This letter should also be sent to relevant search firms and organizations. From this point forward, consider making at least one relevant networking contact (call or lunch) every month.

BUILD ORGANIZATIONAL ENDORSEMENT BY NETWORKING

*Nearly 100 percent of executives and senior managers
are terminated unnecessarily. It's not for the lack of
technical competency, rather it is the lack of
organizational endorsement.*

*If you are marginally competent, yet have widespread
organizational endorsement, you can literally retire
from your company. Conversely, you can be the world's
most technically competent person, but if you do not
have organizational endorsement, you will soon be
terminated.*

*The methodology for effective networking to find a job
is the same methodology you use to build widespread
organizational endorsement inside your company.*

Organizational endorsement? Isn't that just another phrase for "playing politics"? The term, **politics,** whether used in an organizational or governmental sense, seems to evoke an incredibly negative connotation. Indeed, the image that we have of a person who engages in corporate politics is a slippery, manipulative, two-faced, two-timing, back-stabbing, low-life who would lie, cheat, and sell out his or her relatives to get ahead. Why is that? It's probably because we have seen or been burned in the workplace by individuals whose behavior has been labelled "political" and we made up our minds that any behavior that looked like "schmoozing" with executives more senior than ourselves was bad and should be avoided. Yet, we also know intuitively that if our relationships were better with the decision makers above us we would be better able to do our jobs and contribute to the growth and profitability of our organization. On that basis alone, you would think that every one of us would be flocking to our boss's offices in an attempt to strengthen our relationships. Well, that may be perfectly justified and probably long overdue. However, lest you just wander down to your boss's office and saunter in unannounced to spend your "coffee break" with her or him in idle conversation, remember busy senior executives do not have time for idle, aimless conversation. They have way too much to do, and their schedules are crammed, with every minute of the day counted as precious. Rather, you need to have a specific, goal-oriented strategy and outcome clearly in mind before you meet during your prearranged appointment. Most senior managers prefer knowing your agenda ahead so they are not surprised and so they also carve out the time necessary to deal with the issues. By the way, you may need to justify the meeting in the first place when you are face to face with the executive or you may need to convince the executive's assistant of the importance of the meeting. Clearly, you need to be able to quickly present the essential points that you wish to cover as summary highlights and not get drawn into a full-blown discussion if you are not ready. Most individuals will be interested in having you justify spending the time on this matter and will also understand that you may not have all your data ready at this time. Do not try to handle important issues with senior executives "on the fly" in chance hallway encounters. These impromptu meetings undermine both your credibility and depreciate the importance of the topic you are championing.

Creating a Broader Focus _____

But before we get too deeply into the specific tactics of building endorsement, let's look at what we believe are the causes of "political discomfort." First and foremost, we are taught technical skills in school but not interpersonal skills nor how to build and sustain organizational endorsement. Figure 11-1 reflects the interconnectedness of technical knowledge, task skills, and interpersonal skills.

For the vast majority of us, our early training and schooling were fairly traditional; we earned liberal arts or technical degrees learning highly specialized subjects in our respective disciplines, such as finance and accounting, psychology, engineering, production management, research, marketing, and distribution—all technical knowledge—and then demonstrated proficiency in it—task skills—through some form of testing or internship. Although many of these topics may have touched on the concept of interpersonal skill building or gaining organizational endorsement, none of the thousands of executives we've dealt with in the past remembers anyone or any course equipping them to effectively maneuver through their organizations. The focus of our early training and times in which we have been mentored have largely been spent on enhancing our technical knowledge and task skills and not on how are you going to get people rallied around a particular point. To be effective in our roles inside companies, we

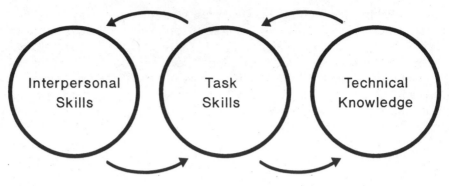

Figure 11-1. Skill set integration.

need to fully integrate effective interpersonal and organizational endorsement skills with our current strengths—our technical skills. Even individuals who have graduated from our outplacement program and successfully connected in new jobs seem to revert to their old habits of not building endorsement from others in their new jobs unless they really work at it. Tragically, the very people who understood that they got zapped because they blew up their work relationships get caught up once again in the push to make a contribution immediately. They seem to have forgotten that it is better to slow down ever so slightly to build solid relationships (e.g., endorsement) so they might have unqualified understanding and support for their efforts later. The unsuccessful executives, managers, supervisors, and individual contributors are the people who are fixated on the task skills and the technical knowledge. Successful people are those who effectively balance these three dimensions: technical knowledge, task skills, and interpersonal skills. Indeed, the truly effective executives and managers know that building solid relationships and gaining organizational endorsement is the very first step to truly contributing to a company, its employees, and its customers.

Recontextualize Company Politics

One of the first things you need to do, as we see it, is to recontextualize how you view this concept of politics. Rather than perceiving this as unproductive "ring kissing" that doesn't get the job done, we ask you to shift your thoughts and feelings on this matter. Even if all the people whom you know who "kiss up" are not trustworthy and are ineffective, you do not have to operate in the same manner. Take the best of intentions and possibilities from positive politics and learn from it. Think of this activity not as politics but as "partnering." Your goal, then, is to function as a partner with more senior executives, learning from them and helping to get their personal and departmental needs met. You can borrow the working definition of **partnership** we use with our clients: "We have a strong, vested interest in their success. To achieve this outcome, we will do everything in our power to help them be successful with the utmost integrity, diligence, and creativity." Within the context of integrity, we include being honest, ethical, open, straightforward, genuine, approachable, helpful, friendly, responsive, respectful, flexible, supportive, emotionally stable, and always looking for both what is **wanted** and **needed** in relationships and projects.

Just because someone else was "politicing" badly does not mean you have to compromise your integrity and core beliefs. Interestingly, even the dictionary recognizes the potential derogatory nature of politics in one of its definitions. "Politician: one who is more concerned to win favor or to retain power than maintaining his principles." However, a synonym to politician is **statesman,** whose definition is more laudatory: "suggests the eminent ability, foresight, and unselfish devotion to the interests of his country." You might think it a might presumptuous to consider yourself a "statesperson" given your age, education, training, rank, or role—so think of yourself as a "statesperson in training." What kind of nobility do you think Abraham Lincoln, Jack Kennedy, Winston Churchill, Franklin Roosevelt, Harry Truman, and other great men and women exhibited **before** they became well known? What kind of compassion did Mahatma Gandhi, Martin Luther King, Jr., or Mother Teresa exhibit **before** the causes they championed gained popularity (or notoriety)? Our challenge to you is to determine the kind of person you want to become, then operate as if you have already achieved that level of personal power, confidence, assertiveness, boldness, nobility, compassion, openness, genuineness, straightforwardness, approachability, or integrity. So, just because you haven't been operating in these arenas the way you'd like to, doesn't mean you can't. **The extent to which you are committed to something is the extent to which you will achieve it.** Learning how to operate effectively through the political mazes that confront every single one of us in business is important, yea, it is critical. For if you have something important to contribute or to communicate, then it is incumbent upon you to be interpersonally skilled enough to build the endorsement you need to be given the opportunity to do so. Without the solid interpersonal skills used in networking and in endorsement building, you might be the best contributor on the planet, but your talents will go unutilized. How tragic. What a waste.

Next Steps . . . Your Postsearch Strategy

Once the dust settles on your successful career search campaign, it may be very appropriate to step back and reexamine what happened and commit yourself to a course of action that will always keep your network healthy and your in-company organizational endorsement high.

One of the insights you might have gained during your search was the importance of networking in your own organization, as well as with search firms, target companies, and personal and professional acquaintances. Granted, your situation may be different now that you are connected (or even if you are still employed), but we recommend that you maintain your networking contacts on an ongoing basis:

1. Commit to taking a contact (search firm account executive or professional colleague or friend) to lunch at least once a month. This will help you promote yourself in a nonthreatening manner, and you will maintain your visibility appropriately.

2. Continue to be a networking source to others in need. Do you remember how gratifying it was to receive support from others when you were "casting about" for leads or even a friendly voice on the other end of the phone? Now it's your turn. We recommend that you make some time available for people who are trying to network with you. However, guard against overextending yourself by providing too much support, as you don't want to create the impression that you're carrying on your campaign or that you are not busy. We think it's great to help out, but clearly your job is to build endorsement and contribute to the growth and profitability of your new or current organization.

3. Two to three weeks after you accept the new position, send a mailing to 50 to 100 contacts, including companies, search firms, and personal contacts indicating your changed status. For correspondence samples, refer to the sample letters in Secret 9.

4. Add value to other job seekers when they call—more than merely providing names. Inquire about the status of their search and don't be afraid to ask penetrating questions. Be a friend to a stranger. **Caution:** Do not "bowl people over" with your keen careering insights, no matter how correct they may be. Earn the right to volunteer information by asking what role the caller wants you to play, then provide your observations and recommended action steps which have worked for you.

A Checklist: Growth Questions Designed to Strengthen Your Endorsement and Networking Abilities

As you strengthen your networking skills and build organizational endorsement in your current or new employer, you may find it helpful to review some questions designed to stimulate your thinking and personal growth. If you are interested in discovering how you could have achieved more at your current or previous employer, what you could have done differently, and perhaps why you didn't—great! The following questions are for your insight and personal growth. However, we understand you may be "burned out" on all these introspective exercises, and you may not be interested in going through this additional process of self-discovery at this time. That is fine, but we do recommend that you go through this process sometime soon, for all these are valid questions your networking contacts may ask you whether you are employed still or not. Answer the following questions candidly and completely.

1. What constitutes success in this job? In this company? Who is successful in the organization, both technically and politically?

2. What is the best way to approach these successful persons to learn from them? What do you have or can do for them which might interest them in spending time with you?

3. What is your personal operating and interpersonal style? What is the style of your greatest proponent or advocate? The style of your greatest opponent? What conclusions can you draw from any style differences that might be present?

4. What is the reason for your leaving your organization?

5. If asked, what would **others** say is the reason for your leaving?

6. Why are you leaving versus someone else?

7. What things did you do at your former company to make yourself indispensable?

8. What things could you have done **differently?** Why didn't you?

9. What signs were visible that indicated the company and/or you were in trouble?

10. What did you do to protect yourself inside the organization *and* hedge your bets outside in the marketplace? Did you feel you did all you could do? Why or why not?

11. What did you gain by protecting your position? What did you lose?

12. If you did not do anything "protective," what did you gain by not taking "protective" measures? What did you lose?

13. Are you as proactive in your job search as you could be? Why or why not? What barriers are present that prevented you from being as proactive?

14. If you were a "victim of organizational politics," what can you do to strengthen your networking skills and gain greater endorsement next time?

15. What are your five-year career and life goals? Ten-year goals?

16. What experiences, on the new job and off the new job, will be instrumental in achieving your goals?

17. What specific action will ready you to achieve your five- and ten-year goals?

18. How do you plan to keep your network alive and healthy and yourself appropriately active in the marketplace?

19. What are the top five responsibilities in your new or current job?

20. What are the top five challenges or demands in your new or current job?

21. Who are the greatest **proponents,** supporters, or advocates for you in this new or current position? Why?

22. Who are the greatest **opponents,** the people who will resist or challenge you the most? Why?

23. In what three ways can you contribute to your opponents? To your proponents?

24. In what three ways can these people and functions contribute to you?

25. What functions do you know least well? Who is in charge and when will you learn more about each one?

26. If you did not receive the kind of position, responsibility, or authority that you wanted on this move, what experiences are you missing? Who in the organization can help you gain that knowledge? What project or assignment do you need in order to gain the experience to qualify you for greater opportunities?

27. What is **needed** and **wanted** by your boss, your boss's peers, your coworkers, your subordinates (if appropriate), and other parts of the organization?

28. What are you willing to change in order to develop a strong, healthy relationship with the people you work with?

Starting a New Job (or Rebuilding the Current One): Your First Few Months

- Operate more as a "consultant," creatively solving problems and resolving conflicts or confusion.

- Learn how to **contribute value** to everyone with whom you come in contact. If you don't feel you are adding value, then do some research and figure out how you can help.

- Identify those individuals whom your function impacts and meet them. Get to know their needs, interests, and motivations better. Learn about their roles and responsibilities. It is critical to your own success that you know what seems to work best (as well as not so well) with your colleagues.

- Do not talk much about how things were managed at your former employer, and do not be too quick to volunteer solutions which, at first glance, look just like something you encountered previously. If you don't stop and ask questions, you run the risk of being embarrassed by your incomplete recommendation.

- If you are replacing a person, you may wish to ask the following questions to key people:
  - How did you view the other person?
  - What was done well?
  - What was not done well?
  - If you could have anything you want from this position, what would it be?

- Volunteer to either chair or contribute for a high-visibility task force to solve a difficult problem for your company. Ideally, this would be a multifunctional team which would also allow you to make a major presentation to senior management.

- Be proactive in identifying and executing a strategy that will be credited for generating significant revenue or contain significant costs.

- Learn to gain support and endorsement of others (superiors, peers, and subordinates) by informing and involving them in your thoughts, feelings, ideas, and intentions. Do not confuse your need to use people as sounding boards with consensus decision making, it is not. Your colleagues will be pleased that you asked for their input and support. Involvement fosters commitment.

Signs That Your Company May Be Going To Downsize

Here are some of the things employees have reported seeing just prior to downsizing decisions in their companies. One or two may not mean much, but several signs appearing together could mean that you want to avoid major personal expenditures, bid to safer jobs, update your résumé, contact your network, and begin considering your employment options.

- Bosses seem distracted and under a lot of pressure.
- There is a lot of talk among employees about job security issues.
- The company is always "reorganizing."
- Needed equipment is promised but never appears.

- Company rejects ideas that might cost some money but which will save more.
- Preventive maintenance programs are dropped.
- There are frequent changes of plant managers or other front office people.
- Salaried vacancies are not replaced—jobs are combined.
- Corporate or division managers visit a lot more than usual.
- Open door policies seem to go away.
- Bosses pick up job duties previously performed by their subordinates.
- Equipment is transferred out and not replaced by other equipment or with other products.
- "Difficult to please" customers are dropped.
- Large accounts are lost and not replaced.
- The company has recently been acquired by a new firm.
- There are no new products in a long time.
- Profitable customers are transferred to other plants.
- Night shifts and afternoon shifts are cut back.
- Research lab people in the plant are assigned to quality control duties.
- Research people are being let go or not replaced.
- Quality circle teams are deemphasized.
- Groups of strangers in suits are touring the plant.
- The word is out that the facility is not profitable.

ANNOTATED BIBLIOGRAPHY

While we previously identified many of the following books in *In Search of the Perfect Job,* we feel that they are good enough to recommend again. These resources will provide additional insights and support in the areas of careering, entrepreneurial, management skills, and personal development.

Careering

Bolles, Richard N.: *What Color Is Your Parachute?,* Ten Speed Press, Berkeley, CA, 1993. This 1972 classic, with its annual updates, is especially good for people who may be exploring a radical departure from their fields or have absolutely no idea what career direction to take. If you are searching for some answers, then you will probably find these introspective exercises thought provoking and the numerous directories and agencies which are included here valuable resources.

Kleiman, Carol: *100 Best Job$ for the 1990's & Beyond,* Dearborn Financial Publishing, Chicago, IL, 1992. As a business columnist for *The Chicago Tribune,* Ms. Kleiman has identified and described the 100 career positions which she feels are the "best" for the long haul. If you are just starting out in your career, this book may be helpful for you as a number of careering trends are identified and each position is briefly described.

Krannich, Ronald L., and Caryl Rae Krannich: *Network Your Way to Job & Career Success,* Impact Publications, Woodbridge, VA, 1989. This well-written book provides solid counsel on how to develop, expand, and use networking as a vehicle for finding jobs. Networking trends, abuses, and strategies prove to be an important part of the reader's insights.

Lauber, Daniel: *The Complete Guide to Finding Jobs in Government,* Planning Communications, River Forest, IL, 1990. If you are interested in exploring career opportunities in the public sector, this book is a valuable resource. It could be considered an insider's guide to getting connected in government with its practical ideas and identified agencies.

Levering, Robert: *A Great Place to Work: What Makes Some Employers So Good and Most So Bad,* Random House, New York, 1988. Not only has

Levering identified a number of successful and "attractive" companies through in-depth interviews, but he has also highlighted some of the factors that most employees would love to experience in their employers. This is an enjoyable and easily read book filled with keen insights.

Lloyd, Joan: *The Career Decisions Planner,* John Wiley & Sons, New York, 1992. We highly recommend this thought-provoking book if you are interested in conducting a reality check on your career and if you are committed to taking charge of how your career and life look. Filled with exercises that both reveal and instruct, you will find that you will be guided on the path to meaningful self-discovery.

Lowstuter, Clyde C., and David P. Robertson: *In Search of the Perfect Job,* McGraw-Hill, New York, 1992. This highly practical and complete career counseling guide offers proven strategies within the 12-step approach to job changing for executives, managers, seasoned professionals, and first-career young professionals. Packed with interactive exercises and worksheets, self-assessment tests, instructive case histories, sample résumés and letters, and offer-negotiation tips, this book "walks you through" every critical stage of the job search process from résumé development, search firm contacts, powerful interviews, to effective offer negotiations.

_____: *$ix Figure Networking,* RL Communications, Deerfield, IL, 1994. Subtitled *Your Inside Track to the Perfect Job!,* this lively and informative six-audiocassette album is filled with highly practical job hunting advice which will equip you to effectively make those professional and personal connections necessary to unlock the hidden marketplace. If you follow these proven methods you **will** accelerate your job-hunting efforts and help create your ideal job!

Sibbald, John: *The Career Makers: America's Top 100 Executive Recruiters,* Harper Row, New York, 1990. America's most effective and reputable recruiters are identified, profiled, categorized by areas of competency and assignments so that professionals looking for work and companies looking for talent can "supposedly zero in on" the right firm for them.

Smart, Bradford: *The Smart Interviewer: Tools and Techniques for Hiring the Best!* John Wiley & Sons, New York, 1989. For the dedicated job changer, this book is a "must buy," as industrial psychologist Dr. Smart presents strategies and checklists for interviewers evaluating job candidates. Although written to employers, job changers can greatly benefit from the many hiring factors which can "make or break" a candidate.

Tarrant, John: *Perks and Parachutes: Negotiating Your Executive Employment Contract,* Linden Press/Simon & Shuster, New York, 1985. Every executive should have this comprehensive guide to employment contracts on a bookshelf and be knowledgeable as to its contents. This fast-reading book will walk you through many contract concerns and considerations, including highlighting actual case histories and sample contracts. In addition, it teaches psychological tactics and bargaining strategies.

_____: *Stalking the Headhunter: The Smart Job-Hunter's Guide to Executive Recruiters,* Bantam Books, New York, 1986. Timeless in its advice, this book identifies a number of strategies you can use in networking with search firms so you can improve your chances of being contacted and considered for a better job.

Entrepreneurial

ABC's of Borrowing, SBA Publications, Denver, CO, 1989. This publication provides an insider's look at why some small-business people cannot get SBA loans while others, who have no trouble getting loans, find that there are obligations they hadn't previously considered.

Connor, Dick: *Increasing Revenue from Your Clients,* John Wiley & Sons, New York, 1989. If you follow the logical, straightforward advice this book offers, you will create new business and increase revenue from your existing clients while protecting your consulting relationships from competitors. If you are launching a business, the ideas contained herein will help you in establishing your practice.

Diamond, Michael R., and Julie L. Williams: *How to Incorporate: A Handbook for Entrepreneurs and Professionals,* John Wiley & Sons, New York, 1987. This is a practical "how to" guide through the often confusing maze of incorporation options and your obligations under each. The material covers special agreements and forms of incorporation to securities laws, stockholders, and dividends. Subchapter "S" and "C" corporations, partnerships, and proprietorship are all included.

Goldstein, Arnold S.: *How to Buy a Great Business with No Money Down,* John Wiley & Sons, New York, 1989. If you are interested in buying an existing business with a minimum financial exposure, you will find this book helpful and enlightening. The author has some good advice on how to purchase businesses without putting any money down and how to determine the worth of a business.

Greenbaum, Thomas L.: *The Consultant's Manual: A Complete Guide to Building a Successful Consulting Practice,* John Wiley & Sons, New York, 1990. This book instructs you in every aspect of launching and marketing a successful consulting business with particular emphasis on the development of the business plan and the focus of your business.

Jones, Constance, and The Philip Lief Group: *The 220 Best Franchises to Buy,* Bantam Books, New York, 1993. This book lives up to its subtitle of *The Sourcebook for Evaluating the Best Franchise Opportunities.* It is filled with solid information and the detail on each of the franchises is "user friendly," as it gives you a pretty complete picture of trends which have influenced each company and some of its issues.

Keup, Erwin: *Franchise Bible: A Comprehensive Guide,* The Oasis Press, Grants Pass, OR, 1991. Not only does this book deal with the myriad number of issues you might encounter as you consider purchasing a franchise, but it also addresses the perspective of a company exploring the potential of franchising its business. The book's worksheets and the strategic thinking that is generated are well worth its price.

Kuriloff, Arthur H., John M. Hemphill, and Douglas Cloud: *How to Start Your Own Business . . . and Succeed,* McGraw-Hill, New York, 1993. Unique because of the inclusion of an IBM-compatible disk, this "how to launch your own business" text is among the better entrepreneurial sourcebooks. The advice is applicable to both manufacturing and service businesses with the software skewed somewhat toward retail.

Levinson, Jay Conrad: *Guerilla Marketing Attack: New Strategies, Tactics & Weapons for Winning Big Profits from Your Small Business,* Houghton Mifflin, Boston, MA, 1989. This "handbook" is jammed with solid, practical, easily applied advice on how to effectively market your business' goods and services. This book is particularly beneficial to the entrepreneur who is not an expert in marketing as it identifies numerous common sense options with their pros and cons.

Lindsey, Jennifer: *Start-Up Money: Raise What You Need for Your Small Business,* John Wiley & Sons, New York, 1989. This book shows you how to successfully consider and access all of today's available start-up capital from offshore investors to incubators, technology transfer, licensing arrangements, venture capital, limited partnerships, strategic alliances. There is a wealth of practical information for first-time entrepreneurs, as well as seasoned venture capitalists.

Shenson, Howard L.: *How to Develop and Promote Successful Seminars and Workshops,* John Wiley & Sons, New York, 1990. For anyone contemplating launching a seminar business or conducting only a single workshop, this book is must reading. Shenson, the consultant's consultant in workshops, has taken the guess work out of developing and sustaining a successful practice. You are practically assured of success if you follow his advice carefully and provided you have solid technical skills, a burning personal commitment, and consistently add value to your audiences.

Smith, Jeanette: *The Publicity Kit,* John Wiley & Sons, New York, 1991. This well-written book shows you how to effectively create, launch, and manage a comprehensive public relations campaign at little or no cost. Topics span all forms of media from newspaper, to radio, television, special events, public service, and how to handle bad news.

Weinstein, David A.: *How to Protect Your Creative Work: All You Need to Know about Copyright,* John Wiley & Sons, New York, 1987. This book would prove to be invaluable for the person developing creative material and who wants to legally protect and safeguard it. Weinstein, an experienced copyright attorney, explains what works can and cannot be protected, how to register your work, and all the important copyright documents and forms.

Management Skills and Personal Growth _____

Alessandra, Tony, Phil Wexler, and Rick Berrera: *Non-Manipulative Selling,* Prentice-Hall Press, New York, 1987. This easy-to-read book provides practical relationship-based tools and approaches for anyone who wants to or needs to persuade anyone of anything. The authors' consultative selling strategy shows the reader how to take away much of the pressure to sell and replace it with the privilege of adding value to others.

Below, Patrick J., George L. Morrisey, and Betty L. Acomb: *The Executive Guide to Strategic Planning,* Jossey-Bass, San Francisco, 1987. George Morrisey, author/coauthor of more than 15 books on management technology, teamed up with his coauthors to offer a comprehensive, straightforward, and practical approach to strategic planning to senior managers. George is a good friend, and we have personally benefitted from his keen insights and commonsense approach which always generates results far more than expected. We heartily recommend this book.

Bennis, Warren: *On Becoming a Leader,* Addison-Wesley Publishing Company, Reading, MA, 1989. While countless books and articles have been written about leadership, Warren Bennis once again delivered a book which is interesting, crisp, believable, and motivational, as he helps the reader develop leadership mastery, enhance strategic thinking, and build organizational endorsement.

Blackman, Jeff: *Opportunity $elling,* Blackman and Associates, Glenview, IL, 1994. Created and produced by one of the most innovative sales consultants, this six audio-tape cassette program is designed as a business growth system to help you significantly improve your selling prospects and potential. The six tapes explain in detail how to open, probe, reveal, translate, negotiate, and create The Yes. You can secure his program directly: (708) 998-0688.

Blanchard, Kenneth, William Oncken, Jr., and Hal Burrows: *The One Minute Manager Meets the Monkey,* Quill, New York, 1989. This version of the "One Minute Manager" incorporates one of the most enduring and most easily understood symbols of management practice, that being Bill Oncken's monkey-on-the-back theory of management. We heartily recommend that you sit down and take the time to spin through this deceptively simple, yet powerful book. You'll find yourself returning to it often as we have.

Block, Peter: *Stewardship,* Berrett-Koehler Publishers, San Francisco, 1993. Block proposes that organizations which practice stewardship and create working partnerships and open relationships will be more balanced, responsive, empowered, and nimble to meet the challenges of an increasingly competitive marketplace. It's an excellent book for those who want to raise their social awareness in the workplace.

Bucholz, Steve, and Thomas Roth: *Creating the High-Performance Team,* John Wiley & Sons, New York, 1987. There is a wealth of great ideas and commonsense approaches in this very well laid out book. Not only do the premises and worksheets challenge your thinking, they also effectively guide and motivate you into a new way of thinking with a great deal of respect and support. This book is a super "coach" in providing strong leadership, creating a positive work culture, and leading your team to higher performance and interdependence.

Byham, William C., and Jeff Cox: *Zapp! The Lightening of Empowerment,* Fawcett Columbine, New York, 1988. *Zapp!* is a light-hearted little book with a powerful leadership message which distills many management and personal growth concepts and practices while presenting them in an entertaining style. If you are a crusty realist and are able to push through the book's allegorical style, you will discover some interesting insights that you can begin to immediately apply.

Covey, Stephen R.: *Principle-Centered Leadership,* Simon & Schuster, New York, 1990. Described as a long-term, inside-out approach to developing people and organizations, *Principle-Centered Leadership,* recognizes the extent to which core beliefs influence the quality of our lives, both on and off the job, in leadership and personal situations. In this book Covey promotes a more balanced, more rewarding and more effective life.

Cox, Danny, and John Hoover: *Leadership When the Heat's On,* McGraw-Hill, New York, 1992. Written in an engaging style, this book is loaded with highly practical, commonsense ideas, tips, and strategies which will both provoke insights as well as provide some tactics you can immediately use to manage yourself and others when the pressure's on in your organization or team. There are many lists in the form of questions, observations, and guidelines which everyone can benefit from exploring.

Crosby, Philip B.: *Leading—the Art of Becoming an Executive,* McGraw-Hill, New York, 1990. Written in a "user-friendly" manner, Phil Crosby provides a roadmap for those interested in mastering effective leadership and executive skills. The major principles of an executive profile, executive focus, leading, relationships, quality, and finance are all solid performance benchmarks and standards. Through the use of numerous examples of client successes and challenges, you will find yourself growing without effort, stress, or strain. In fact, you may be motivated to change.

DePree, Max: *Leadership Jazz,* Doubleday, New York, 1992. We concur with the book's cover flap—this **is** a brave book. In this his second book, Max masterfully reveals nuance after nuance which gently enlighten and lift us as to how to live and lead in harmony, in and out of the workplace. This is a beautifully written book and we are all privileged to have one of America's business leaders so sensitively share of himself.

Gordon, Dr. Thomas: *Leader Effectiveness Training,* Wyden, New York, 1977. If you haven't read and digested this classic communication/managerial book, track it down today. Written in 1977, the power and practicality of the concepts have stood the test of time and proven themselves ageless. If you are committed to working more effectively with people on and off the job while generating more balance, joy, and creativity, then this is a must read!

Hill, Napoleon: *Think and Grow Rich,* Fawcett Crest, New York, Revised edition, 1960. This is one of the most influential books ever written on personal empowerment and wealth accumulation. "Whatever the mind of man can conceive, he can achieve" is the concept for which Napoleon Hill became known and that personifies the potential of the human mind to create great things seemingly out of nothing but passion, focus, and a burning commitment to a worthwhile goal. Every person serious about personal growth needs to know and apply these 13 powerful principles.

Land, George, and Beth Jarman: *Breakpoint and Beyond,* HarperBusiness, New York, 1992. This thoughtful and truly fascinating work challenges all of us to tap into our potential creativity by breaking with the past and mastering the future. The authors uncover those hidden patterns which can accelerate individual and organizational contribution through the Power of Creative Growth, the Power of Future Pull, and the Force of Connecting.

McNally, David: *Even Eagles Need a Push,* TransForm Press, Eden Prairie, MN, 1990. This delightfully written, easily read book by one of our good consulting friends was born out of life's hard lessons. While this book is an autobiographical, motivational, and inspirational mix and can be read strictly for pleasure, Dave has also developed a number of practical exercises for you to gain breakthrough insights similar to his own, albeit without all the struggle.

Robbins, Anthony: *Awaken the Giant Within,* Summit Books, New York, 1991. International peak performance consultant, Tony Robbins, helps you apply numerous strategies and approaches to take immediate control of your mental, emotional, physical, and financial destiny. In this second book, Tony digs deeper into his own experiences to create the models which truly help people operate more effectively and live more powerfully and confidently. You definitely want to read this book with a highlighter in hand.

Wellins, Richard S., William C. Byham, and Jeanne M. Wilson: *Empowered Teams,* Jossey-Bass, San Francisco, 1991. You definitely should be interested in this book if you are interested in learning about and following proven strategies which help organizations develop and sustain self-directed work teams. Written out of the experiences the authors/consultants have had with Development Dimensions International (DDI), this is a great book as it not only establishes the benchmarks for successful empowered teams, it also shows you how to realize this level of team synergy and performance potential.

INDEX

About the Authors

Clyde C. Lowstuter and **David P. Robertson** are the authors of the nationally acclaimed *In Search of the Perfect Job,* which has assisted thousands of job seekers worldwide. Messrs. Lowstuter and Robertson and their team regularly consult with clients throughout the United States, Canada, Europe, and Puerto Rico. They are successful entrepreneurs and the cofounders of Robertson Lowstuter, Inc., an international executive career coaching and development consulting firm with several divisions. Their firm specializes in empowering individuals to be more effective contributors in their organizations. In addition to this incisive book on networking, they also created and produced *$ix Figure Networking,* a dynamic, highly insightful audiotape learning system which enables listeners to network at new performance levels.